Information: Protection, Ownership and Rights

To Sandra and Carol
and our parents

EMPLOYMENT LAW LIBRARY

Information: Protection, Ownership and Rights

Adrian Chandler LLB, LLM, PhD

Head of Resources, Faculty of Law
Associate Director of the Industrial Law Unit
University of the West of England, Bristol

James A Holland LLB, PhD

Head of Degree Studies, Faculty of Law
Director of the Industrial Law Unit
University of the West of England, Bristol

Series editor: John Bowers MA, BCL, Barrister

BLACKSTONE PRESS LIMITED

347. 462 C

First published in Great Britain 1993 by Blackstone Press Limited,
9–15 Aldine Street, London W12 8AW. Telephone 081-740 1173

© A. Chandler and J. Holland, 1993

ISBN: 1 85431 210 3

British Library Cataloguing in Publication Data
A CIP catalogue record for this book is available from the British Library

Typeset by Kerrypress Limited, Luton, Beds
Printed by BPCC Weatons Ltd, Exeter

Contents

0.1 Defining who is an 'employee' — 0.2 Foundations of the contract
— 0.3 Terms of the contract — 0.4 Variation of contract —
0.5 Wrongful dismissal and wrongful repudiation — 0.6 Unfair dismissal
— 0.7 Remedies — 0.8 General bibliography

1.1 How will a duty of confidentiality arise? — 1.2 What makes
information confidential? — 1.3 The duty owed by employees — 1.4 The
duty owed by former employees — 1.5 Distinguishing trade secrets from
other information — 1.6 Liability of third parties — 1.7 Checklist —
1.8 Bibliography

2.1 What constitutes a restraint of trade? — 2.2 How is reasonableness
determined? — 2.3 Drafting and interpretation — 2.4 Implied and
indirect restraints — 2.5 Restraints during employment —
2.6 Preparatory actions — 2.7 Associated companies — 2.8 The effect
of dismissal — 2.9 Garden leave — 2.10 Checklist — 2.11 Bibliography

Preface

It has always seemed strange to us that no text has attempted to draw together the various proprietary rights relating to information arising in the employment context. Although there are some excellent texts dealing with the specialist areas of intellectual property, confidential information and data protection, their impact and interrelation within the sphere of employment is barely addressed.

It has been estimated, for instance, that 80 per cent of patents emanate originally from the work of employees; confidential information abounds in companies; and rights to gain access to personal information held by employees have burgeoned in the 1980s. This level of activity brings with it problems both of maintaining secrecy and of establishing rights of ownership, use and access.

Our aim in this book has been to integrate those aspects of intellectual property rights and employment law which stand on common ground. In order to do this we have divided the text into three main sections: part I deals with the protection of confidential information; part II deals with intellectual property rights; and part III deals with the maintenance of confidential files. By a touch of serendipity this division roughly correlates with the title of the book: protection, ownership and rights. Where appropriate we have incorporated practical checklists either at the end of, or at suitable points in, each chapter.

We have not attempted to produce a general text on intellectual property and associated rights, merely to clarify their impact on employment law issues. We have, however, sought to summarise and explain the general principles wherever relevant.

Originally we had thought to produce precedent clauses which could be used by practitioners and employers in drafting contracts. With this in mind, together with a deal of curiosity to see how companies perceived the need to protect their secrets, we undertook two industrial surveys. The first was conducted by one of our research assistants, Miss Jane O'Brien. In this we asked companies two things: first, to detail how computer-held information relating to employees was collated and used, and secondly, what were their policies regarding medical reports and records. The results of this survey appear throughout the text in part III.

In the second survey we asked companies to send us their standard employment contracts, or at least those extracts which related to the protection and use of confidential information and intellectual property. The results of this survey appear mainly in parts I and II. Having conducted this survey it appeared quite obvious to us that producing *one* 'model' clause on, say, confidentiality, was pointless. The different needs of the companies participating was a striking feature, even as between companies of the same size. Styles of drafting, company structures and demands of the market-place all contributed to the variety. Whereas one company felt secure with a clause which lasted two sentences, another company preferred the detail of two pages. We therefore abandoned the idea of 'model clauses' in favour of providing appropriate commentaries on the range of clauses utilised by companies and the efficacy of their wording.

Most of the companies which participated in these surveys were kind enough not only to answer our unsolicited requests by providing us with their standard contracts, but also sent explanatory notes on recent occurrences relating to their contracts. All but a handful of companies wished to remain anonymous in the text. Therefore we have decided that the best line to take is to preserve the confidentiality of all participants by ensuring that no company is identified.

Throughout the text we will refer to these surveys as the *ILU survey* because they were conducted as part of the activities of the Industrial Law Unit in the Faculty of Law of the University of the West of England at Bristol. No distinction will be made between the two surveys, though the statistical evidence used in part III was mainly compiled by Jane O'Brien in relation to the first questionnaire.

We owe a debt of gratitude to a number of people. First, to our colleagues and friends at Bristol and around the country who have patiently ploughed through some of our earlier drafts and benefited us with their advice and criticism: Professor Alan Bensted at Bristol, Professor Gerald Dworkin at King's College, London and Professor Robert Grime at Southampton University. Secondly, the help provided by John Bowers as general editor of this series has been very much appreciated. It hardly needs stating that any mistakes that still appear in the text are down to our obstinacy or incapabilities. Thirdly, we would like to express our gratitude to Jane O'Brien for the professional way in which she conducted the first of the ILU surveys and for her compilation and analysis of all the data. And to Alistair MacQueen, Jonathan Harris and Heather Saward at Blackstone Press we would like to say thanks for all their support, faith and interest in the book; as well as for their friendship and lack of pressure over deadlines!

One of the enjoyable features of this research has been the enthusiastic cooperation of all the legal and personnel officers who provided us with data, contracts and comments for inclusion in the text. Though they remain anonymous in this work their help is valued greatly.

Adrian Chandler
James Holland

Table of Cases

Table of Statutes

Table of Statutory Instruments

1   Introduction: the Contract of Employment

In order to discuss the various information and intellectual property rights which touch upon the employment relationship we begin with a short description of the contract of employment. This introduction will outline the various features of the employment relationship, the discussion being pitched primarily at the matters considered in later chapters. Our aim is to demonstrate how the specific rights dealt with later in the text fit into the general picture of the employment relationship.

We have adopted the Harvard reference system in citing textbooks and articles whereby the author's name is followed by the year of publication and page number if appropriate. A short bibliography appears at the end of each chapter. Any references to the *ILU survey* relate, as we described in the preface, to the two surveys of companies we conducted through the Industrial Law Unit in the Faculty of Law at the University of the West of England, Bristol.

The book's theme of 'information' is divided into three parts. Leaving aside this introduction, Part I deals with the protection of confidential information and trade connections through the device of express and implied terms. Part II covers the more obvious intellectual property rights of patents, copyright and design rights. These possess a common feature in that the arguments centre more on ownership and rights of exploitation. Finally, Part III reverses the picture and is concerned with employees' rights of access to information and the consequent obligations imposed on employers.

Of course, there can be extensive overlaps between these topics. Hence, the trade secret so closely guarded by a company may, at some time, enter the public domain in the form of a patent; there will be specific rights relating to that information both before and after the granting of the patent. The more nebulous rights of confidentiality present in the development stages, for instance, may change to distinctive rights of ownership. Equally, there may be both copyright and confidential information rights relating to a drawing or a document. Hence, as the division of the topics is for the convenience of structure and analysis, we have tried wherever possible to note the overlap that may exist regarding the specific rights.

To this picture must be added the concerns and attitudes of employment law. Thus to say that s. 39 Patents Act 1977 allows employees the right of ownership to any inventions made outside the course of their employment duties merely begs the question: how does employment law define an employee's 'duties'? In this respect the introduction stands as an extended glossary for the rest of the work. More detailed explanations of the topics touched upon may be found either in later chapters or in other works in this series.

This introduction will assume the following format:

0.1 Defining who is an 'employee'.
0.2 Foundations of the contract.
0.3 Terms of the contract.
0.4 Variation of contract.
0.5 Wrongful dismissal and wrongful repudiation.
0.6 Unfair dismissal.
0.7 Remedies.
0.8 General bibliography.

The final part of this introduction examines the question of remedies available to employers and employees arising out of incidents within or related to the contract of employment. This section will address in particular the remedies available which relate to later chapters in this book, e.g., injunctions. In one sense it is a little strange to present the remedies before analysing the substantive issues. We have adopted this approach in order to avoid repetition when making appropriate references, throughout the book, to the range of remedies available.

The first problem confronting anyone dealing with employment law is: How does one determine whether a worker is an employee or independent contractor? The distinction is significant for many general reasons such as liability for tax and National Insurance contributions, matters of vicarious liability, the acquisition of statutory rights such as unfair dismissal compensation, redundancy pay, maternity rights and so on. Of particular importance to this book, however, is the fact that all the matters addressed in the ensuing chapters centre around the presence of a contract of employment. Many of the subjects covered *can* apply to independent contractors as well, but employees are usually presumed to be covered by the particular provisions whereas independent contractors will generally have to agree liability.

0.1 DEFINING WHO IS AN 'EMPLOYEE'

The problems associated with defining the term 'employee' or 'servant' have been with us for centuries; arising long before the application of contract terminology to the employment relationship. The assessment of the presence and extent of responsibilities closely followed the analytical line as to whether the putative employer had 'control' over what the individual did and the manner in which it was done. This seemed a natural path to take. The greater the degree of control, the more likely it was that there was a contract *of* service rather than a contract *for* services, that the person was a servant rather than an independent contractor or agent. Thus the primary method of establishing the nature of the relationship has traditionally been that of a 'control' test; and even now this is still a method of analysis used widely.

0.1.1 Control test

The courts are concerned to find who it is that determines the operation of the contract; who exercises the discretion? This is achieved by what may be termed a *'Who, what, where, when and how' test*. That is to say: first, to what extent does the 'employer' control who does the work? The contract of employment is a contract of personal service, so if the worker can delegate the task or send replacements this essential element of personal service will be missing. Next, does the 'employer' control what work is done, e.g., the order in which jobs are undertaken? Thirdly, what control does the 'employer' have over the place of work. If work is done at home or on the worker's own business premises this will point away from an employment relationship. The fourth point is similar but relates to the hours worked. The final point is: can the 'employer' control how the work is to be performed? With skilled workers it becomes unrealistic to suppose that control can be exercised here. In truth, though, the courts have approached this by asking does the 'employer' have the *right* to control activities rather than asking whether control is *physically* exercised.

0.1.2 Integration test

The integration test developed to cope with the problems of controlling *how* a job is to be done. 'Integration' was never accurately defined and the test only ever really applied to fringe occupations. The formula applied was: if the worker was fully integrated into — 'a part and parcel' — of the enterprise then there was likely to be a contract of service. This meant investigating whether the worker took part in administrative duties, management decisions, or undertook other tasks. If some degree of mutuality was present, with the 'employer' providing benefits such as holiday pay, this would tend to indicate a contract *of* service. However, where a person performed only a single task, usually for only a short time, this raised the presumption of a contract *for* services.

These tests (the control test and the integration test) tend now to be subsumed into a more general balancing exercise which goes by various names: the economic reality test, the mixed test, and the multiple test. The question of who is or is not an employee is generally one of fact, not law.

0.1.3 Economic reality test

This test recognises that it is the combination of features and the degree of emphasis that matters more than one simple checklist. So the modern approach demands that all the factors for and against the presence of an employment relationship are put into balance. Two key questions are then posed. These are:

(a) Are these workers in business on their own account? Here one looks to the financial risk and input of capital as regards equipment and varying profits. Any company, when set against an individual, will obviously have injected more capital and have taken more sizable financial risks, so the emphasis has to be on the level provided by the worker: is it higher than one would normally expect from an employee? This entrepreneurial aspect of the test was emphasised in *Ready Mixed Concrete (South East) Ltd* v *Ministry of Pensions and National Insurance* [1968] 2 QB 497 and, with surprising results, *O'Kelly* v *Trusthouse Forte plc* [1984] QB 90.

(b) Is there a mutual obligation to provide work and perform tasks as directed? Here one looks to matters such as the provision of sick and holiday pay, set hours and whether workers doing the same tasks are usually classed as employees. This aspect of mutuality was emphasised in *Nethermere (St Neots) Ltd* v *Gardiner* [1984] ICR 612 where homeworkers, who largely regulated their own workload, were nevertheless found to be employees on the basis that in many respects they were treated the same as their full-time equivalents.

These are the guiding forms of analysis adopted by the courts, but in the end the exercise is one of balancing these features. Whatever the parties wish to call themselves it is clear that the relationship will always be analysed under an objective test (*Young and Woods Ltd* v *West* [1980] IRLR 201). Nevertheless, the expressed wishes of the parties will be taken into account.

0.1.4 Types of employee

Specific occupations still cause problems. Traditionally, for instance, Crown servants have not been classed as 'employees', but that now appears to be changing (*R* v *Lord Chancellor's Department, ex parte Nangle* [1991] ICR 743). Equally, directors will not be classed as employees unless there is a contract of employment to that effect. In many cases, however, a director's duty as a fiduciary will create a greater burden of responsibility and accountability than if there were a contract of employment. And even consultants might be classed as employees if they become integrated into the business.

Part-time workers are an interesting category. On the whole, full-time work exists where the employee works 16 or more hours per week or has worked between eight and 16 hours per week for the last five years; anything less will be part-time work. Part-time workers qualify for relatively few rights under employment legislation; though under common law no real distinction is drawn between full-time and other work.

Thus, whereas part-time workers do not qualify for unfair dismissal or redundancy rights, they will nevertheless be caught by provisions relating to a wide range of duties such as confidentiality, patents, copyright, and possibly even restraint of trade. As regards these common law duties, the courts have become increasingly aware that the standard expected of part-time workers (especially where restrictions are imposed on their activities) must inevitably be less than that expected of full-time workers; but the residual elements of the duties must nonetheless be present. Equally, recent European case law (though not UK case law for the moment), together with proposals for a new Directive relating to part-time workers, may soon change the statutory position so that part-time workers gain at least pro rata rights with full-time employees.

0.2 FOUNDATIONS OF THE CONTRACT

The contract may be made orally or in writing (or in any combination) and may be open-ended or for a fixed term. Express terms, statements made by the parties (e.g., in advertisements or job descriptions), collective agreements if incorporated into the contract, works rule books, custom and practice, and a wide range of implied terms will all determine the terms of the contract. Unfortunately, employment contracts are treated with far less respect than other contracts. Good evidence of agreed terms is often difficult or impossible to come by and most employees do not receive written contracts or even written evidence of their contracts. To quote Sam Goldwyn, the result is that when it comes to a dispute these verbal contracts are often not worth the paper they are written on.

0.2.1 Written statement of terms and conditions

Most employees have the right, under s. 1 Employment Protection (Consolidation) Act 1978, to receive from their employer a written statement of terms and conditions. This must be supplied within 13 weeks of commencement. At the moment, certain classes of employee are excluded from this right, e.g., part-time employees and persons working wholly or mainly abroad. The contents should include: when commencement date occurred; the scale of pay; the sick pay scheme, if any; hours of work, including a statement as to the status of overtime, and holiday entitlement; pension scheme arrangements, if any; notice requirements; disciplinary and grievance procedures; and the expiry date of a fixed-term contract.

The written statement is *not* the contract, however. Rather it is very strong prima facie evidence of the terms. Industrial tribunals and courts will accept such evidence only if there is nothing in the contract proper to contradict this. Thus written or oral evidence of agreed terms, express or implied, will prevail. For example, in *Robertson* v *British Gas Corporation* [1983] ICR 351 a written statement which had been issued subsequent to the conclusion of the contract was held to be ineffective in altering the terms of that agreement. Any change in the contents of the written statement should be communicated within four weeks. Other documents may be referred to by the statement, e.g., disciplinary procedure, collective agreements. Originally it was a criminal offence not to issue written statements but now, should the employer fail to comply with s. 1, s. 11 Employment Protection (Consolidation) Act 1978 allows reference to be made to an industrial tribunal to determine what the parties ought to have stated, as per their agreement, in the document. However, this is almost a right without a remedy because the tribunal will not make the contract for the parties; it will simply record what the evidence reveals was agreed between the parties.

Written statements are a useful way of informing employees of the general terms of the contract. They are no substitute for a properly drafted contract. Indeed, in the areas we cover in this work written statements are often not relevant at all. Where rights of information are concerned, enforcement rights tend to centre on the written contract or the range of implied terms.

0.3 TERMS OF THE CONTRACT

Terms may be express or implied. The implication of terms in a contract of employment does not necessarily follow the traditional contract lines and often the courts are seen to operate from a set of presumptions.

Specific legislation on employment issues first arose out of the problems of the Black Death in the 14th century and the responses to the shortage of labour produced by this calamity. The Ordinance of Labourers of 1348 and then the Statute of Labourers 1351 set limits on the movement of labourers and on wage increases, the effects of which were to last for centuries. The Statute of Artificers 1562 and later the Settlement Laws and Poor Laws were equally to have an effect on judicial attitudes to 'labourers', 'servants' and later 'employees'. It was not until late in the 19th century that actions such as disobedience to lawful orders on the part of an employee ceased to be criminal offences. When judges had to analyse the structure of the contract of employment it was hardly surprising, then, to find that they drew upon many of the old and established feudal notions of service. This history has influenced the judicial view of the employment relationship, especially as regards notions of loyalty and commitment to the enterprise. Its impact can still be felt in the analysis of the rights and obligations which are dealt with in this book.

0.3.1 Express terms

The extent of express terms, reached orally or in writing, will vary a great deal. In drafting a contract one might look for the following, in addition to those mentioned for inclusion in a written statement:

(a) *Job title* and general statement of duties.
(b) Clauses explaining *continuity of employment*.
(c) *Confidentiality clause*. During the currency of the contract an employer's 'secrets' will be protected by the implied terms relating to confidentiality and fidelity. However, an express term can serve to detail the nature of the confidential information and also serve as a warning to employees. Without

such a clause there may be circumstances where junior employees who somehow come into contact with confidential information are not bound by any duty of confidence because it was not made obvious to them. Confidentiality clauses are also frequently drafted to protect against the use or disclosure of information once the relationship has terminated. It is a matter of some debate whether such clauses are effective and we will deal with this point extensively in chapter 2. For the moment we can say that it is advisable to insert properly drafted clauses of this nature in the contract — certainly as regards employees who are likely to handle confidential information.

(d) *Dedication to enterprise clause.* Sometimes referred to as a 'whole time and attention' clause, this spells out that the employee owes a duty of fidelity to the company. In the ILU survey these clauses frequently took the form of re-stating that which the law would imply anyway, i.e. that during the employer's time employees would devote all their efforts to furthering the employer's interests. But some clauses went further, forbidding any form of 'moonlighting' activities or financial involvement with other enterprises.

(e) *Restraint of trade clause.* Such clauses endeavour to prevent an employee working in a particular job or industry for a set time, and usually within a defined area, after the contract has ended. The effect of restraint clauses is therefore far more dramatic than any preservation of confidentiality clause. Many employers seek to rely on both types of clause in order to protect against disclosure of secrets and/or to prevent the former employee poaching the employer's trade connections. The presumption with restraint of trade clauses is that they are void unless: (i) they seek to protect a legitimate interest; and (ii) they are shown to be reasonable by reference to time, area and the market setting.

(f) Details of 'perks', e.g., car, health insurance.

(g) 'Contracting-out' clause regarding unfair dismissal and redundancy payments rights in relation to the non-renewal of a fixed-term contract.

0.3.2 Implied terms

Terms will only be implied where they are *necessary* for the business efficacy of the contract, not simply because it would be *reasonable* to imply them. Employment contracts are rarely thought out by the parties and there is therefore great scope for implying terms.

The generally established implied terms as to duties owed may be summarised as follows:

(a) *The duties incumbent on the employer:*

(i) The duty to *pay* the employee for being ready and willing to work.

(ii) A limited duty *to provide work.* The implied duty of the employer is limited to providing *pay.* Only in exceptional cases will there be a duty to provide work. The major exception is: where lack of work leads to an effective wage reduction as where pay is related to commission or piecework.

(iii) A duty to *indemnify* the employee.

(iv)   Duties relating to *safety*. In *Wilsons and Clyde Coal Co. Ltd* v *English* [1938] AC 57 these duties were said to relate to the provision of safe fellow employees, equipment, premises and the system of work. There are also statutory duties relating to defective equipment and compulsory insurance in addition to the responsibilities created by the Health and Safety at Work etc. Act 1974 which impose criminal liabilities in this field.

(v)   The duty of *mutual trust and confidence*. This is a rather nebulous duty and much of the case law has arisen in the context of unfair dismissal claims based on constructive dismissals. Just as employees have found that duties of obedience and loyalty can be vastly extended beyond the perceived agreement by implied terms, so too is an employer bound by an element of reciprocity. Thus there will be a serious breach of contract if the employer victimises the employee, acts capriciously towards the employee, maliciously undermines an employee's authority in front of subordinates, harasses the employee and so on. The list is open-ended. What the courts are looking for is conduct which makes further continuance of the relationship impossible. This will not always be the same as a finding of unreasonableness; especially if express terms allow the employer to take that particular action. Thus it may seem unreasonable to move employees across the country every two or three years, but it is unlikely to constitute a breach if a mobility clause has been incorporated in the contract.

(vi)   A duty to *provide proper information* to employees regarding matters affecting rights under the contract. This arises out of a recent decision of the House of Lords in *Scally* v *Southern Health and Social Services Board* [1992] 1 AC 294 where new employees were not informed of their rights to enhance their years of pension entitlement. The implications of this decision are that employees should be advised of all major terms at the start of the relationship, and should also be expressly notified of changes that occur during the currency of the contract. To most companies this will be an example of good practice anyway, and the rules regarding written statements apply the same logic. However, whereas the written statement stipulations are ignored by many companies without penalty, there is now the financial incentive of court action to encourage employers.

Terms may also be imposed by statute. For example, terms relating to sex discrimination and equal pay will automatically become part of the contract and cannot be evaded even by express agreement. The most important of these terms, for our purposes, relates to notice periods. There are requirements for the provision of minimum periods of notice laid down in s. 49 Employment Protection (Consolidation) Act 1978 which broadly give one week's notice for each year of service. The contractual periods may be longer, but not shorter.

(b)   *The duties incumbent on the employee*:

(i)   A duty to act in *good faith*. This is a wide and undefined duty which relates to the loyalty and fidelity that can be expected of an employee. This duty has had a major bearing on matters such as confidentiality, spare-time working, employees competing with their employer, and pre-1977 patent law. Its operation can be seen in the following examples:

(1) A duty *not to disrupt* the employer's business interests (*Secretary of State for Employment* v *ASLEF* (No. 2) [1972] 2 QB 455). This case concerned workers observing their contracts to the letter under a 'work-to-rule'. The disruption that followed was held to be a breach of contract. The duty was also described as the more burdensome 'duty to promote the commercial interests of the employer'. On similar lines, in *British Telecommunications plc* v *Ticehurst* [1992] ICR 383 the Court of Appeal further classified the withdrawal of goodwill (as part of industrial action) as being a breach of the implied terms of the contract. The action involved choosing methods of operation which might cause the most inconvenience to the employer. Ticehurst's actions were held not to be 'in honest exercise of choice or discretion for the faithful performance of her work but in order to disrupt the employer's business . . .'. The employers were therefore held to be entitled to refuse her the right to remain at work.

(2) A duty of *honesty*. This incorporates actions other than theft or fraud. In *Sinclair* v *Neighbour* [1967] 2 QB 279 a betting-shop manager habitually left IOUs in the till — though he always repaid them. He was expressly forbidden to do this, but he continued. The summary dismissal was held to be justified. It was said that a breach occurred where further continuance of the relationship would prove impossible. That was the case here. Again, in *Denco Ltd* v *Joinson* [1991] ICR 172 the use of an unauthorised password to gain access to a computer was found to constitute gross misconduct, analogous to dishonesty.

(3) A duty *to account for secret profits* (*Boston Deep Sea Fishing and Ice Co.* v *Ansell* (1888) 39 ChD 339). Most cases involve high-ranking employees taking bribes or having undisclosed interests which affect the employment relationship. Strictly speaking, however, this duty extends to such things as the undisclosed gift from a client of a bottle of whisky at Christmas time.

(4) A duty to *disclose misdeeds*. There is no obligation to incriminate oneself. When asked direct questions, however, there is a duty not to mislead. An intermediate area exists here under the provisions of the Rehabilitation of Offenders Act 1974. In general, this Act allows certain criminal convictions to be 'spent' after an appropriate length of time so that they do not have to be declared. What has also developed recently is the idea that there is a duty, at least incumbent on senior management whose responsibilities are affected by the actions, to notify the employer of serious breaches by fellow employees even when that involves self-incrimination: *Sybron Corporation* v *Rochem Ltd* [1984] Ch 112.

(5) A duty not to disclose *confidential information* (*Thomas Marshall (Exports) Ltd* v *Guinle* [1979] Ch 227). This duty arises during the course of the relationship and, in some cases, will continue to operate after its termination (*Faccenda Chicken Ltd* v *Fowler* [1987] Ch 117).

(6) A duty to surrender *inventions*. Sections 39 to 43 Patents Act 1977 deal with this point extensively. As regards most employees any invention

arising out of the employee's normal duties will belong to the employer (*Harris's Patent* [1985] RPC 19).

(7) A duty *not to compete* with the employer (*Hivac Ltd* v *Park Royal Scientific Instruments Ltd* [1946] Ch 169. This duty relates to actions during the currency of the contract. Competition cannot be prevented once the contract has been determined, subject to a valid restraint of trade clause.

(ii) The duty to *obey lawful orders*. This is an essential element in the relationship. 'Lawful' in the employment context means 'contractually justified'; such orders do not necessarily have to be reasonable as well. For instance, in *Cresswell* v *Board of Inland Revenue* [1984] ICR 508 the issue was whether an alteration in how a job was done (here, the introduction of computers) could be enforced as a lawful order. It was held that employees are expected to be adaptable in performing their duties. If the change was merely as to how the job was done, rather than a change to the job content itself, modern employees are expected to respond favourably. It must be said, however, that the extravagant use of even an express term may amount to an abuse of power so as not to constitute a lawful order, e.g. excessive demotions under a disciplinary procedure.

(iii) A duty to provide *personal service* and to be ready and willing to work. Illness is not a breach of this duty, but things such as taking part in industrial action will amount to a breach.

(iv) The duty to exercise *reasonable skill and care*.

(v) The duty to *take care* of the employer's property.

0.3.3 The Transfer of Undertakings (Protection of Employment) Regulations 1981

Where a business is sold, all the contractual and statutory rights concerning employees which are noted in this chapter and throughout the book will be transferred as well. Employees will maintain these rights and obligations only if they are 'employed [by the transferor] immediately before the transfer'. The term 'immediately' is now given a loose interpretation (*Litster* v *Forth Dry Dock and Engineering Co. Ltd* [1990] I AC 546).

The transfer of the whole or part of a business is covered by the Transfer of Undertakings (Protection of Employment) Regulations 1981 provided the transfer satisfies the test of the business being sold as a 'going concern'. This requires an examination of whether business contracts, name and goodwill have been transferred as opposed to mere sale of assets.

0.4 VARIATION OF CONTRACT

Under strict contract theory a contract cannot be varied unilaterally. It can be varied by agreement, notably where a contract is subject to 'alteration from time to time agreed with the XYZ union'. Thus, if an employer seeks to change the rate of pay or the place of work, or to insert a new restraint of trade clause the employee is not bound in law to accept such an alteration unless the instruction is lawful, i.e., contractual. This is particularly apposite to s. 39 Patents Act 1977 where the *current* duties of an employee may be relevant to the question of an invention's ownership. To consider the full impact of all this one must look to the possible consequences of a unilateral variation.

0.4.1 The employee stays in the job

(a) Even if there is no express term permitting variation the order may still be lawful because the employee's duty of fidelity and cooperation makes it so.

(b) If the employee acquiesces in the alteration it will eventually be deemed a legitimate change in the contract. The more immediate the effect of the alteration the sooner the employee needs to show some objection.

(c) The employee may object and sue for damages (*Rigby* v *Ferodo Ltd* [1988] ICR 29).

(d) The employee might obtain a declaration or possibly an injunction to prevent the unlawful variation.

0.4.2 The employee refuses to accept the new terms and resigns

If the employer's actions constitute a repudiation of the contract, the employee can lawfully accept the repudiation by resigning and sue for damages related to notice period. The employee may, as an alternative or additionally, claim there was a constructive dismissal for the purposes of unfair dismissal (see below). Further, any restraint of trade clause in the contract will become inoperative in the light of the employer's repudiation (*General Billposting Co. Ltd* v *Atkinson* [1909] AC 118).

0.4.3 The employee is dismissed

The employer might take direct action when met with a refusal to accept the order and dismiss the employee. If the dismissal is without notice there will be a potential claim for wrongful dismissal. Whether or not the employee is given notice he or she might possibly claim unfair dismissal. In such a case the employer is likely to argue business reorganisation as a defence to this action (see 0.6.4).

The irony is that the employee seems at the moment to be better protected against unilateral variations by the law of contract rather than the law of unfair dismissal.

0.5 WRONGFUL DISMISSAL AND WRONGFUL REPUDIATION

0.5.1 Wrongful dismissal

At common law an employer can dismiss an employee for any reason provided proper notice is given. Proper notice is determined according to the terms of the contract, subject to the minima stated in s. 49 Employment Protection (Consolidation) Act 1978.

A dismissal without notice or with inadequate notice will constitute a wrongful dismissal unless the employee had committed a serious breach of the contract to which the employer was responding. Payment in lieu of notice, unless allowed for in the contract, will also constitute a technical breach of contract. For the most part this is an irrelevancy, given that damages for wrongful dismissal would amount to the same sum. However, the technical breach may have the effect of invalidating post-termination terms such as restraint of trade clauses (see *Rex Stewart Jeffries Parker Ginsberg Ltd* v *Parker* [1988] IRLR 483, which we will cover in chapter 2).

0.5.2 Wrongful repudiation by the employer

A serious breach of contract committed by the employer will amount to a repudiation which the employee may accept as terminating the contract. The employee will have effectively been 'dismissed' and will be able to recover damages, which again are limited to the notice period.

0.6 UNFAIR DISMISSAL

Although s. 54 Employment Protection (Consolidation) Act 1978 states that every employee has the right not to be unfairly dismissed, there are certain conditions to be met.

0.6.1 The employee must qualify for the right

The right generally only applies to full-time employees who have at least two years' continuous employment. Further, the employee must be aged below 65 or 'normal retirement age' for that grade of employee in that company. The employee must also not ordinarily work outside Great Britain. This is satisfied by what is termed the 'base of operations' test (*Todd* v *British Midland Airways Ltd* [1978] ICR 959), which amounts to an investigation of where the company's headquarters are, what currency the employee is paid in, whether the employee pays UK tax and National Insurance, and whether the employee physically reports to the UK offices. Pilots, sales representatives and seconded employees may all be affected by this provision.

The employee must present any claim within the three month limitation period which begins at the effective date of termination (EDT). The EDT is defined as: (a) the date the notice period expires, if the employee is given notice (whether or not all the notice is worked); or (b) the date of dismissal, if the employee is summarily dismissed or dismissed with payment in lieu.

0.6.2 The employee must have been dismissed

The employee must prove that he or she has been dismissed under s. 55 Employment Protection (Consolidation) Act 1978. There is usually no dispute about this, but the definition includes:

(a) Termination of the contract by the employer with or without notice.
(b) The expiry and non-renewal of a fixed-term contract.
(c) Resignation by the employee because of the employer's repudiatory conduct, i.e., conduct which strikes at the root of the contract. This is referred to as a 'constructive dismissal'.

0.6.3 Constructive dismissal

The key case here is *Western Excavating (ECC) Ltd* v *Sharp* [1978] QB 761, which established that an employee is entitled to resign and claim unfair dismissal only if:

(a) the employee can point to the employer's actions being a serious breach of contract (an employer who is merely acting unreasonably is not necessarily in breach of contract, but the two can overlap substantially);
(b) the employee responds quickly; and
(c) the resignation is obviously related to the employer's conduct.

Examples of constructive dismissal actions are: harassment, victimisation, unwarranted demotion or disciplinary sanctions, unilateral variation in contract terms, destruction of mutual breach and confidence. Note, it is usually one breach that is in issue but the idea of a 'last straw' can also apply so that a history of incidents can be drawn together. If the employee qualifies and has been dismissed, the question of fairness still has to be assessed. Constructive dismissals may be fair or unfair in the same way as ordinary dismissals.

0.6.4 How is fairness decided?

This involves a two-stage process:

(a) *Was the dismissal for a fair reason?* Under s. 57 Employment Protection (Consolidation) Act 1978 the burden of proof transfers to the employer to show a defence under one of the following as the reason or principal reason for dismissal:

(i) *Capability* or qualifications. Capability covers both incompetence and inability owing to ill-health.
(ii) *Conduct.* Disobedience to lawful orders, theft, assault, absenteeism, and even conduct outside the contract which affects the relationship.
(iii) *Redundancy.* This arises in three situations: (1) where there is a cessation of business; (2) where there is a closure of the employee's particular workplace; (3) where there is a cessation or diminution in the requirements for employees to do 'work of a particular kind'.
(iv) *Statutory illegality.*
(v) *Some other substantial reason.* This is a catch-all category. The major example is that of a business reorganisation falling short of redundancy.

The *standard of proof* is governed by the House of Lords decision in *W. Devis and Sons Ltd* v *Atkins* [1977] AC 931. This means that employers (or employees for that matter) can only rely on evidence known to them at the date of dismissal. Notwithstanding this, the failure to allow a proper appeal (although obviously an action which naturally follows the decision to dismiss) will most likely make a dismissal unfair (*West Midlands Co-operative Society Ltd* v *Tipton* [1986] AC 536).

(b) *Was the dismissal fair in all the circumstances?* The tribunal will now look to the substantial merits of the case, having regard to the size and administrative resources of the company. There are two principal points: first, does the decision to dismiss fall within the range of reasonable responses open to a reasonable employer? See *British Leyland UK Ltd* v *Swift* [1981] IRLR 91. Some employers may not have dismissed in these circumstances, but if the decision falls within an acceptable range then this points towards reasonableness. Secondly, since the House of Lords decision in *Polkey* v *A. E. Dayton Services Ltd* [1987] AC 344, particular attention is now being paid to procedural factors such as: proper use of warnings, retraining and supervision schemes, the operation of just hearings and the assessment of alternative solutions. In the case of sickness dismissals, the employer should investigate the nature of the illness and the likely length of absence, assess the impact on the business (the importance of the employee's position), take account of medical evidence, and consider alternative work. This will often mean that the employer will have to obtain appropriate medical reports. In such situations, the Access to Medical Reports Act 1988 may be relevant (see chapter 6).

With a redundancy dismissal the tribunal will be concerned to discover whether the redundancy was implemented fairly. Thus if selections for redundancy are not made in accordance with existing agreed or customary arrangements concluded with the relevant trade unions or the selection criteria are not objectively justifiable then there may be an unfair dismissal for reason of redundancy. The employer should also ascertain whether suitable alternative employment is available. In the case of 'some other substantial reason', e.g., business reorganisation, the tribunal will examine whether the employer has shown a business need to reorganise and considered alternative courses of action.

Dismissal for any reason other than those noted above is unfair. Particularly inadmissible reasons include sex and race discrimination, dismissal because of pregnancy (though there are exceptions regarding incapability), and dismissal because of trade union membership or refusal to belong to a trade union.

0.7 REMEDIES

In all actions detailed in this book an employer will be entitled to sue for damages where 'information' belonging to the employer has been used or disclosed contrary to business needs. Thus actions by employees in breach of a valid restraint of trade covenant or the unlawful disclosure of confidential information will generate such a right. Equally, damages may be recovered for infringements of intellectual property rights. In most cases, however, damages are not the primary remedy sought by employers. Thus, as regards patent rights, the aggrieved party will usually begin entitlement proceedings to ascertain ownership: damages will really only be relevant where a breach has already occurred.

An award of damages will secure recovery of loss of profits resulting from the breach or infringement. The employer might alternatively (not in addition) choose to claim an account of profits rather than damages. Such a course of action will be appropriate where the plaintiff has not suffered direct loss or where the estimation of the defendant's gain is greater than the plaintiff's loss. An account of profits is ordered on principles of unjust enrichment and is calculated on the basis of the profits from the sales of any product which are attributable to the confidential information. Where the product has resulted from a mixture of confidential and non-confidential information the apportioning may of course prove difficult. This factor tends to deter applications for account.

As regards confidential information, what the employer requires most is to prevent either the initial misuse of the information or at least the continued misuse. Restraint of trade clauses are not inserted to gain monetary compensation, but to prevent harm being occasioned by unfair competition. There is the practical point that most employees or former employees will not be worth suing. Damages will be more appropriate if a party such as a rival company has become liable, e.g., for knowingly receiving and using confidential information, inducing a breach of contract or infringing a patent. Consequently, we have concentrated below on some of the alternative remedies ranging from dismissal through to *Anton Piller* orders.

0.7.1 Breach of a contract of employment: the employer's remedies

As well as suing either an employee or former employee for damages or for the recovery of any secret profit, an employer may choose to dismiss an existing employee. At common law the range open to the employer is:

(a)   A lawful dismissal *with notice* for any reason.

(b)   A lawful dismissal *without notice* where the employee has repudiated the contract, e.g., where the employee has unlawfully set up in a rival business whilst still in employment. In justifying a summary dismissal, an employer may rely on evidence discovered after the date of dismissal which relates to the employee's conduct during the currency of the contract (*Boston Deep Sea Fishing and Ice Co.* v *Ansell* (1888) 39 ChD 339).

(c)   Hold the employee to the notice period when he or she seeks to leave in breach of this provision (a '*garden leave*' injunction) (*Evening Standard Co. Ltd* v *Henderson* [1987] ICR 588).

(d)   Seek an injunction to prevent breach of confidential information, or to enforce a restraint of trade covenant, or to prevent an employee making unauthorised use of inventions belonging to the company.

It should also be noted that an employee who is dismissed without notice may have an action for wrongful dismissal unless the employer can show that the employee had repudiated the contract. The amount of damages will relate to the notice period, or the remainder of a fixed term if there is no break clause in the contract. The employee who continues in employment may of course sue the employer for damages relating to any breach, e.g., an unlawful wage reduction (*Rigby* v *Ferodo Ltd* [1988] ICR 29).

0.7.2 Unfair dismissal

As well as common law rights relating to dismissal there are the statutory provisions relating to unfair dismissal. The remedies are:

(a)   *Reinstatement* and *re-engagement*. If requested by the employee on the originating application (IT1) the employer can only refuse to reinstate or re-engage an employee who has been unfairly dismissed where it is reasonable to do so. An employer's failure to comply may lead to further compensation.

(b)   *Compensation*. The two main elements are the basic and compensatory awards. They are assessed on different grounds. The basic award is calculated by reference to length of service. It is almost identical to the redundancy entitlement. The calculation works on the following formula:

Age factor × length of service × week's pay.

The maximum basic award is £6,150 (1992–3 figure).

The compensatory award is based on what is just and equitable. It is calculated on net payments. *The maximum award is £10,000 (1992–3 figure).*

The relevant principles for calculating the compensatory award were laid down in *Norton Tool Co. Ltd* v *Tewson* [1972] ICR 501. These include: (a) immediate loss of wages; (b) future loss of wages; (c) loss of fringe benefits; (d) loss of employment protection rights; (e) loss of pension rights. Both the basic award and the compensatory award may be subject to a number of deductions, e.g., in relation to contributory fault, *ex gratia* payments made, or failure to mitigate loss.

0.7.3 Injunctions

Two types of injunction need to be noted here: the interlocutory and final injunction. They are relevant to all aspects discussed in all parts of this book, but particularly to parts I and II. Injunctions are not available as of right.

An injunction (of perpetual effect or limited in time) may be granted at the conclusion of a full action. Though a plaintiff may have a remedy of damages as of right, there exists the additional or alternative discretionary remedy of such an injunction. If damages will compensate the plaintiff fully an injunction will not be granted. The court will not grant an injunction which amounts to an order for specific performance of an employment contract. As far as the subject-matter of this book is concerned interlocutory injunctions have greater prominence than their final cousins. For, despite the fact that the interlocutory injunction really does not decide the merits of the case at all, the granting of such injunctions can effectively determine the issue. For instance, if the lifespan of a restraint of trade clause is one year, it is unlikely that the full action will be heard before its expiry. Thus where an employer is faced with an employee or former employee who is about to divulge confidential information, breach copyright, destroy the novelty of a patentable invention and so forth, the effectiveness of an injunction can come into play. Even in advance of any breach it is possible to obtain a *quia timet* (because he fears) injunction.

Almost inevitably where an interlocutory injunction is granted the plaintiff will have to undertake to pay any damages due should the final action determine that the injunction was not justified. In some cases the court will require proof that this undertaking can be honoured.

The decision of the House of Lords in the patent case of *American Cyanamid Co.* v *Ethicon Ltd* [1975] AC 396 has established the principles as regards *inter partes* applications for prohibitory interlocutory injunctions. In these cases evidence is normally given by affidavit, to the exclusion of cross-examination. The employer does not have to show a prima facie case to obtain an injunction preventing, for example, the breach of a restraint of trade or confidentiality clause. The test is whether there is a triable case showing a prospect of success at the full hearing and, if there is, whether the 'balance of convenience' favours the granting of the injunction. This aspect has been described as a shorthand phrase for 'the balance of the risk of doing an injustice' or 'the balance of hardship'. It seeks to make allowance for any uncompensatable damage that may arise. The balance of convenience will generally favour the employer's case. Thus, preventing an employee from effectively working at all whilst the issue is being determined may be more damaging than any effect on the employer. But preventing the disclosure or further use of confidential information would most likely not have such a dramatically adverse affect on the employee's employment prospects. Further, the court will not grant the interlocutory injunction if damages at the final trial would be an adequate remedy and the defendant would be in a position to pay them.

In *Lawrence David Ltd* v *Ashton* [1989] ICR 123 the Court of Appeal stated that the *American Cyanamid* principles will not apply to restraint of trade cases if the full action can be tried before the period of the restraint has expired. Where the case cannot be heard in time the court must effectively determine the issue at the interlocutory stage.

Equally, there is little point in granting an interlocutory injunction concerning confidential information where there can be no further material damage to the employer. For instance, if the employee discloses information publicly this action will potentially undermine the 'novelty' of a future patent application. The employer's main concern here would be to meet the requirements of s. 2(4) Patents Act 1977 which allows for the preservation of 'novelty' provided the patent application is made within six months of the disclosure.

Thus the protection of confidentiality, or the novelty of a future patent application, will more easily justify a *quia timet* injunction on the basis that once the information is lost any recovery of the position, even by an award of damages, might prove impossible.

0.7.4 Anton Piller orders

Anton Piller orders (from *Anton Piller KG* v *Manufacturing Processes Ltd* [1976] Ch 55) represent the final link in a chain of orders which seek to deal with physical evidence. These orders were once described as one of the law's two nuclear weapons. In any action a party may seek discovery, inspection or delivery up of documents, drawings etc. Orders 24 and 29 of the Rules of the Supreme Court 1965 allows such applications to be made *inter partes*. Delivery up and destruction will be particularly important in the case of intellectual property infringements.

Anton Piller orders were developed in intellectual property actions and represent the extreme limits of such processes to regain property because they are granted on an *ex parte* application by the plaintiff. The element of surprise is a key factor.

Anton Piller orders do not come in any standard format, but the effect (to varying degrees) is to allow the plaintiff immediate access to the defendant's premises to search for and seize documents and other evidence such as information stored on computer. The purpose behind such orders is to prevent dishonest defendants dealing with the evidence in a manner prejudicial to the case. The employer may seek an *Anton Piller* order against an employee or former employee where the safeguarding of evidence is believed necessary.

Circumstances have to be exceptional for an *Anton Piller* order to be made. There must be an extremely strong prima facie case, the extent of possible damage must be serious, there must be clear evidence that the other party is likely to disobey any court order, and the items to form the subject of the order must be clearly identifiable. An order might be made, for instance, where an employee is secretly making 'pirate' copies of the employer's copyright work and selling them abroad.

Care must also be taken where the right of inspection (and consequent search) might actually reveal the other side's trade secrets etc. An undertaking for damages will be required and the court demands that the applicant comes with 'clean hands' so that all matters even remotely relevant to the case must be disclosed. The order must be served by an independent solicitor who must explain the effect of the order to the defendant and inform the defendant of the legal right to seek legal advice before complying with the order.

Abuse has generated a judicial backlash. In *Lock International plc* v *Beswick* [1989] 1 WLR 1268, for instance, such an order was refused. Hoffmann J noted that the making of such an order 'can only be done where there is a paramount need to prevent a denial of justice to the plaintiffs'. Recently, in *Universal Thermosensors Ltd* v *Hibben* [1992] 3 All ER 257, the defendants were awarded £20,000 for the extraordinary manner in which the order was executed (at 7.10 a.m. to a woman alone in the house). The points noted above take account of the new guidelines which have resulted from this case.

0.8 GENERAL BIBLIOGRAPHY

Anderman, S.D. (1992), *Labour Law: Management Decisions and Workers' Rights* (London: Butterworths).

Bean, D. (1991), *Injunctions*, 5th edn (Longman Practitioner Series) (Harlow: Longman).

Bowers, J. (1990), *Employment Law* (London: Blackstone Press).

Chitty, J. (1989), *Chitty on Contracts*, 26th edn by A. G. Guest (London: Sweet & Maxwell).

Gee, S. (1990), *Mareva Injunctions and Anton Piller Relief* (Harlow: Longman).

Harvey, R.J. (ed.) (1984), *Industrial Relations and Employment Law* (London: Butterworths).

Smith, I.T., and Wood, Sir John C. (1989) *Industrial Law*, 4th edn (London: Butterworths).

Upex, R. (general ed.) (1992), *Sweet & Maxwell's Encyclopedia of Employment Law* (London: Sweet & Maxwell).

PART I

PROTECTING BUSINESS INTERESTS

The pervading themes explored in this part are twofold: the protection of information and the safeguarding of business interests against unfair competition.

Every business, from the small back-street engineering company to the large multinational, will generate business secrets and trade connections. The business secret may take the simple form of customer lists, discount concessions, or manufacturing know-how. The information may not, in effect, be unique to that particular enterprise; but it still holds some value to the employer. Equally, the information may take the form of formulae, inventions, secret recipes, or technical data and drawings. To the officious bystander these items may seem to have greater inherent value. Notwithstanding this view, all the items noted above are at least *capable* of attracting the protection of the law. The size and importance of the company are not the determining features; nor will the perceived value of the information be conclusive of any classification of secrecy.

Although confidential information comes in a variety of configurations it will usually take the form of oral or written disclosures to an individual or select group. The entrusted person or group will fall under a duty to preserve that level of secrecy provided the law regards the information as truly 'confidential'. Thus, once the information has passed this test of confidentiality, protection may be gained against its unauthorised use or disclosure. That protection will usually take the form of injunctions directed at employees, but third parties may equally be placed under a duty to preserve the confidentiality of the information.

Protection may be obtained under general equitable notions, but we will be most concerned with the security afforded by the express and implied terms of a contract. Chapter 1 therefore attempts to investigate and analyse the situations which will give rise to the duty of confidence and the manner in which that duty is enforced. Attention will be focused on the duties arising during the currency of the contract of employment as well as those which continue to operate after its demise.

In many cases information which has taken a more tangible form, such as a drawing, a document or manufactured item, may attract more definite rights of ownership via copyright or patent protection. These matters will be discussed in part II. But rights of confidentiality stand alongside these intellectual property rights, providing at least supplemental security; and, in many instances, the *only* effective safeguard against exploitation of information by others.

Employers may also be anxious to guard against more direct forms of competition. They may wish to ensure that an employee does not have the opportunity to utilise any confidential information or exert influence over the employer's trade connections. Restraint of trade clauses thus enter into the fray.

Restraint of trade clauses seek to prevent an employee from working in a particular field; they curtail the employee's opportunity to gain employment. Their effect on a former employee's career is therefore much greater than any confidentiality agreement. Hence the courts subject such clauses to stringent analysis. The viability of these clauses depends on the presence of a legitimate interest deemed worthy of protection and the reasonableness of their drafting. The paradigms of 'legitimate interests' are confidential information and trade connections.

Used effectively, a restraint clause frustrates competitive ventures, but justification rests on the prevention of *unfair* competition only. Mere rivalry attracts no judicial intervention.

Chapters 1 (confidential information) and 2 (restraint of trade) therefore concentrate on issues of conservation: the preservation of an employer's accumulated confidential information; and the maintenance of competitive edge.

1 Confidential Information

Confidential information comes in a variety of forms and levels of significance. Matters such as trade secrets, business plans, customer discounts, personal details, manufacturing processes, official secrets and so on may all fall within this classification. In different circumstances, information which to one employer would not merit any form of protection may, to another employer, be seen as highly confidential. Any classification is therefore open to a large element of subjective as well as objective assessment. This chapter seeks to explore how those assessments correspond and what level of protection the law provides for information which can be classed as confidential.

As will be seen in this chapter, the law demands that in certain circumstances a person must observe the confidentiality of information imparted to him or her. Rights to confidentiality are more nebulous than patent rights, design rights or copyright; often the information is intangible and proof of breach is not always straightforward. The information does not have to be contained in a document but it must have an identifiable source. Confidentiality may extend for only a limited period or forever; but the law will not protect all 'secrets'. Anyone claiming that a person has breached one's confidence must show three things:

(a)   that the law would class the information as possessing the necessary quality of confidence about it;
(b)   that the information was imparted in circumstances which conveyed an obligation of confidence; and
(c)   that there was unauthorised use of that information.

We shall explore these factors throughout the course of the chapter. All of the factors are relevant to employment contracts; and all of them must be proved before the person disclosing the secret will be liable. If you take away one element then the rest cannot stand on their own.

As well as this three-stage test for breach of confidence there are two main areas of concern that arise in relation to employment contracts: first, what duties are owed by employees *during* the currency of the contract? Secondly, can such duties *continue* once the contract has ended? This chapter will therefore adopt the following lines:

1.1 HOW WILL A DUTY OF CONFIDENTIALITY ARISE?

1.1.1 General basis of the right

In *Attorney-General* v *Guardian Newspapers Ltd* [1987] 1 WLR 1248, 1263 Browne-Wilkinson V-C summed up this area in this way: 'The principles upon which the law of confidential information is based have never been clarified and remain, to my mind, obscure'. Considerations of what is meant by confidence (or confidentiality) raise the spectre of equitable concepts, fidelity and fiduciary relationships. The issues themselves range from problems of copying information, through disclosure to outright competition from employees.

The origins of the right to protect confidential information have been ascribed at various times to property rights, contract, bailment, equity, tort and good faith. This jurisdictional difficulty arose in the earliest cases and has not been resolved satisfactorily. Indeed some have commented that it matters little in practical terms what the conceptual pigeon-hole is. Occasionally, though, it may matter — in balancing the remedies of specific performance, injunction and damages, or in questioning 'clean hands' — whether the claim is founded in common law or equity. It certainly matters in that by reason of equitable principles parties who are not involved in the contract may still be held to observe the confidence.

Many of the problems of classification arise because the notion of confidentiality pervades familial, contractual and non-contractual relationships alike. The variety of facts thereby inherent have inevitably led to a wide range of explanations to justify or deny liability. The general law of confidence, with its dual role of protecting rights in contractual and non-contractual relationships has therefore struggled to determine clear guidelines. The tendency in the 20th century has been to view the basis of liability as resting on equitable concepts. In *Saltman Engineering Co. Ltd* v *Campbell Engineering Co. Ltd* (1948) 65 RPC 203 Lord Greene MR said, at p. 211 '. . . the obligation to respect confidence is not limited to cases where the parties are in a contractual relationship'. Lord Denning has contributed to the debate. In *Seager* v *Copydex Ltd* [1967] 1 WLR 923 (a case concerning the design of a carpet grip disclosed in confidence during the course of negotiations for the manufacture of the grip) he said, at p. 931:

The law on this subject does not depend on any implied contract. It depends on the broad principle of equity that he who has received information in confidence shall not take unfair advantage of it.

Little wonder then that with this level of disagreement the Law Commission (1981) has recommended treating this area as *sui generis*. As Finn states (1977, p. 130) the rule of confidentiality 'has not evolved primarily from the law of trusts. Rather it has grown up somewhat haphazardly.' Broad equitable notions probably underlie even any contractual analysis, the court enforcing an obligation that already exists independently of the contractual terms.

1.1.2 Basis in the employment relationship

Some of the earlier cases touched on the duties owed by servants. In *Yovatt* v *Winyard* (1820) 1 Jac & W 394, for instance, an assistant, a journeyman, had copied medicinal recipes from his master's books. He was enjoined from using them on his own account both because his actions were a breach of the contractual obligation of confidence and also, it seems, an express agreement. The basis for this obligation is not explained and is presumed without reference to authority. But there is no reason to expect that embryonic labour law should have solved the conceptual dilemma witnessed in more general cases. The case is, however, one of the earliest authorities for the application of such duties to the employment relationship.

Throughout the 19th century the duty of confidence expected of an employee was presumed as self-evident by the courts. For the first satisfactory explanation of the basis and mechanism of application we have to wait until the late 19th century (*Lamb* v *Evans* [1893] 1 Ch 218 and *Robb* v *Green* [1895] 2 QB 315). The more discernible analysis laid in this area owes a great deal to Kay LJ (who heard both cases) and Bowen LJ, who not so long before had enunciated principles of fidelity as relevant to the employment field, in *Boston Deep Sea Fishing and Ice Co.* v *Ansell* (1888) 39 ChD 339 and those of the implied term in general contract law as seen in *The Moorcock* (1889) 14 PD 64.

Lamb v *Evans* concerned canvassers employed to place traders' advertisements in a directory. At the expiration of their contract they sought to use the information gained by taking up employment with a rival. They were prevented from using the information. Strictly this case can be seen more as a principal-agent relationship. Its almost universal acceptance in employment law analysis seems now to make this a matter of insignificance. In *Robb* v *Green* (a clear employment law case) the employee-manager copied lists of customers and used the list after termination of his employment. An injunction was granted to prevent this activity. The boundaries between contract and equity are by no means clearly drawn in these cases. In *Vokes Ltd* v *Heather* (1945) 62 RPC 47 Lord Greene MR unequivocally supported the view that the express and implied terms of the contract determined the matter; that there were not two separate obligations in equity and contract. Subsequent cases, such as *Bents Brewery Co. Ltd* v *Hogan* [1945] 2 All ER 570, *Hivac Ltd* v *Park Royal Scientific Instruments Ltd* [1946] Ch 169, *Wessex Dairies Ltd* v *Smith* [1935] 2 KB 80, and *Faccenda Chicken Ltd* v *Fowler* [1987] Ch 117, reinforce this contractual approach.

The duty of confidence is correlated with the duty of fidelity by most authors and in the decisions of many cases, though some commentators do perceive a distinction. The key point here is that if the duty of confidentiality *is* merely a branch of the duty of fidelity then the expectations placed upon the employee are probably more general and more burdensome than if the duty exists *sui generis*. This divergence of opinion is therefore of practical significance as it helps to explain judicial perceptions of the extent to which an employee is lawfully permitted to gain an 'unfair advantage' over the employer.

In contrast to the development of confidentiality in other areas the contract theory has dominated the employment law analysis. Unfortunately this does not quantify matters any more rigorously and still begs a number of questions. For instance, we will see that there undoubtedly exists an *implied contractual* duty of confidentiality which has been subjected to detailed scrutiny by the courts; it is less clear whether an express term preserving confidence is a contractual duty *simpliciter* (as is suggested in the recent case of *Attorney-General* v *Barker* [1990] 3 All ER 257) or is the contractual expression of a wider duty of confidentiality. For, taken to the extreme exhibited in *Attorney-General* v *Barker* (discussed below at 1.4.3), if the express term is to be examined in the same vein as any other term (e.g., as to pay) then many of the traditional tests applied to confidentiality become irrelevant.

The analysis offered in this chapter takes the line that the duty of confidentiality (appearing by means of express or implied terms) is subject to different considerations than are applied to most other terms.

1.1.3 What circumstances will convey an obligation of confidence?

The mere fact that someone has come into possession of information does not mean that a duty of confidentiality has arisen. The information must be imparted in circumstances which convey an obligation of confidence. The recipient of the information must accept that the information is to be treated as confidential before any duty will be imputed to that recipient. This is tested objectively: Would a reasonable person, standing in the shoes of the recipient, have realised that the information was being given in confidence?

The employer's rights are to prevent *disclosures* by employees or others and, in the event of unauthorised disclosures occurring, to prevent the further use of the information. It is a *sine qua non*, therefore, that the person receiving the information must be subject to a duty to preserve confidentiality before any rights or liabilities can apply.

If the information is disclosed for business purposes then, provided it is clear that the recipient is receiving information which is confidential (preferably by express notice), it will be assumed that the recipient is bound by the confidence so that the information can only be used in the context of the relationship (*Seager* v *Copydex Ltd* [1967] 1 WLR 923). Thus subcontractors, consultants or companies taking part in joint ventures will be so covered. As regards employees, a duty of confidentiality is imputed in nearly all cases. The employee will not be allowed to reveal the employer's confidential information to anyone who is not authorised to receive it, e.g., rival companies or trade unions. Nor can the employee make copies of the information or deliberately memorise it for use after leaving the company.

Thus the major problem with assessing whether or not there is a duty will arise in the case of third parties. The liability of third parties will only originate where the person in possession has obtained the information directly or indirectly from the 'owner' (*Saltman Engineering Co. Ltd* v *Campbell Engineering Co. Ltd* (1948) 65 RPC 203). The 'owner' of the information does not have rights in the information as against the world, as would be the case with copyright or patent rights. Rather, the rights regarding confidentiality are aimed at preventing unauthorised disclosure; they do not create a monopoly on the idea itself, for an idea or a process can be thought of by more than one person. Thus the bright idea, unprotected by other rights such as patents or copyright, cannot belong exclusively to the employer. Any persons may discover for themselves the secrets of, say, a revolutionary compact disc player by their own independent research or by a process of reverse engineering. There can be no breach of confidence in such circumstances; hence the importance of intellectual property rights such as patent protection.

Employers may also find themselves having to entrust another party with their confidential information. The circumstances in which the other party acquires the information make a difference. In pre-contract negotiations, for example, information will often have to be exchanged and such communications have given rise to a duty of confidence (*Seager* v *Copydex Ltd* [1967] 1 WLR 923). If a contract develops, further secrets may have to be divulged or received. Equally, the exchange of information may arise in relation to licensing agreements or joint ventures to develop products or processes, or in relation to the marketing or advertising of a product.

But where third parties come by the information accidentally, acquiring it indirectly from someone other than the owner, or by industrial espionage, the presence of an imputed duty will depend very much on the third party's actions, actions in bad faith tending to impose a duty on the recipient. And where a person or company receives a document marked 'confidential' this does not mean that a duty has effectively been imposed. If further negotiations ensue or use is made of the information the position may then alter to one of confidence.

Assuming that employment contracts are remote from the influence of equitable principles regarding confidentiality then there are two principal ways in which an employee will acquire a duty of confidentiality. First there is the device of express terms inserted in the contract. Secondly, the range of implied terms may supplement (or stand in the place of) the express terms.

1.1.3.1 Express terms of the contract
In the Industrial Law Unit survey (ILU survey) nearly every contract supplied included a confidentiality clause of some form; many of them of great detail

and length. Such express terms are important in a number of respects. The most obvious is that the employer can set out in clear terms what the responsibilities of the employee are as regards information gained in the course of employment. This is not as trite as it sounds. In a number of cases employees have been held free to use information because the contract did not make the confidentiality point clear. For instance, in *United Indigo Chemical Co. Ltd* v *Robinson* (1932) 49 RPC 178 an injunction to restrain the former employee from using 'secret processes' learned during employment was refused on the grounds that access to the information was freely available within the company and he had never been told that what he had learned was to be regarded as confidential. Terms appearing in the survey therefore frequently adopted the following lines:

> *You shall not, except as authorised by the Company or required by your duties hereunder, use for your own benefit or gain or divulge to any persons firm company or other organisations whatsoever any confidential information belonging to the Company or relating to its affairs or dealings which may come to your knowledge during your employment.*

Or

> *It is important that all employees safeguard confidential information about the Company's activities. You must ensure that you do not discuss or divulge any such matters to an unauthorised person at any time.*

Or

> *The employee shall not either during his appointment or at any time for one year after its termination: disclose to any person(s) (except those authorised by the Company to know or as otherwise authorised by law); use for his own purposes or for any purposes other than those of the Company . . . any confidential information belonging to the Company.*

There were many other variations, and many other additional definitions and further responsibilities detailed to which we shall return in considering the nature of the duties owed by employees and former employees.

It has been stated by judges that the law will imply into contracts of employment the obligations necessary for the protection of confidential information. In most cases this is true, but, as seen above, the inclusion of such a clause is recommended as an additional precaution. It also has the practical advantage of standardising personnel practice. Certainly one would expect such clauses to appear in contracts with scientific, research, technical and other skilled or professional employees.

The advantages of the inclusion of such clauses are:

(a) Setting out matters in a clear form makes obvious to the court the employer's 'subjective' assessment regarding the importance of confidentiality.

(b)   In borderline situations it may be that a clear policy will convince a court that certain information deserves to be labelled 'confidential'.

(c)   Such clauses serve as a warning to employees.

There is also a possible drawback: once a term has been spelled out, any drafting errors may bind the employer when the more nebulous implied term might have accommodated the need better. There are two problems hidden in this statement. The first is: Will the courts analyse the wording of the agreement to the point that anything omitted may not later be included, e.g., the term prevents 'disclosure' of the information but does not cover 'use'? To this one has to say that there are cases where this analysis has been applied (*Thomas Marshall (Exports) Ltd* v *Guinle* [1979] Ch 227).

The second problem is related to the first: Does the presence of an express term preclude reliance on implied terms such as fidelity? Somewhat paradoxically, the answer to this appears to be no: *Triplex Safety Glass Co.* v *Scorah* [1938] Ch 211 and *Thomas Marshall (Exports) Ltd* v *Guinle* again. In the latter case the deficient express term failed to achieve the protection required but Megarry V-C nevertheless granted an interlocutory injunction on the basis that the request to restrain 'the disclosure or use of confidential information or trade secrets, seems to me to be fully supported by the implied duty of fidelity and good faith'. The courts therefore feel free to supplement express terms with wider implied duties.

1.1.3.2 Implied terms of the contract

As we noted in the introduction, terms will be implied into any contract, including the contract of employment, where they are *necessary* for the working of the contract. They are not implied merely because it would be reasonable to do so. Once accepted as part of the contract, however, the exact formulation of that duty will be subject to a test of reasonableness.

The law must still perceive a duty of confidentiality arising before it will take any action. As seen in *Robb* v *Green* [1895] 2 QB 315 and *Lamb* v *Evans* [1893] 1 Ch 218, the courts have long been prepared to imply an obligation of confidentiality irrespective of the presence or absence of express terms. The existence of that duty is therefore treated as axiomatic in the employment relationship. The most common ground for this is that a violation of confidence is a breach of the duty of fidelity or good faith which is an intrinsic part of every employee's contract. Indeed, the courts treat this so seriously that even the *possibility* of a breach of confidence may prevent employees working for others in their spare time (*Hivac Ltd* v *Park Royal Scientific Instruments* [1946] Ch 169).

The extent of that duty is often said to depend on the level of seniority of the employee. Such a statement can mislead, however, for most employees who would be likely to come in contact with confidential information will be expected to behave in a similar manner. It is unrealistic to think of 'fidelity' and 'super fidelity' in the abstract. To say that a financial manager owes a greater duty of fidelity than a manual worker is a statement of the obvious, and to this extent therefore the duty of confidentiality does vary with status.

But to say that a senior researcher owes a substantially (or even measurably) higher level of confidentiality than that expected of a junior researcher is to create a distinction without any real difference.

The implied duty may be expressed as a *negative* responsibility, i.e., a duty not to use or disclose confidential information acquired during the course of employment (*Thomas Marshall (Exports) Ltd* v *Guinle* [1979] Ch 227), not to make unauthorised copies of documents (*Robb* v *Green* [1895] 2 QB 315), and not to deliberately memorise documents for further use after the relationship has ended (*Johnson and Bloy (Holdings) Ltd* v *Wolstenholme Rink plc* [1987] IRLR 499). There may also be a *positive* duty to disclose to the employer information discovered by the employee which the employer has a right to know about, e.g., where an employee detects patterns in the market which might have an adverse or beneficial effect on the employer's business. We will return to these matters below (1.3.4).

As seen in *Thomas Marshall (Exports) Ltd* v *Guinle*, implied terms relating to fidelity and good faith will be implied very easily: they are effectively a 'fall-back' for missing or badly drafted express terms. However, the duty of confidentiality owed by an employee whilst the contract subsists is now different in nature from that owed by former employees. The case of *Faccenda Chicken Ltd* v *Fowler* [1987] Ch 117 drew a clear distinction between the responsibilities owed in these circumstances. It was said in that case that the only implied term which continues after the contract has ended is that the employee must still respect the employer's trade secrets to the same extent as when the contract subsisted. We have grave doubts on a number of matters raised in the Court of Appeal's decision in *Faccenda Chicken Ltd* v *Fowler*, but the central analytical point concerning the continued protection of trade secrets is clear and has set the pattern for all subsequent decisions.

1.2 WHAT MAKES INFORMATION CONFIDENTIAL?

Anyone seeking an injunction to restrain the use or disclosure of confidential information will be called upon to specify the secrecy element; to give clear particulars of the information. It will not suffice for an employer merely to say that there is some confidential information in need of protection. In *Thomas Marshall (Exports) Ltd* v *Guinle* [1979] Ch 227, Megarry V-C provided guidelines as to how confidentiality is to be assessed. He said:

> It is far from easy to state in general terms what is confidential information or a trade secret. . . . Plainly 'something which is public property and public knowledge' is not confidential (see *Saltman Engineering Co. Ltd* v *Campbell Engineering Co. Ltd* (1948) 65 RPC 203 per Lord Greene MR at p. 215).

So there is a prerequisite that the information must not be in the public domain already. Megarry V-C continued:

> If one turns from the authorities and looks at the matter as a question

of principle, I think . . . that four elements may be discerned which may be of some assistance in identifying confidential information or trade secrets which the court will protect. I speak of such information or secrets only in an industrial or trade setting.

Those four elements were:

(a)   Does the employer believe that the information is of a kind whereof a disclosure would harm the business?
(b)   Does the employer believe the information is secret, i.e., that it has not become public knowledge?
(c)   Are these reasonable beliefs? For instance, what has the employer done to protect the secrecy of the information?
(d)   The information must be judged in the light of the usage and practices of the particular industry or trade.

To this list must be added a fifth point:

(e)   The maintenance of secrecy must not offend the public interest. That is to say, you cannot claim that unlawful activities merit protection.

1.2.1 What kind of information is capable of attracting protection?

The range is extensive. The list would include chemical formulae; customer lists, sales figures, drawings, industrial designs, fashion designs, details of an invention currently under development, information contained in computer programs, discount concessions given to customers, delivery route plans, research papers, financial and other reports; and, of course, State official secrets. All of these items of information are *capable* of being classed as confidential. The information may be of a technical, commercial or even personal nature. Francis Gurry's description that the information must have the basic quality of inaccessibility (1984, p. 70) has also received judicial support.

In *Potters-Ballotini Ltd* v *Weston-Baker* [1977] RPC 202 it was argued that where foreign companies were willing to pay for the information in question, this indicated that it *was* confidential. On the particular facts the point was dismissed out of hand, however. It is a pity this line was not developed further. It is suggested that this is one very good yardstick (though not a conclusive one) for valuing the information and separating it from employees' skill and knowledge. As was argued in the case, the Japanese are not usually willing to pay for information which by diligence and research they might easily find for themselves. The weakness of this argument, of course, is that companies are also willing to pay for expertise in employees.

Unlike a patent, confidential information does not have to be novel to draw protection. It is the security of secrets that matters, not inventiveness. Thus, a company has the right to protect all information which relates to the running of a business provided the company has not already made the information public knowledge. Disclosures can certainly prove disastrous to a business. For instance, the disclosure of information prior to a patent application can destroy the 'novelty' of that patent. This is so vital an aspect of patent law that certain limited exceptions to this disclosure principle have had to be developed, e.g., s. 2(4) Patents Act 1977 allows the patent to stand where the patent application is made within six months of the employee's breach of confidence.

Whilst the employment relationship continues, the employer can rely heavily on the duty of fidelity to ensure that secrets are protected. The grade of that secret (trade secret or merely confidential) does not really matter. The employee will be expected to observe the duty of confidentiality in either case. As seen in the four points furnished in *Thomas Marshall (Exports) Ltd v Guinle* [1979] Ch 227, however, this does not mean that the employer has an absolute and automatic right to the preservation of information held. Thus an employer who takes no steps to preserve the confidentiality of information or who takes inadequate steps to inform employees that they are under such a duty may suffer accordingly.

We have noted that once the employment has been terminated the classification of information as a 'trade secret' or 'other confidential information' will matter very much (*Faccenda Chicken Ltd v Fowler* [1987] Ch 117). We will discuss the practical effect of this distinction in some depth below. For the moment, certain points need to be noted by way of introduction.

The first is that the courts do not seem too certain what they mean by the term 'trade secret'. In 19th and early 20th century cases the term trade secret was used loosely to describe the demarcation between information which attracted protection and an employee's general skill and knowledge, which did not. Trade secrets attracted protection by the device of extending the implied duty owed during employment to conduct post-termination. Trade secrets were also classed as a legitimate interest which provided the justification for enforcing restraint of trade covenants: see *Herbert Morris Ltd v Saxelby* [1916] 1 AC 688.

The antithesis of a trade secret was the employee's 'know-how'; the aptitude, dexterity, manual and mental ability: the skill and knowledge of the industry which an employee gained from experience. An employee's skill and knowledge could be taken freely from job to job. Use of this 'know-how' could not logically be restricted; otherwise every time employees changed job they would theoretically have to be treated and act like raw recruits. This distinction still holds true in that an employee's general skill cannot be the subject of a confidentiality clause, nor will the use of such skill be prevented by a restraint of trade clause. Thus an employee's knowledge of organisational and business *methods* is not generally protectable (*Ixora Trading Inc. v Jones* [1990] FSR 251 regarding the business methods and techniques of establishing bureaux de change).

That was the traditional distinction. More recently the term 'trade secret' has been used to distinguish highly confidential information from low-level (but still confidential) information. Such a distinction may be valid, but it is not always clear in a judgment *how* the court is applying the term 'trade secret'. Equally, many of the older authorities are often cited to authenticate the 'high-level/low-level' classification, when these decisions stand for no such thing. As we have noted, the classifications are unimportant during the currency of the contract; but on termination they may become critical.

1.2.2 What is expected of the employer?

An employer can exercise a great degree of control in this area. Reliance on the implied terms is probably safe in most situations during employment, though it will not guarantee safety (where, for example, security is lax). So even during the currency of the employment relationship an employer is well-advised:

(a) To ensure that employees are informed of their duty in respect of confidential information.

(b) To ensure that any changes in company policy, or changes in responsibility or status of the individual, or changes in access to information, are made clear to the employee.

(c) To restrict access to information which the employer believes is confidential.

(d) To detail in writing any information which might or might not normally be classified as confidential in that industry but which the employer has special reason to regard as such. Any classification should not be too restrictive; a detailed and closed list might be deemed to exclude other information.

The ILU survey revealed an extensive use of express terms to bring the duty of confidentiality to the attention of the employee. A number of companies stated that it was policy to reissue these terms, for emphasis if nothing else, whenever an employee changed duties or status. We have no evidence regarding levels of security employed, but some companies did issue a detailed explanation of what was meant by 'confidential information'; in each case the list was declared as not being exhaustive as a definition. For instance:

> *any manufacturing process, formula, design, program, calculation, method, specification or any other trade secret of the Company . . . any other confidential information not comprising a trade secret but relating to the business of the Company . . . including but not limited to their plans, procedures, products, equipment, sales, prices, contractual terms and trade connections.*

And

> *information of a confidential or secret nature . . . which may be made known to me by the Company or any customer or supplier of the Company . . . or which may be learned by me during my employment, including, in particular, information which relates to: research and development, and technical programmes and operations; manufacturing formulae, processes and techniques; marketing and sales policies and plans; prices (including discounts, rebates and commissions) and costs; customers . . .*

1.2.3 Information in the public domain

Once information is in the public domain it is no longer confidential and so not protectable. This general statement is subject to a number of explanatory caveats. Megarry V-C was anxious to point out in *Thomas Marshall (Exports) Ltd v Guinle* [1979] Ch 227, for instance, that just because an item has been constructed from materials which themselves are in the public domain does not mean the preparatory information fails the confidentiality test, for the ingenuity in constructing the finished item may be the confidential information, not the final product *per se*. The fact that competitors or others might eventually ascertain how and why the information was used to produce an item, e.g., the basis for combining certain features, does not destroy confidentiality — at least in the meantime.

So, publication of material will not always have the effect of depriving the employer of protection. For instance, once a patent has been granted that document will have become public knowledge — although protected by the patent system. Employers may legitimately wish to impose a duty of confidentiality on matters not contained in the patent, e.g., on the manufacturing know-how which went into the invention and which cannot be included in the patent. And this applies to products which have not been patented too. For instance, in *Weir Pumps Ltd v CML Pumps Ltd* [1984] FSR 33 information had been supplied by Weir to the CEGB in the form of drawings and pumps. CML overhauled and repaired the pumps and thereby gained access to the drawings. CML then produced spare parts for the pumps. There were problems ascertaining copyright so that the question of protecting the confidentiality of the information became particularly important. It was held that the information supplied by Weir was still under protection. The publication of the drawings for a limited purpose did not destroy the confidentiality because the protection which was sought related to the combination of features.

Equally, where the information is in the public domain, in the sense that it could have been discovered by careful research through the literature, a person who has received the information without undertaking that research may still be restrained from using it (*Schering Chemicals Ltd v Falkman Ltd* [1982] QB 1). In *Speed Seal Products Ltd v Paddington* [1985] 1 WLR 1327 the Court of Appeal identified two aspects of disclosure which are of relevance here:

(a)   Where information is published by the confider, the confidant is released from his previous duty. Thus if the *full details* have indeed been published, e.g., regarding a process in a patent specification then *that* information ceases to be confidential (*O. Mustad and Son v Dosen* [1964] 1 WLR 109).

(b)   Publication by a stranger does not necessarily release the confidant (*Cranleigh Precision Engineering Ltd v Bryant* [1965] 1 WLR 1293), especially if there is any evidence of connivance between the confidant and the stranger.

The validity of this last point, however, was questioned by Lord Goff of

Chieveley in *Attorney-General* v *Guardian Newspapers Ltd* [1990] 1 AC 109. His lordship tended to the view that *Cranleigh Precision Engineering Ltd* v *Bryant* was really founded on the 'springboard doctrine' (see below) and was not good law on the disclosure point: that once a secret had been published it ceased to be a secret. It would be unsound, therefore, to assume that protection might continue to operate in these circumstances.

Clearly, if one is set to argue that the information is still deserving of protection (despite some form of publication) then that specific 'secret', its unique attributes, must be capable of being precisely identified. It will not be enough simply to assert that the method of construction is different or something which the business does not want revealed.

During the currency of the contract, therefore, an employee will not be free to disclose information even if it has entered the public domain, provided there is still an element of confidentiality attached to the processes behind the product or service. The confidentiality might, for instance, be founded on the reason why certain microchips were rejected rather than why one was chosen. But the duty of fidelity is so fundamental to the employment relationship that it is not understating the position to say that the employee will be bound by practically any confidence *during* the operation of the contract.

1.2.4 The springboard doctrine

The term 'springboard' arose in *Terrapin Ltd* v *Builders' Supply Co. (Hayes) Ltd* [1967] RPC 375 where Roxburgh J stated, at p. 391, that:

> . . . a person who has obtained information in confidence is not allowed to use it as a springboard for activities detrimental to the person who made the confidential communication, and springboard it remains even when all the features have been published or can be ascertained by actual inspection by any member of the public . . . I think it is broadly true to say that a member of the public to whom the confidential information had not been imparted would still have to prepare plans and specifications . . . Therefore, the possessor of the confidential information still has a long start over any member of the public. The design may be as important as the features.

The springboard doctrine is used by the courts in two ways. The first context in which the term appears is where an individual is making use of information which he or she has 'taken' from the former employer (*Roger Bullivant Ltd* v *Ellis* [1987] ICR 464). Here the Court of Appeal had to deal with a managing director who, despite the presence of a restraint of trade clause, resigned his employment and launched a competing business. He took with him various documents containing technical and commercial information including trade secrets and a card index of customers.

There is no doubt about the secrecy of the information in such instances, and the fact that the lists *could* have been compiled legitimately from other sources is irrelevant. The aim of the courts is to prevent the abuse of the confidence as against the employer. In this sense the courts use the term to denote the length that any injunction should last — which will be until the employee has ceased to gain any advantage from the information. As Nourse LJ commented (at p.477G): 'the injunction should not normally extend beyond the period for which the unfair advantage may reasonably be expected to continue'. On the facts of this case that time period was judged according to the length of time stated in the restraint clause. As Sir Donald Nicholls V-C pointed out recently in *Universal Thermosensors Ltd* v *Hibben* [1992] 3 All ER 257, dishonest copying of information does not ipso facto mean that the court will impose restrictions but a defendant will have 'a difficult row to hoe'.

Frequently in the ILU survey we came across clauses which not only made no attempt to provide a time-limit in relation to the information but which positively stated that the obligation of confidentiality would last for ever. This prompts a degree of suspicion that the restriction relates more to the prevention of competition *per se* and not to the protection of information. The unlimited time span would probably be justified in relation to some trade secrets, but otherwise there must be an element of doubt about the efficacy of these terms.

The second context in which the term 'springboard' appears is when the information has entered the public domain but the background knowledge of the product or process gives the employee an advantage or head start over those who also have access to that publicised information. In this instance the information is really a mixture of public and secret material and the advantage lies in relation to both the general market and the former employer. Obviously the court is mainly interested in protecting the employer's position, but in effect such injunctions also benefit the wider market by preventing the introduction of a very well-informed extra competitor — a person who fully understands the hidden depths of the information. The employee will not be allowed to take advantage of such an edge to take the appropriate short cuts in development of the product. In *Cranleigh Precision Engineering Ltd* v *Bryant* [1965] 1 WLR 1293 the defendant was the managing director of Cranleigh Precision. He invented an above-ground swimming-pool which was not eventually patented by his employer. Some years later he came across another similar Swiss patent. He did not inform his employer of this and sought to exploit this for his own benefit. He then left Cranleigh after forming his own company. He was found to have acted in breach of contract and an injunction was granted to prevent use of this patent *in conjunction with* the (unpublished) information belonging to his former employer.

In *Potters-Ballotini Ltd* v *Weston-Baker* [1977] RPC 202 some constraint was placed on the longevity of the springboard. Whilst still in employment a group of employees formed a company designed to compete with the employer once it was established. As regards the duration of the springboard the Court of Appeal (in a self-acknowledged cursory exploration of the topic) stated that once the advantage had disappeared the employee would no longer be bound by any relevant confidences. That period will vary with the nature of the information (its life span, and how long some form of reverse engineering would take to reveal the secrets) and the nature of the market itself — the more active the level of research in the market the greater chance that the springboard will be short-lived.

The usefulness of this alternative springboard doctrine seems now to have been affirmed by the Court of Appeal in *PSM International plc & McKenzie plc* v *Whitehouse & Willenhall Automation Ltd* [1992] IRLR 279. A managing director, during his notice period, established his own rival company in breach of express confidentiality and restraint clauses. An injunction was granted on the basis of the need to protect the confidentiality of the information and the breach of the express terms. The springboard doctrine was not specifically relied upon by the company, but Lloyd and Neill LJJ gave tacit approval to its efficacy (see also 1.4.2). A further point of interest here is that the court was prepared to issue an injunction which affected both future and *existing* contractual arrangements.

There is still some doubt in this area about the exact scope of the springboard doctrine and even Megarry J noted in *Coco* v *A.N. Clark (Engineers) Ltd* [1969] RPC 41, that the idea of 'springboard' was actually very difficult to apply in practice. But as a general point it serves to enforce the sanctity of the duty of confidentiality, even where the owner of the information has placed *some* of the relevant information in the public domain.

It was common practice in the ILU survey to state that information which entered the public domain would cease to be regarded as confidential *provided* the release was at the instigation of the employer and/or that it did not emanate from the employee.

1.2.5 The maintenance of secrecy must not offend the public interest

'There is no confidence as to the disclosure of iniquity': unequivocal words from Sir William Page Wood V-C in *Gartside* v *Outram* (1857) 26 LJ Ch 113 at p. 114. Public interest is therefore a limiting factor in the duty of confidence. It is a balancing exercise and only if the court is sure that it is in the public interest that the information should be disclosed will the courts allow this to occur. 'Whistle-blowers' are welcomed with a degree of caution.

Where there is some wrongdoing, an employee who discloses this will consequently not be acting in breach of confidence (*Lion Laboratories Ltd* v *Evans* [1985] QB 526). The disclosure should be to the appropriate bodies rather than to the world at large and there must be some substance to any allegations made. The classic case in this area is *Initial Services Ltd* v *Putterill* [1968] 1 QB 396 where an ex-employee disclosed to a newspaper agreements which were illegal as being restrictive trade practices. The disclosure was held not to be a breach of confidence. In most cases, however, newspapers are not the appropriate body; one would instead look to the police, regulatory or professional bodies or even royal commissions.

The defence of public interest may apply to all types of information and many different activities. Criminal behaviour on the part of the employer is not a prerequisite. Health and safety matters which are hazardous or endanger the public, the practices of religious sects, the activities of local authorities or other such organisations, tax evasion schemes and conduct which misleads the public are all capable of falling under this exception to the sanctity of confidentiality. However, mere incompetence or even negligence in an organisation (especially if there is no continuing danger) will not *per se* meet the criteria for public interest disclosure; nor will the public interest extend to revealing secrets which might be beneficial to the community as a whole, but which have been suppressed for commercial reasons, e.g., the apocryphal everlasting lightbulb. The most recent example of this area in operation came in *Re a Company's Application* [1989] Ch 477 where a former senior employee sought to disclose information to the Financial Intermediaries, Managers and Brokers Regulatory Authority (FIMBRA). Scott J allowed the disclosure. FIMBRA was an appropriate body for such disclosures, even if the employee was motivated by malice.

1.3 THE DUTY OWED BY EMPLOYEES

Founded on express and implied terms, the identification of the employee's duties is a straightforward exercise. The case law provides well-trodden paths regarding disclosure of information and the quality of the information which may gain protection. Closely linked with the duty of confidentiality are the rules covering the soliciting of clients and customers. Again, reasonably clear guidelines can be offered as to employees working for rival firms or generally moonlighting, during or after the relationship. We will deal with these anti-competition aspects in the next chapter (2.5). For the moment we can say that an employee will be forbidden from competing with the employer during the currency of the contract.

What follows is therefore an examination of what is expected of the employee as regards the use of information. How is the employee's duty formulated? We shall explore the following:

    (a)   What information is protected.
    (b)   The role of honesty.
    (c)   The extent to which the duty alters with the employee's status.
    (d)   The extent to which the duty requires positive action on the part of the employee.
    (e)   The duty to disclose details about oneself and others.

1.3.1 What information is protected

The general extent of this topic has been discussed above. One question which was left unanswered, however was: Can trivia be the subject of a duty of confidentiality? One would think not; though defining trivia might prove difficult. It has been said that what has been called 'trivial tittle-tattle' is unprotectable. So the fact that the company mouser is a tabby called Henry is hardly deserving of protection. Or, to borrow a phrase from Scott J regarding

MI5's secrets in *Attorney-General* v *Guardian Newspapers Ltd* [1990] 1 AC 109:

> Could the duty of non-disclosure be thought to apply to the contents of the daily menu in MI5's London offices? . . . It is obvious that, as a general proposition, a duty of confidence will not be imposed so as to protect useless information.

This does not mean that information must be complex in order to attract protection. As was noted in *Coco* v *A.N. Clark (Engineers) Ltd* [1969] RPC 41, the simpler the idea the more likely it is to require protection. In the same case, however, Megarry J also noted that 'equity ought not to be invoked to protect trivial tittle-tattle, however confidential'. This latter view received tacit approval in *Church of Scientology of California* v *Kaufman* [1973] RPC 635 regarding the publication of material by a former student of the sect when Goff J refused to give protection to material which he termed 'absurd' (and note the same point made again some years later in *Attorney-General* v *Guardian Newspapers Ltd* by Lord Goff: 'The duty of confidence applies neither to useless information, nor to trivia' — Lord Griffith was of the same opinion).

Unfortunately, the assessment of 'trivia', like one's grasp of 'general knowledge' in quiz programmes, or one's evaluation of whether a belief is merely a delusion, is apt to be influenced by subjectivity. In different contexts information may be trivial or important. What biscuits the chairman has with tea strikes a chord of irrelevancy — unless the information reveals that the company produces biscuits and these are either 'test' biscuits or biscuits from another manufacturer. And when pieces of information are put together the sum might be greatly more significant than the parts. Or to borrow a phrase from the cases, the individual pieces of the jigsaw might now reveal a discernible picture.

The discussions in all courts in *Attorney-General* v *Guardian Newspapers Ltd* concerning trivia appear to have been *obiter*. It is therefore still unclear whether trivia can be protected, even if it can be defined. The safest presumption to make is that any item of information which does not relate directly to the interests of the business is unprotected. If there is doubt, then company documentation which seeks to define more precisely what is confidential is an advisable precaution. During the currency of the contract, however, any doubt is likely to be decided in favour of the employer.

1.3.2 The role of honesty

As seen in the introduction, an employee is expected to act with honesty (*Sinclair* v *Neighbour* [1967] 2 QB 279). With regard to confidentiality the most obvious example of this is that the employee will not be permitted to copy or memorise confidential documents for use after the contract ends (*Robb* v *Green* [1895] 2 QB 315). A number of companies in the ILU survey included such a duty as a specific term of contract, usually accompanied by a 'delivery-up' term along the lines of:

> *Immediately upon ceasing to be employed by the Company the employee shall deliver to the Company all books, records, computer software, memoranda, lists and other documents relating to the business of the Company.*

It has also been held that liability will exist even though the reason for the disclosure is not founded on financial gain or malice (*British Steel Corp. v Granada Television Ltd* [1981] AC 1096). Oddly enough it is less clear whether a duty of confidentiality is placed upon a person who obtains information by reprehensible means and then seeks to make use of it. The field ranges from obtaining stolen documents, temporary borrowing and unauthorised reading, through to acquisition of information not contained in any document, e.g., by eavesdropping or deceit. The Law Commission gave this matter consideration in its report and, despite an earlier Court of Appeal observation that there might be a duty in such cases, the Law Commission reluctantly concluded that information gained in this manner was probably not impressed with an obligation of confidence simply by reason of its means of acquisition. It has since been argued forcefully by commentators that this may reflect the case law but is unlikely to be followed.

We would argue that the acquisition of information by reprehensible means on the part of an employee does convey a duty of confidentiality. The foundation of the duty in equity should demand this; equally, if an employee can be prevented from working for competitors because of the *possibility* of a breach of the duty of confidentiality (as in *Hivac Ltd* v *Park Royal Scientific Instruments Ltd* [1946] Ch 169) all the more should the dishonest employee be caught and the information protected. Copying and deliberately memorising lists (see *Roger Bullivant Ltd* v *Ellis* [1973] ICR 535) have been held to be actions which put the employee under a restraint in the utilisation of that information. In the area of unfair dismissal cases such as *Denco Ltd* v *Joinson* [1991] ICR 172 have shown the importance that the courts place on the gaining of access to confidential information. The employee was a trade union shop steward who gained access to computer files using another employee's identity code and password. The employee claimed this was an accidental, isolated incident. The information would have been of use to the trade union in negotiations. This was found to constitute gross misconduct, analogous to dishonesty. The EAT held that it was irrelevant that the employers had not proved that the purpose of access was for illegitimate reasons.

Thus the method of the acquisition should not be the determining aspect, other than in cases where the employer's negligence promotes casualness and makes nonsense of the tag of secrecy. However, as a precautionary measure, it is suggested that any express term should specifically include a phrase to impose a duty of confidentiality on employees who receive information from whatever source and by whatever means. Specific reference should be made to this in disciplinary procedures. And, following statements by the EAT in

Denco Ltd v *Joinson*, there should be clear indications placed in areas of restricted access or alongside computers to the same effect.

The question of criminal liability for 'hacking' and 'eavesdropping' is now covered by the Computer Misuse Act 1990.

1.3.2.1 To what extent is the employee's 'pure heart' a defence to the charge of breach of confidence?

If honesty is a requirement placed upon the employee we need to ask whether it may also be a defence to charges of breach following disclosure. If the employee acts with a 'pure heart but empty head', is this still a breach and can the employer prevent further use of that information?

Even if an employee's negligent disclosure of information were not to stand as a breach of the duty of confidence it is difficult to envisage an employee escaping liability under the duty of care principles. Such negligent actions could lead to the employee's dismissal. There appear to be no cases dealing with employees *losing* vital bits of information; but the Law Commission (1981, para. 4.14) touched upon such possibilities and concluded:

> Where the parties are in a contractual relationship, there is no doubt that the confidant is in breach of his contractual obligations if the information is disclosed as a result of his failure to take reasonable care of it.

From the tenor of the argument it seems most likely that the reference to 'contractual obligations' related to the implied duty to take reasonable care of the employer's property, and not the duty of confidentiality. By focusing on reasonableness, considerations of honesty are removed; the honest fool is not protected. As in the unfair dismissal concept of misconduct, when the analysis rests on care or conduct the employee's *mens rea* is irrelevant. What we cannot be sure of, however, is whether honesty is pertinent to discussions on the contractual duty of confidentiality, and assuming it is, whether, like the duty of care, the standard to be expected turns on the status of the employee in the organisation. This is particularly relevant to the next section.

Whether third parties could benefit from the information is both more important and more debatable (see 1.6).

1.3.2.2 Disclosure or use may have occurred because the employee was aware of his actions, but unaware that the information was confidential

We can start with the proposition that very little judicial sympathy is given to a recipient of confidential information who has become aware of the nature of the information. The case law has generally focused on third-party recipients, but similar principles would most likely apply to employees. The cases regarding third parties show that liability tends to be strict, once the duty of confidence has been proved. Treating the range of confidential relationships alike, therefore, it is probable that the employee's honesty is again deemed irrelevant.

Such a conclusion may, however, be drawn too hastily. The more extreme the employer's casualness in protecting his information or failing to notify the employee of its nature, the more easily it can be argued that he is less deserving of, and is indeed deprived of, protection. The employee's honesty is brought into play via the employer's inadequacies. Thus an employer's failure to warn employees of the importance of the information may prove fatal to the employer's case, at least as regards junior employees. Equally, a failure to protect the information adequately and so allow easy access to it may defeat the employer's claims of confidentiality.

The supporting case authority, however, must be viewed with some degree of caution as it concerns duties relating to employees having left employment. The pervading duty of fidelity might well alter the analysis during employment. To counter this Jones has argued (1970, p. 463) that one of the most influential cases on the application of strict liability was incorrectly argued, viz. *Seager v Copydex Ltd* [1967] 1 WLR 923 where it was held that once a confidential relationship had been established liability followed even from unconscious use of the material. Jones argues that the belief of the parties should not have been treated as irrelevant, but should have been judged against standards of reasonableness. He finds support for this in the judgment of Megarry J in *Coco v A.N. Clark (Engineers) Ltd* [1969] RPC 41.

Further, in *Faccenda Chicken Ltd v Fowler* [1987] Ch 117 it was noted that one of the distinguishing marks showing whether items of information might fall to be protected by the courts was the degree of attention paid to the employer's attitude to the secrecy of the information. Those actions and the seniority of the employee's position were to be vital elements in the assessment.

Thus if the definition and classification of confidential information can rest on such tests, so too the employer's actions must be relevant in determining breach of the duty. The 'pure heart and empty head' employee does not gain exemption because of his stupidity *per se*; rather, the general circumstances excuse this lack of thought. There is still room for constructive knowledge to be argued successfully, notably where the employee's status is sufficiently senior that he or she is deemed to have understood the full ramifications for the business.

1.3.3 The extent to which the duty alters with the employee's status

If confidence is simply a parasite of fiduciary notions then the formulation of the duty takes on strict, if not absolute, characteristics. Moreover it becomes vital to inquire whether the duties of confidence are thereby confined to employees acting in a fiduciary capacity, or extend to employees at large. We will deal with fiduciary responsibilities below (see 1.4.4).

Senior employees are sometimes classed as being in a fiduciary position and so subject to very strict restraints on their activities; though no judge or writer makes any attempt to define 'senior' or its euphemisms. But what of junior employees (equally undefined, but for present purposes presumed to be those below director or senior management status)? First, are they subject to the duty of confidentiality; and if so, is that duty either similar to or part of fiduciary notions? For generally one might assume that the more an employee is placed under the roof of 'fiduciary' the more diffuse his obligations to the enterprise become, and the more he takes on the mantle of positive duties of disclosure of information etc. The corollary is, of course, that if 'low trust' employees are exempt from such strict obligations the duty of confidentiality becomes something of a mere shell.

One major difficulty in this area is that 'the employee's duty of good faith' and 'fiduciary' are terms which are used interchangeably. Thus when the phrase 'good faith' is found in reference to an agent or 'low-trust' employee one can never be too sure of its boundaries. Though there is a deal of overlap they are not the same concept; if only as regards the element of honesty required in most definitions of good faith. However, in this area in particular, the judges do not seem to wish to differentiate. A practical difficulty also arises in that there are few examples to be found of employees who fall outside the limited 'fiduciary' classification disclosing vital information to others. Their lack of opportunity may account for this. Regarding confidential information and the affected class of employee, Gurry states (1984, p. 180):

> There are a number of general statements in the cases which suggest that the existence of the employment relationship suffices to establish that information has been imparted in confidence and that every employee will, therefore, be bound by an obligation of good faith.

Such a sweeping statement is perhaps too strongly put in the light of the authorities; though Gurry's arguments are often linked to fidelity and loyalty points. In *Bents Brewery Ltd* v *Hogan* [1945] 2 All ER 570, for instance, a divisional manager circulated a questionnaire on pay and conditions to other managers on behalf of his trade union. This was held to be a breach of his duty of fidelity. One will find comments in the case about the duties of 'an employee' but the tenor of the decision is one related to position, status and the potential fiduciary position of a manager. Perhaps this is all one might expect from the cases. After all, if strangers to a relationship can be caught by obligations of confidentiality, *a fortiori* employees must be similarly affected.

What is not so easy to discern is that if all employees owe a duty of confidentiality, how can that standard alter according to status? How can one keep something more, or less, secret because of one's position? Clearly this is impossible. The only differences can be: first, that senior employees have access as of right to more confidential information; secondly, that junior employees might be able to avail themselves more easily of the 'pure heart and empty head' defence noted above. Thirdly, though the duty not to disclose or make use of information might be the same for all employees, senior employees may have an additional duty to *surrender* information acquired by them as employees.

1.3.4 To what extent the duty requires positive action on the part of the employee

An employee acquiring information from a source outside employment is obviously not breaching the employer's confidence when use is made of it; arguably the employee is breaching the general duty of *fidelity* if the information would be valuable to the employer. As regards confidentiality *simpliciter* there have been cases where a positive duty to surrender information has been postulated for those in fiduciary positions. For example, in *Sanders* v *Parry* [1967] 1 WLR 753 an assistant solicitor acquired information regarding a level of dissatisfaction amongst the firm's clients and was held to be under a duty to disclose this to the employer; and *Industrial Development Consultants Ltd* v *Cooley* [1972] 1 WLR 443 is along the same lines, with the employee setting up in business to deal with a company with whom the former employer had failed to obtain a contract.

More interestingly, in *General Nutritions Ltd* v *Yates* (1981) *The Times*, 5 June 1981, an employee who was not in any fiduciary position, but in a position of 'trust', was held accountable for breach of confidence. She was employed as a general manager, her duties being to service customer accounts. She added names to the company index which she had acquired from other sources unconnected with her employer. Following her dismissal she attempted to impart this additional information to her husband for his business purposes, thereby causing loss to her former company. An injunction was granted to restrain the use of the information.

There is thus clear authority for the proposition that an employee (at least a senior employee) owes not only a duty *not to disclose* the employer's confidential information, but also a positive duty to surrender information relevant to the relationship.

A handful of companies in the ILU survey sought to impose such positive duties as an express term of the contract. The most clearly stated ran:

> *I will promptly disclose to the Company any and all inventions, discoveries, improvements, trade secrets, processes, techniques and know-how whether or not patentable, made or conceived or first reduced to practice or learned by me, either alone or jointly with others, during the period of my employment with the Company, whether or not in the course of my employment.*

We would have grave doubts about the application of such a term to junior employees or employees whose jobs are unrelated to research. Those misgivings would relate particularly to: (a) the width of the clause as taking into account matters alien to the relationship; and (b) even in connection with creative and inventive employees, the extent to which the clause seeks to override s. 39 Patents Act 1977. We will discuss this latter point more fully in chapter 3.

1.3.5 The duty to disclose details about oneself and others

We can start with the basic premise that there is no obligation to incriminate oneself. In employment law this becomes: once having committed a breach of contract it is not a further breach to fail to volunteer this fact to the employer. In the absence of fraud, such as employees' deceit in response to direct questions, there is no duty to volunteer information regarding misdemeanours (*Bell* v *Lever Brothers Ltd* [1932] AC 161). A short time after this case, however, a general manager was faced with the misconduct of an employee (who was also the managing director) which had a detrimental effect on the business. It was held that the general manager was under a duty to notify the employer of such breaches (*Swain* v *West (Butchers) Ltd* [1936] 3 All ER 261). When these two principles were combined in the case of *Sybron Corporation* v *Rochem Ltd* [1984] Ch 112, the finding was that there is a duty, at least incumbent on senior management whose responsibilities are affected by the actions, to notify the employer of serious breaches by fellow employees even when that involves self-incrimination. Here an employee (a 'zone controller') failed to report the misdeeds of his subordinates. Any report would have implicated the employee. Nevertheless, the lack of disclosure was held to be in breach of contract.

We have noted the limited effects of the Rehabilitation of Offenders Act 1974 regarding statements of 'spent' convictions in the introduction and we will return to the questions regarding an employee's declarations as to health in chapter 6.

Any disclosure of information during the currency of the contract is likely to amount to a breach of contract; a serious one if the effect is potentially or actually to cause harm to the enterprise. In either case disciplinary actions may be taken by the employer. Further, an employee who commits a serious breach of contract may be lawfully dismissed with or without notice and any dismissal will be for the fair reason of misconduct (whether this is fair depends upon the circumstances, especially the procedure involved). Realistically, however, these responses strike at the symptom and not the cause. What the employer requires is the prevention of use or disclosure of the information and to recover any lost profit. The remedies available will therefore include:

(a) Suing the employee for damages or for an account of profits.

(b) Seeking permanent and interlocutory injunctions to prevent use or disclosure of the information. An injunction will only be granted where the court considers that the award of damages would not be an adequate remedy.

(c) Obtaining an *Anton Piller* order. This order is somewhat Draconian in its effect and execution and will therefore not be granted lightly. The court will have to be convinced that the defendant is unlikely to obey any court order.

(d) Requesting delivery up and/or destruction of documents.

1.4 THE DUTY OWED BY FORMER EMPLOYEES

Most disclosures or use of information are likely to occur once the employee has left the company. It is here that the real battle lines are drawn.

The courts are wary of imposing the same level of duty on former employees as is placed on existing employees. Partly this is because once the employee has left then any restraint on the exercise of that person's skill, expertise, technical competence or general ability to earn a living has to be treated with great caution. That caution surfaces particularly in the doctrine of restraint of trade, which is the subject of the next chapter.

Courts will therefore examine the character of the information for which protection is sought, the level of security utilised by the employer, and how identifiable that information is when set against the general mass of information in a company (or indeed, when set against the employee's own skill and knowledge). In establishing whether information is capable of being protected the same rules seen in *Thomas Marshall (Exports) Ltd* v *Guinle* [1979] Ch 227 apply here as during the subsistence of the contract.

1.4.1 The decision in *Faccenda Chicken Ltd* v *Fowler* [1987] Ch 117

No discussion these days can be made of this area without reference to this case. Both Goulding J, in the High Court, and then the Court of Appeal took the opportunity to restate the ambit of former employees' liabilities regarding confidential information. The decision of the Court of Appeal, and particularly that of Neill LJ, has been the subject of debate since that time. We have reservations concerning the decision which we detail below.

1.4.1.1 The case
Fowler was employed as a sales manager for the company. He established a system of selling fresh chickens from refrigerated vans. Subsequently, he resigned and set up a similar business in competition with Faccenda Chicken, taking a number of Faccenda's employees with him. It was alleged that Fowler and the others had used and disclosed sales information, derived from Faccenda's operations, in their new business. The information related to routes taken to supply customers, their addresses, delivery times and pricing policy. The company sought an injunction to prevent the disclosure of this information. In the High Court Goulding J identified *three* classes of information:

(a)   Information which is of a trivial character or is easily accessible from public sources.

(b)   Information which the employee must treat as confidential during the currency of the contract but which becomes part of the employee's skill and knowledge.

(c)   Specific trade secrets.

The first category Goulding J deemed unprotectable; the second, protectable only by an express stipulation in the contract 'restraining the servant from competing with [the employer] . . . after the termination of employment'; the third was automatically protected even though the relationship has ended. The sales information in *Faccenda* fell into the second category and, as there was no restraint of trade clause, could not be protected. The specific weakness in this classification lies in assimilating ordinary confidential information with skill and knowledge; and assuming that both could be protected by an express term.

The Court of Appeal came to different conclusions. Having described the duty expected of an employee whilst employed as being based on good faith or fidelity, Neill LJ then explained the position regarding post-employment duties. First he established that the obligations owed by an employee are subject to the rules of contract and not those of equity. Secondly, he stated that:

> The implied term which imposes an obligation on the employee as to his conduct after the determination of the employment is more restricted in its scope than that which imposes a general duty of good faith. It is clear that the obligation not to use or disclose information may cover secret processes of manufacture such as chemical formulae (*Amber Size and Chemical Co. Ltd* v *Menzel* [1913] 2 Ch 239), or designs or special methods of construction (*Reid and Sigrist Ltd* v *Moss* (1923) 49 RPC 461), and other information which is of a sufficiently high degree of confidentiality as to amount to a trade secret. The obligation does not extend, however, to cover all information which is given to or acquired by the employee while in his employment, and in particular may not cover information which is only 'confidential' in the sense that an unauthorised disclosure of such information to a third party while the employment subsisted would be a clear breach of the duty of good faith.

Consequently the court decided that the information in question did not amount to a trade secret and was therefore not protected once employment had ended.

We have cited this at length because of its impact on both the protection of information and on the efficacy of confidentiality clauses in employment contracts. If confidentiality matters to a company at all, it is often the level of protection which an employer can attain *once the relationship has ended* that is of vital importance to the organisation. We would also respectfully seek to disagree with the analysis offered by the Court of Appeal in *Faccenda Chicken Ltd* v *Fowler*.

The effect of the *Faccenda* decision has been that whilst trade secrets or the equivalent of trade secrets gain the continuing and automatic protection of the courts once the contract has ended, nothing else survives the termination of the contract; and this is so even if an express clause seeks to restrict the employee's use or disclosure of the information. Our disagreement is as follows:

(a)   This approach is not a natural application of previous authorities; it is a departure from those precedents. The exclusion of express terms as a safeguarding device for information which cannot be classed as a trade secret is both novel (which may not be a bad thing) and provides a licence to employees to exploit their former employer's confidences.

(b)   There appears to be a confusion as to the distinction to be drawn between 'trade secrets', 'confidential information' and 'know-how' which would cast doubt on the decision. As Rideout has commented (1986, p. 183): 'The fact that [the Court of Appeal] finds itself [drawing a distinction between trade secrets and confidential information] for the first time in 150 years of the existence of the contractual duty of fidelity might suggest to the suspicious that this has not been the line of distinction recognised hitherto'.

(c) The analysis of the overlap with restraint of trade clauses is not adequately explored; indeed, there is a lack of recognition of the functions that different restrictive covenants perform.

1.4.1.2 The use of precedents and the relevance of express and implied terms

Neill LJ cited in aid of this interpretation two principal cases: *Printers and Finishers Ltd* v *Holloway* [1965] 1 WLR 1 and *E. Worsley and Co. Ltd* v *Cooper* [1939] 1 All ER 290. These are referred to as authority for the proposition that express terms which seek to restrict use and disclosure of the information have no effect following termination. But in *Printers and Finishers Ltd* v *Holloway* Cross J never took this line. On the contrary, Cross J made the point that an employee can be prevented from using trade secrets 'even though he has entered into no express covenant with regard to the matter in hand'. Effectively this is simply reiterating the equitable duty.

There was no express covenant in *Printers and Finishers Ltd* v *Holloway*; this was the problem. The information (some printing instructions) was not classed by the court as a trade secret and therefore gained no protection. But later in the case Cross J stated that:

> the proper way for the plaintiffs to protect themselves would be by exacting covenants from their employees restricting their field of activity after they have left their employment . . .

This clearly envisaged that protection may be gained for information which is not a trade secret by means of an express covenant. Cross J, in using the term 'restrictive covenant', may have been talking about an express confidentiality clause or a restraint of trade clause (preventing the employee from working in that business for a set time). This is not clear; but what is clear is that *some* form of restriction was thought possible. Thus, with respect, Neill LJ's conclusion that an express term is of no avail does not logically follow.

E. Worsley and Co. Ltd v *Cooper* presents the same problems. This time the case centred on paper merchants. Again there was no express term. No warning was ever given to the employee that the source from which the paper came was to be regarded as confidential. Indeed the employee could not help but know the source; the employee had generated most of the information and carried it in his head. It was held that the information was not in the nature of a trade secret but information 'which a determined and persistent trade rival, with sufficient skill and knowledge of the paper business, could have ascertained at the cost of considerable inquiries of considerable length' so that the injunction was refused. A point touched upon, that price lists and sample books had also been taken, was not developed. Thus the distinction drawn is the old one we have touched on before (and we will address again below) of trade secrets as set against skill and knowledge.

Finally, if more technically, this aspect of *Faccenda* is *obiter dicta*. There was no express term relating to Fowler and the others, thus the whole question really centred on whether the information they used was a 'trade secret' which would be automatically protected by a continuing implied term.

1.4.1.3 The classification of 'trade secrets'.

We have noted in 1.2.1 that the term 'trade secret' has had more than one meaning in the past hundred years. Originally, the term 'trade secret' was used loosely to describe the demarcation between information which was confidential and an employee's general skill and knowledge. The antithesis of a trade secret was the employee's 'know-how'. Use of this 'know-how' could not be the subject of a restriction. That was the traditional distinction.

What the Court of Appeal did in *Faccenda Chicken Ltd v Fowler*, without any real explanation, was to distinguish highly confidential information from low-level (but still confidential) information. In post-termination cases the low-level information became relegated to the ranks of trivia and an employee's general skill and knowledge. With respect, this cannot be right. Indeed, a number of the older authorities were cited to enforce the 'high-level/low-level' classification, when these decisions stand for no such thing (e.g., *Herbert Morris Ltd v Saxelby*).

Returning to *Printers and Finishers Ltd v Holloway* [1965] 1 WLR 1, it is not clear whether Cross J classified the printing instructions given to the employee as low-level confidential information or something which had become a part of the employee's know-how. If Cross J meant that this information had become part of the employee's know-how, this reflects the old distinction between trade secrets and experience. It would not be surprising that the know-how was not protected. This is the most likely explanation.

If on the other hand the learned judge meant to draw a distinction between the various classes of information then this would give some force to Neill LJ's later classification. But it does not follow that supporting the classification also gives support to the proposition that express terms are *a fortiori* an irrelevancy. The origins of this idea stem from no other source than *Faccenda* itself.

1.4.1.4 The relationship with the doctrine of restraint of trade

We will deal extensively with restraint of trade clauses in chapter 2. For the moment we should say that a restraint clause is far more Draconian than any confidentiality restriction in that it seeks to limit the rights of employees to obtain employment elsewhere. An effective restraint clause will prevent an employee, for a specific length of time, usually within a defined geographical area, setting up in a competing business, working for another employer, or soliciting former trade connections once the employment relationship has come to an end. As will be seen, when faced with such a clause the courts will presume the restraint to be void unless, *inter alia*, it seeks to safeguard a *legitimate interest*. One such legitimate interest is the protection of confidential information.

It would seem peculiar, therefore, that Cross J in *Printers and Finishers Ltd v Holloway* [1965] 1 WLR 1 would think it permissible to have a restraint of trade clause based on the protection of confidentiality, but not allow a less Draconian express confidentiality clause to apply in the same way.

We will argue more extensively in chapter 2, therefore, that:

(a)   either an express confidentiality clause *can* protect information which is more than know-how but less than a trade secret; or

(b)   confidential information *cannot* be protected by any means whatsoever once the employment relationship has ended unless it amounts to a trade secret.

It also seems puzzling, as has been noted in more than one case since *Faccenda Chicken Ltd* v *Fowler*, that if the implied terms give automatic protection to 'trade secrets' (and nothing else can be protected) why should Cross J (in the passage cited above in 1.4.1.2 and expressly approved by Neill LJ in *Faccenda*) have advocated inserting an express clause at all? What would be the point of such a clause?

1.4.2 The case law since *Faccenda Chicken Ltd* v *Fowler*

Faccenda Chicken Ltd v *Fowler* has not been reviewed directly by the House of Lords. In *Attorney-General* v *Guardian Newspapers Ltd* [1990] 1 AC 109, their Lordships made reference to *Faccenda*, but not as regards these issues. Many other cases have dealt with the principles enunciated in *Faccenda* and an overall impression might be that there is tacit approval for the decision and its classification. This, however, is by no means clear, and the major practical point as to the efficacy of express restrictive covenants has not been tested.

Our review of the case law is somewhat condensed, but the following authorities reveal the general trend. We can begin with *Roger Bullivant Ltd* v *Ellis* [1987] ICR 464 which concerned the taking and copying of various documents containing technical and commercial information including trade secrets and a card index of customers. Nourse LJ (who was also a member of the Court of Appeal in *Faccenda*) stated (at p. 473E emphasis added):

> What is now clear [in reference to *Faccenda*], *at all events in cases where there is no express agreement between the parties*, is that confidential information whose misuse is actionable at the suit of the employer may fall into one of two distinct classes.

The 'two distinct classes' were: (a) trade secrets, and (b) confidential information which is protectable during the currency of the contract. His Lordship also spoke of the low-level information as being available for use 'if and only to the extent that it is inevitably carried away in the employee's head'. And on the facts the injunction was ultimately refused, not because protection was unavailable, but because the restraint clause had run its course already (one year) and that was held to be the logical life span of the information too.

The most direct attack on the *Faccenda* decision has come from Scott J in *Balston Ltd v Headline Filters Ltd* [1987] FSR 330. It is respectfully submitted that the analysis is very persuasive. Scott J's reservations concerning *Faccenda* were that Goulding J's second category of information covered both general skill and knowledge *and* confidential information which fell short of a 'trade secret'. Scott J said (at p. 347): 'I do not think the Court of Appeal can have intended to exclude all information in Goulding J's second category from possible protection by a restrictive covenant'. More importantly, he added that:

An express restrictive covenant would not be needed to protect third category trade secrets; the implied term would do that. Neill LJ must, therefore, in my view, have been contemplating the protection by an express restrictive covenant of confidential information in respect of which an obligation against use or disclosure after the determination of the employment could not be implied.

This would mean, as has also been suggested by Purvis and Turner (1989, p. 3), that there are in fact *four* categories of information:

(a) *Trade secrets*, which will gain automatic protection by the continuing effect of the implied term.
(b) *Confidential information*, falling short of such protection but which may be the subject of a reasonable restrictive covenant (either a confidentiality clause or restraint of trade clause).
(c) *Skill and knowledge*, which inevitably become part of the employee's experience and cannot be protected.
(d) *Trivia*, which, except in rare cases noted above on 1.3.1, cannot be protected.

In *Systems Reliability Holdings plc v Smith* [1990] IRLR 377 Harman J noted that the comments in *Faccenda* on the efficacy of express confidentiality clauses were in fact made *obiter*, and expressed both surprise that this should be taken as the law as well as stating a preference for the views expressed by Scott J in *Balston Ltd v Headline Filters Ltd*.

Other Court of Appeal cases have not commented specifically on this point, though there is a standard assumption that *Faccenda* has established the general position on confidential information. Instead they have concentrated on extending the boundaries of what is meant by 'trade secret'. The traditional scientific secrets in this category are being augmented by more commercial secrets.

The names and preferences of customers, for instance, are capable of being classed as so highly confidential that they amount to trade secrets — or at least attain the same level of protection (*Lansing Linde Ltd v Kerr* [1991] 1 WLR 251). In the same case Butler-Sloss LJ commented that the term 'trade secret' has to be 'interpreted in the wider context of highly confidential information of a non-technical or non-scientific nature'. More recently, in

PSM International plc v *Whitehouse* (1992) 1 WLR 279 the Court of Appeal noted two points of interest: first, as had been recognised by Cross J in *Printers and Finishers Ltd* v *Holloway* [1965] 1 WLR 1, there was a difference between the typical confidential information cases which involved using or disclosing information, and those of the 'copying and taking' variety (such as *Robb* v *Green* [1895] 2 QB 315 and *Roger Bullivant Ltd* v *Ellis* [1987] ICR 464) where the information in question is more in the nature of tangible property and could be protected under the springboard doctrine. It was suggested that the 'springboard doctrine' could be used as an alternative method of protecting information which did not qualify as a trade secret. Secondly, *PSM International plc* v *Whitehouse* was distinguishable from *Printers and Finishers Ltd* v *Holloway* because in *PSM* there was an express term of confidentiality.

The Court of Appeal has also confirmed that information which is carried away in the employee's head does not automatically belong to the employee (*Johnson and Bloy (Holdings) Ltd* v *Wolstenholme Rink plc* [1987] IRLR 499). An employee may have no difficulty in retaining knowledge of valuable research findings but that is more akin to memorising the information than the acquisition of ordinary skill and knowledge.

Finally, returning to the High Court, Mummery J in *Ixora Trading Inc.* v *Jones* [1990] FSR 251 at first appeared to follow the *Faccenda* attitude towards express terms, but cited in support cases where the definition of trade secret was given in contrast only to 'employees' skill and knowledge'. The position taken by Mummery J is not clear because he quoted extensively from Scott J's decision in *Balston Ltd* v *Headline Filters Ltd* and only refused to give force to the express covenant on the grounds that it was drafted too widely in relation to the particular information.

The thrust of these cases, therefore, is that the principles enunciated in *Faccenda* regarding the efficacy of express terms have not been fully tested by either the Court of Appeal or the House of Lords. What *Faccenda* has achieved is that the inquiry into what constitutes a 'trade secret' and how accurately or convincingly the employer has identified the confidential information in need of protection has been given new life.

1.4.3 Excursus

For obvious reasons we have concentrated on the *Faccenda* decision in this analysis. An interesting contrast can now be drawn between Gurry's words of 1984, that 'It is trite law that the courts will enforce an express obligation of confidence, whether written or oral . . . . The exercise of the express contractual jurisdiction usually presents few problems' with the *Faccenda* decision made only one year later. Gurry's words related as much to former employees as to those in service (1984, pp. 28 and 60).

That aside, there is one recent decision of the Court of Appeal we have not yet addressed: *Attorney-General* v *Barker* [1990] 3 All ER 257. Barker had been an employee in the royal household. His contract contained an express undertaking not to 'disclose, publish or reveal . . . any incident, conversation or information concerning any member of the royal family or any guest or visitor . . . or any incident, conversation or information relating to [his] employment in royal service' either during or after his period of employment. Barker later set up a company and sought to publish a book concerning his employment experiences. An injunction had previously been granted against Barker covering the United Kingdom and worldwide activities; the injunction against the company related only to the UK. The case centred on Barker's attempt to have the personal worldwide ban lifted and the Attorney-General's cross-appeal to have the worldwide ban applied to the company. Barker failed and the Attorney-General succeeded.

The case is puzzling because it was decided on purely contractual grounds. Nourse LJ, for instance, stated that the case was governed by 'well-settled principles of contract law and practice which are not at all affected by any recent developments in regard to implied obligations of confidentiality'. Lord Donaldson MR said, 'It is a simple case of someone who has entered into a negative covenant for a consideration where the covenant is not limited territorially and is not limited in time'. No mention was therefore made of *Faccenda*.

The case may be peculiar to its facts. It has received no comment, it has not been analysed in any other case, nor has it been reported elsewhere. Equally it may signal an alternative approach to the protection of information, viz., that if the pleading is limited to breach of an express contractual term rather than breach of confidence the courts will review it in that light alone. We can only await the outcome of this.

1.4.4 Fiduciary duties

Directors stand in a fiduciary position and, as we noted earlier, senior employees are sometimes said to do so too. 'Senior employee' has not, however, been defined; it probably is impossible to do so accurately. The label of 'fiduciary' carries with it expectations of higher standards of conduct, or at least accountability.

The label of 'fiduciary' can affect the general duties owed by employees as regards furthering the employer's interests, disclosing misdeeds or as regards the imposition of positive duties, but as regards the duty of confidentiality such a label has traditionally made no real difference. The information, for instance, must still be confidential to attract protection. It is submitted, however, that if *Faccenda* is correct as regards the strength of express and implied terms after determination of the contract it is at least arguable that fiduciaries may not be treated in the same way as ordinary employees. Thus a fiduciary who profits from information received as a fiduciary may be liable as constructive trustee for the use or disclosure even if the information did not stand as a 'trade secret'.

1.4.5 The practical effects of *Faccenda Chicken Ltd* v *Fowler* and drafting strategies

1.4.5.1 Practical effects
The following table sets out the effects of the two approaches side by side for comparison. The left-hand column takes the assumption that *Faccenda*

is correct on all grounds. The right-hand column is based on the assumption that *Faccenda* is open to doubt and suggests an alternative interpretation. The suggestions we make in this 'alternative approach' do not in fact advocate any dangerous policy as regards drafting practice; indeed, and rather oddly, this second alternative, based as it is on the assumption that *Faccenda* is misleading, will probably prove to be the more cautious strategy to follow.

The Faccenda *approach*	*The alternative approach*
(a) During the employment relationship all information, with the probable exception of trivia, will be protected by the implied term of good faith.	(a) The same as point (a) opposite.
(b) After determination of the contract information falls into *two* classes: trade secrets (or their equivalent) and other information.	(b) After determination of the contract information falls into *four* classes: trade secrets (or their equivalent), confidential information, skill and knowledge; and trivia.
(c) Trade secrets, or other highly confidential information which amounts to a trade secret, will be protected automatically once the employment relationship has ended. The implied term of good faith witnessed during the currency of the contract, will continue with the same force.	(c) The same as point (c) opposite.
(d) No other confidential information will be protected once the relationship has ended. The presence of an express confidentiality clause in the contract which endeavours to obtain protection cannot alter this.	(d) Confidential information falling short of a trade secret but which is distinct from the employee's general skill and knowledge and trivia may be protected by a reasonable express clause.
(e) Where information has been taken, copied or deliberately memorised the distinction between trade secrets and other confidential information appears more hazy and seems to be treated in a special category because of the bad faith involved. Thus the breach during employment may be seen to have a *continuing effect* after determination and (usually by means of the springboard doctrine) the information will be protected.	(e) The same as point (e) opposite.

(f) An employee's skill and knowledge, or trivia, cannot be protected once the relationship has ended. The presence of an express confidentiality clause in the contract which endeavours to obtain protection for these forms of information cannot alter this.

(f) The same as point (f) opposite.

(g) Any restraint of trade covenant based on the legitimate interest of safeguarding confidential information will fail unless that information is a trade secret or its equivalent.

(g) Any restraint of trade covenant based on the legitimate interest of safeguarding confidential information will fail unless that information is either a trade secret (or its equivalent) or at least falls within the second level of confidential information noted in (b) above.

1.4.5.2 Drafting practice

There are a number of similarities displayed in the two columns. However, the *Faccenda* approach means that there is little or no point in inserting a clause in the contract which seeks to protect information once the relationship has ended. The implied term will protect trade secrets (or their equivalent) and nothing else can be covered. An express clause might achieve two things, however: first, it may help to determine whether particular information could be regarded by the courts as attaining the level of trade secrets; secondly, it may deter employees.

The alternative approach would mean that the inclusion of an express term would be vital if information falling short of the 'trade secret' category were to be protected. The clause would also serve as a warning to employees and may still aid the courts in determining whether protection is merited. The only possible drawback is that a badly drafted clause, or one worded too specifically and inadequately, might have defined the 'confidential information' too narrowly. The ILU survey revealed inconsistency in drafting practice here. Although many companies used confidentiality clauses, not all contracts sought to protect information once employment had ended. It may be pure coincidence that (of those which we were able to date) most contracts dated after the *Faccenda* decision did not contain a term relating to post-termination conduct, whilst the reverse was true for most pre-*Faccenda* contracts.

The key point as regards drafting practice, however, is that *even if the* Faccenda *approach is correct* there is a great deal to gain and very little to lose by inserting such a clause. For, if *Faccenda* is right the clause will be ignored. If *Faccenda* is wrong and the drafter has not inserted such a clause, protection will be lost for all but 'trade secrets'.

Whichever is the correct interpretation one problem remains: what is the difference between trade secrets and other information?

1.5 DISTINGUISHING TRADE SECRETS FROM OTHER INFORMATION

1.5.1 Defining trade secrets

In *Faccenda Chicken Ltd* v *Fowler* [1987] Ch 117 Neill LJ sought to identify what would make information a 'trade secret'. He listed the following points as a general guide:

(a) *The nature of the employment.* 'Thus employment in a capacity where "confidential" material is habitually handled may impose a high obligation of confidentiality because the employee can be expected to realise its sensitive nature to a greater extent than if he were employed in a capacity where such material reaches him only occasionally or incidentally.'

(b) *The nature of the information itself.* In addition, a limited circulation list for the information may indicate a higher level of secrecy.

(c) *Whether the employer impressed on the employee the confidentiality of the information.* This relates to warnings and security measures rather than mere labelling.

(d) *Whether the relevant information can be easily isolated from other information which the employee is free to use or disclose.*

The courts have obviously become wary of making the criteria too restrictive in deciding what information should be classed as a trade secret. It is undoubtedly fair that the automatic protection available should only be given to high-ranking information. But too stringent an entrance test will effectively mean that the secret is often already covered by copyright, design right or patent protection.

It is clear that the mere designation of information as either 'confidential' or as a 'trade secret' does not determine the matter; though in really borderline cases it may be persuasive. The information must have passed the basic test in *Thomas Marshall (Exports) Ltd* v *Guinle* [1979] Ch 227. As the classification we are dealing with is of a specific nature, the last element of the *Thomas Marshall* test (usage in the trade or industry) is particularly important.

In *Faccenda*, having stated the guidelines noted above, Neill LJ went on to say:

It is clearly impossible to provide a list of matters which will qualify as trade secrets or their equivalent. Secret processes of manufacture provide obvious examples, but innumerable other pieces of information are *capable* of being trade secrets, though the secrecy of some information may be only short-lived.

The practitioner will recognise at once, therefore, that with so many variables available in an industrial or commercial setting any definition is probably foolhardy; and at the same time one feels a degree of frustration that the principles are so open-ended. In the list below we have attempted to identify the forms of information which have the greatest chance of being classified as 'trade secrets'. Case law, however, is treacherous in this area; not least because (as noted above) prior to *Faccenda* the term was used more to distinguish protectable information from employees' know-how. And even after *Faccenda* one cannot be too sure how the courts are using this term given that many of the favourite precedents cited are these older cases (e.g., *Herbert Morris Ltd* v *Saxelby* [1916] 1 AC 688).

Given these caveats our suggestions for classification are:

(a)   The information must provide a competitive edge so that disclosure would cause significant harm to the employer.

(b)   The information must be inaccessible to the rest of the industry.

(c)   There must be proof that serious attempts have been made to limit and safeguard the dissemination of the material within the company.

(d)   The 'pure and applied research' cases tend to cause fewer problems so that it is reasonably safe to give the tag of trade secret to:

(i)   inventions (possessing some degree of novelty, although not necessarily sufficient to gain patent protection — and including inventions which would be entitled to patent protection but for which patent protection has not been sought);

(ii)   technical or design data and specifications;

(iii)   specific technical processes of construction and manufacture;

(iv)   test performance figures for a new product;

(v)   chemical and other formulae;

(vi)   craft secrets;

(vii)   secret recipes.

(e)   Business secrets are more difficult to characterise and classify, but may include:

(i)   manufacturer's 'know-how' (as distinct from the employee's know-how). By this we mean the *particular applications* of technology unique to that company and which are not part of public knowledge. This might extend to things such as specific and detailed 'quality control' procedures developed by the company;

(ii)   customer lists when connected to things such as discount or purchasing policies and which are not otherwise available — we have some hesitancy here, but include this on the basis of Staughton LJ's comments in *Lansing Linde Ltd* v *Kerr* [1991] 1 WLR 251;

(iii)   operative tenders and quotations which have not been published;

(iv)   detailed plans for expansion and market projections;

(v)   computer sofware containing novel features;

(vi)   access codes for computers and secure areas.

Under the *Faccenda* test, anything which does not qualify for the above list is unprotectable after termination of the contract so that no further distinctions need be made: trivia, the employee's know-how, and any other 'business secret' will all be treated the same.

1.5.2 An employee's 'know-how'

Under our suggested interpretation, a further distinction has to be made: between, on the one hand, confidential information which can be protected by an *express* clause and, on the other hand, an employee's know-how and trivia. The mere existence of an express clause does not in itself determine the issue.

Yet again the cases are not clear in this area but certain features can be discovered in identifying an employee's know-how. Anything which relates to general methods of transacting the company's business, rather than information related to particular negotiations or transactions, is unlikely to be afforded protection (*Littlewoods Organisation Ltd* v *Harris* [1977] 1 WLR 1472). Knowledge which relates only to the form of organisation and the procedures employed for the day-to-day management of the company is unlikely to be deemed confidential. The same has been held true recently of nebulous feasibility studies, despite being given the label of a 'maturing business opportunity' (*Ixora Trading Inc.* v *Jones* [1990] FSR 251). The reasoning behind this approach is that what is revealed is the sort of information an employee cannot help but carry away in his or her head; it is a part of the employee's general stock of knowledge.

The rationale for this approach, stemming for the most part from Cross J's comments in *Printers and Finishers Ltd* v *Holloway* [1965] 1 WLR 1, is that such knowledge is not 'readily separable' from the employee's general knowledge and that it is 'inevitably', 'necessarily' or 'naturally' acquired in the course of employment. This accords with the notion that an injunction will not be granted unless there is sufficient particularisation of the information; and methods and practices will be more difficult to identify than facts and figures. There can be no universally applicable rule because the alteration of one factor, such as the level of dissemination of information, could change the outcome.

1.5.3 Drafting practice

As the distinction between secrets and skills is far from easy to draw the most secure line to take is that anything which is not very clearly part of the employee's know-how should be included in an express confidentiality term. All the cases in which confidentiality has been preserved can be viewed as legitimate starting-points. This will hold true on the basis that the distinction between unprotectable know-how and protectable confidences has always been prominent in the courts' approach and, whatever the meaning of 'trade secrets' or 'confidential information' was in the older cases, the information in question was seen as being capable of generating protection, of being something more than skill and knowledge. Material such as general research data, details of drawings, costings, accounting information, customers' credit ratings, the contents of new catalogues, company-produced 'quality maintenance' manuals (if not already a trade secret), restricted circulation memos and minutes of meetings, problems encountered in the development of a product or reasons why certain matters were rejected, and personnel records such as employees' salary packages would therefore probably qualify in this category.

One might also include in an express confidentiality term any item which may be only debatably a trade secret (e.g., customer lists or sales strategies) thereby making allowance for the courts determining that an item of information in a particular situation does not qualify as a 'post-*Faccenda*' trade secret after all. This strategy will provide the greatest scope for protection. In this sense an express term could operate as a fall-back for both ends of the scale. The other alternative sometimes suggested by the courts is for employers to rely more on the insertion of a restraint of trade clause. However, restraint of trade clauses are not a panacea as will be seen in the next chapter.

1.6. LIABILITY OF THIRD PARTIES

Liability for unauthorised use may extend to third parties. The information must of course have originally satisfied the tests for confidentiality and not have been released into the public domain by the employer. By 'third parties' we mean those individuals or companies who receive information from employees or former employees of another company. The term will include companies established by those employees themselves (*Cranleigh Precision Engineering Ltd* v *Bryant* [1965] 1 WLR 1293). Third parties will obviously not attract contractual obligations in receiving this information, so it is here that the courts return to the general equitable foundations of the subject for principles of liability. There may also be liability in tort where the third party has induced an employee to break the contractual obligation of confidence or where there is conversion of a document.

A third party who comes into possession of confidential information may be restrained from using or disclosing that information if the third party knows that the information is confidential. The third party's actual, imputed or constructive knowledge of the breach of confidence is therefore a determining factor under equity. For, once the third party becomes aware that the information has been received in consequence of a breach of confidence there will be liability to the employer, at least for actions from that moment on. Liability relates to the unauthorised use of that information and will take the form of an account of profits and, where appropriate, the application of an injunction.

Where bad faith exists on the part of the third party, equity (accepting the discretionary element) will prevent that person making use of the information or passing it on to anyone else; and an account of profits will be available. Where the recipient has simply closed his eyes to the possibility of breach of confidence it would seem that knowledge will be imputed (*Attorney-General* v *Guardian Newspapers Ltd* [1990] 1 AC 109). A good faith recipient becomes fixed with the obligation of confidence on gaining notice of the breach as regards use of the information after notification. However, it has been the subject of debate (and the authorities are not clear) whether an innocent purchaser for value should be caught by the same principles. The position would be particularly awkward where the good faith recipient has altered his financial position by relying upon the information, e.g., by a capital investment in plant and machinery.

The range of remedies and orders available to an employer are the same in relation to a third party as with an action against a former employee, namely:

(a) Suing for damages or for an account of profits.
(b) Seeking an injunction to prevent use or disclosure of the information.
(c) Obtaining an *Anton Piller* order.
(d) Requesting delivery up and/or destruction of documents.

1.7 CHECKLIST

In the employment relationship many, if not all, employees will come across confidential information of some level at some time. Judging from the ILU survey, the attitude of employers to the protection of such information varies considerably. In many cases there were detailed documents which sought to spell out not only the general duties expected of the employees but even the minutiae of definitions. Others adopted a far more relaxed attitude, either out of lack of foresight or lack of need. Some sought to rely on the operation of implied terms during the currency of the contract and on restraint of trade clauses for post-termination coverage. For reasons explored in the next chapter we would suggest that this latter course of action is a dangerous game to play.

If we assume that, in the employer's judgment, confidentiality needs to be maintained, what approach should be adopted? We would suggest that the points noted below should be included in any company policy on confidentiality. We have divided the checklist into three categories.

1.7.1 General points

Information can only be protected if the law sees it as confidential. The key elements regarding confidentiality are: that the employer believes that disclosure of the information would harm the business; that the employer reasonably believes the information is secret and has acted to protect it; and those views accord with the usage and practices of the particular industry.

Mark documents 'confidential'. The allocation of levels of secrecy to documents does not guarantee anything. However, as a precautionary measure, this approach was adopted by a few companies in the ILU survey. In some cases the grade of employee allowed access to the information was given — a variation on the 'for your eyes only' approach!

There must be justification for protecting the information. The purpose of protecting confidential information must be that of a damage-limitation exercise rather than a method of preventing the employee earning a living.

Care should be taken with summary dismissals. If the employer breaches the contract, e.g., by wrongfully dismissing the employee or wrongfully repudiating the contract, any confidentiality clause may be deemed inoperative.

Apply the same methods of protection to consultants and contractors as with employees.

1.7.2 Protection during the currency of the contract

Make employees aware of the commercial importance of confidentiality. Specific instructions can be provided through documents such as handbooks, works rules, bulletins and so forth, but *protection* resides in the express or implied terms of the contract. Setting out matters in a clear form makes obvious both to the employee and any court the employer's 'subjective' assessment of the importance of confidentiality. By inserting terms in the contract this also serves as a warning to employees.

Define the types of 'confidential information'. We have noted above that in the ILU survey companies did adopt the practice of setting out the types of information that a particular employee might come across and which would be considered as confidential. Any list should be introduced as not being an exhaustive definition. To ensure that such express duties run in parallel with, and not in opposition to, the implied terms this should be clearly spelt out in the contract. In borderline situations it is likely that a clear policy will convince a court that certain information deserves to be labelled 'confidential'.

Maintain the contracts so that clauses are relevant to the grade of employee in question. As a general presumption, more senior employees have access to more confidential information. The relevant contractual term should reflect this. The contracts of employees who are promoted or change job (or place of work possibly) should be monitored to ensure they meet security requirements.

1.7.3 Protection after the contract has terminated

The implied terms protect trade secrets. The implied term of good faith and fidelity will protect a range of highly confidential items of information in all cases. But the definition of 'trade secret' is unclear so that it is advisable for employers to demonstrate the status of particular items of information by means of warnings, by separating the relevant material from non-confidential items, and by limiting access to small numbers of employees.

Insert an express term to operate after termination. We have discussed this point in relation to *Faccenda Chicken Ltd* v *Fowler* [1987] Ch 117. The ILU survey presented no clear picture relating to companies' attitudes on such a policy. As we argued above, however, it is a wasted opportunity *not* to adopt such a policy. As regards borderline trade secrets such clauses will help to define their status; as regards other confidential information there is nothing to lose by inserting an express term of this nature.

Make sure the drafting is comprehensive. Shorthand phrases such as 'a duty not to use information' are easier to read but incomplete. The clause should extend to cover actions such as use, exploiting, disclosure, divulging, distributing, publishing, revealing and selling the information.

Insert a term on delivery up of documents. It should be made clear that all documentation and computer disks are the property of the employer and should be surrendered on leaving. An express prohibition on copying information may also be advisable. These matters could be reinforced at any termination interview.

Be aware of how long the clause should be effective. Most companies in the ILU survey which did use a post-termination confidentiality clause left open the 'expiry date'. It is suggested that an estimation needs to be made of the life span of particular items of information and that this should be stated in the contract. It may well be that, in some cases, the time period can be left open-ended.

1.8 GENERAL BIBLIOGRAPHY

1.8.1 Books

Bowers, J. (1990), *Employment Law* (London: Blackstone Press).

Clarke, L. (ed.) (1990), *Confidentiality and the Law* (London: Lloyds of London Press).

Finn, P.D. (1977), *Fiduciary Obligations* (Sydney: The Law Book Co.).

Gurry, F. (1984), *Breach of Confidence* (Oxford: Clarendon Press).

Harvey, R.J. (ed.) (1984), *Industrial Relations and Employment Law* (London: Butterworths).

Law Commission (1981), *Breach of Confidence* (Cmnd 8388) (London: HMSO).

Mehigan, S. and Griffiths, D. (1991), *Restraint of Trade and Business Secrets*, 2nd edn (London: Longman).

Pearson, H. and Miller, C. (1990), *Commercial Exploitation of Intellectual Property* (London: Blackstone Press).

Reid, B. (1986), *Confidentiality and the Law* (London: Waterlow).

Skone James, E.P., et al. (eds.) (1991), *Copinger and Skone James on Copyright*, 13th edn (London: Sweet & Maxwell).

Upex, R. (general ed.) (1992), *Sweet and Maxwell's Encyclopedia of Employment Law* (London: Sweet & Maxwell).

Wacks, R. (1989), *Personal Information, Privacy and the Law* (Oxford: Clarendon Press).

1.8.2 Articles

Jones, G.H. (1970), 'Restitution of Benefits Obtained in Breach of Another's Confidence' (1970) 86 LQR 463.

Nathan, D. (1991), 'Trade Secrets in the Area of High Technology' [1991] EIPR 305.

Purvis, I. and Turner, B. (1989), 'More Chicken Pieces' [1989] EIPR 3.

Rideout, R.W. (1986), 'Contract of Employment, Confidentiality or Protection of Trade Secrets' (1986) 15 ILJ 183.

Stewart, A. (1989), 'Confidential Information and Departing Employees: the Employer's Options' [1989] EIPR 88.

2 Restraint of Trade

Contracts in restraint of trade exist to restrict another party's activities. Such restraints have been viewed both with suspicion and approbation by the common law for centuries, whether as applied to employment or commercial contracts.

Approbation arose in statutory form dating back to the Statute of Labourers in 1351, constraining even the physical movement of labourers. Suspicion dates back to at least the 14th century and generally arose in relation to organisations which sought to restrict the individual's liberty to work, e.g., guilds or trade unions. Principles of restraint had a profound effect upon trade union law.

By the 17th century the idea of protecting goodwill was recognised as validating limited restraints of trade. Nevertheless, there still existed opposition to general restraints. In 1711 Parker CJ assessed the reason for this opposition as resting on three points: (a) that such contracts caused the covenantee a loss of livelihood; (b) that there could be a loss to the public; and (c) the potential for abuse of position. In 1894 Lord Macnaghten expressed it this way: '. . . and all restraints of trade of themselves, if there is nothing more, are contrary to public policy' (*Nordenfelt* v *Maxim Nordenfelt Guns and Ammunition Co. Ltd* [1894] AC 535). This basic position holds true today. Thus, where the purpose of the contract is merely to obstruct that other's freedom in disposing of his or her labour this will be prohibited. The contract will only be valid if it seeks to protect the employer's business interests. The aim of the courts is to balance the protection of employers' legitimate interests as against an individual's liberty of action; and occasionally to judge this balance in the light of public interest.

In this chapter we will examine the doctrine of restraint of trade under the following general headings:

2.1 What constitutes a restraint of trade?
2.2 How is reasonableness determined?
2.3 Drafting and interpretation.
2.4 Implied and indirect restraints.
2.5 Restraints during employment.
2.6 Preparatory actions.
2.7 Associated companies.

2.1 WHAT CONSTITUTES A RESTRAINT OF TRADE?

A restraint clause seeks to limit the rights of employees to obtain employment elsewhere: it is an anti-competition clause. It has been the subject of debate whether a clause limiting an employee's activities *while the contract subsists* can fall within this doctrine; certainly the most common type of restraint relates to the activities of employees once the contract of employment has come to an end. In this chapter, therefore, we will concentrate initially on the effects of restraint clauses as applied to ex-employees. The significance of restrictions imposed on employees' ventures occurring during the currency of the contract (as with 'exclusive' contracts, see *A. Schroeder Music Publishing Co. Ltd* v *Macaulay* [1974] 1 WLR 1308) is dealt with later in this chapter and has also been referred to in chapter 1.

The archetypal restraint clause therefore seeks to prevent an employee, for a specific length of time, usually within a defined geographical area, setting up in a competing business, working for another employer or soliciting former trade connections once the employment relationship has come to an end. As will be seen, when faced with such a clause the courts will presume the restraint to be void unless the clause is reasonable. The employer must bear the burden of proving the facts from which reasonableness can be inferred (proving the employer has a legitimate interest to protect), and in practice has to show that the clause is reasonable in relation to the particular employee as well (though, more accurately, this can only be a matter for the court).

Consequently, the wording of restraint clauses is likely to be subjected to close scrutiny. Strictly speaking, such meticulous examination demands that restraint clauses can only arise by means of an express term inserted in the contract. In turn, this effectively means that such a clause has to be in writing. It is nevertheless not uncommon to find judicial references to 'implied restraint clauses'. It is submitted that for the most part this is an inexact use of terminology employed to describe the potential effects of similar clauses which constitute restrictive covenants, e.g., terms restricting the divulging of information (see Neill LJ generally in *Faccenda Chicken Ltd* v *Fowler* [1987] Ch 117). However, there may be instances where a clause has the effect of imposing a restraint although couched in other terms. This, it is submitted, can properly be termed an implied restraint (e.g., *Stenhouse Australia Ltd* v *Phillips* [1974] AC 391, to which we shall return).

It is often stated that precedents are useful in this area only as a guide. Each case turns very much on its facts. One cannot say that a one-year restraint, for instance, will always be reasonable. Indeed, in *Dairy Crest Ltd* v *Pigott* [1989] ICR 92, the Court of Appeal made it clear that even authorities concerning the same trade (here a milkman) were not to be regarded as binding precedents. As regards incorporation into the contract of employment, restraint of trade clauses are no different from any other contractual clause. There is no specifically prescribed form of wording required to effect incorporation, nor any specific process of incorporation. This is because the analysis centres on substance and effect rather than form; the key issue is not so much *how* the clause became part of the contract but whether it is effective or not. That effectiveness is determined by the reasonableness of the clause. Nor do the courts inquire into the adequacy of consideration: there is no such thing as a reasonable or unreasonable sum payable for a restraint clause. It would be naïve to think, however, that a large amount of money paid for a restraint (or a ludicrously small amount paid for an extensive restraint), or the respective bargaining powers of the parties, will have no bearing on a judge's decision: see generally *Bridge* v *Deacons* [1984] AC 705.

2.2 HOW IS REASONABLENESS DETERMINED?

At the heart of all that follows is the notion that the employer must be seeking to protect a legitimate proprietary (business) interest. The restraint must afford adequate, but no more than adequate, protection to the employer's interests. So, if the employer is simply endeavouring to prevent the ex-employee from working or competing elsewhere such an attempt will fail. There must be justification for the restraint. That justification is recognised as arising in two key areas:

(a)   to prevent the potential disclosure of confidential information;
(b)   to prevent the employee soliciting or dealing with the employer's clients and connections.

These grounds reveal the legitimate proprietary interest meriting protection. They are the standard touchstones, though a court can always recognise other 'legitimate interests'. For instance, in *Office Angels Ltd* v *Rainer-Thomas* [1991] IRLR 214 the Court of Appeal noted that an employment agency's contacts with temporary workers might be classed as a legitimate interest.

Once 'legitimate interest' has been established the restraint clause can then be subjected to a more particular and extensive analysis based on the ambit of the clause. Reasonableness will be judged as at the date when the restriction was imposed. There are four grounds to be considered:

(c)   reasonableness in terms of the '*market*' in which the parties are operating and the appropriateness in relation to that employee;
(d)   reasonableness in terms of *time*;
(e)   reasonableness in terms of *area* covered;
(f)   *public policy*.

The restraint must do no more than is reasonable to protect the legitimate interest. These points, (a) to (f), are amplified below.

2.2.1 Legitimate interest: preventing the potential disclosure of confidential information

An employer's confidential information is an obvious legitimate interest deserving of protection. We have seen in chapter 1 how that interest may be protected *during* employment. Before noting how the interest is dealt with *after* employment has ended it should be noted that there can be an overlap between the two forms of protection. This arises in cases where the employee has copied or even deliberately memorised lists or formulae etc. As was seen in *Robb* v *Green* [1895] 2 QB 315 and *Roger Bullivant Ltd* v *Ellis* [1987] ICR 464, where such conduct occurs the courts are likely to adopt severe measures to prevent misuse of that information. Further, the employer may be able to obtain an *Anton Piller* order. As we noted in the introduction, this order is somewhat Draconian in its effect and execution and will therefore not be granted lightly.

It may well be that there already exists a confidentiality clause in the contract of the type explored in chapter 1, restricting disclosure of that information both during employment and after the termination of the contract. If such a clause is effective then the necessity for a restraint of trade clause based on protecting confidential information may be reduced. However, the restraint clause may still prove to be useful. First, in practice the clause may serve as a further warning to employees of the significance which the employer attaches to the information as well as the employer's intentions regarding protection of rights. Secondly, the restraint clause offers a form of protection that is perhaps more easily enforceable in that a breach of the restraint clause (e.g. working in that industry) is more easily detectable and policed than the mere act of disclosing information.

Thirdly, if the effect of the confidentiality clause is dubious, the more general restraint clause may yet serve the same general purpose. For instance, it may be difficult to draft a confidentiality clause to define precisely the confidential information to be covered. The restraint clause, justified on the general grounds that there is *some* confidentiality question, could perhaps more easily resolve the problem. As Cross J stated in *Printers and Finishers Ltd* v *Holloway* [1965] 1 WLR 1 at p. 6, employers faced with this problem should 'exact covenants from their employees restricting their field of activity after they have left their employment' rather than ask 'the courts to extend general equitable doctrine to prevent breaking of confidences beyond all reasonable bounds'. However, there is no bar on the insertion of both restraint and confidentiality clauses side by side.

It follows that there must exist confidential information capable of being protected, and in need of protection, in order to justify any restraint (see *Mason* v *Provident Clothing and Supply Co. Ltd* [1913] AC 724). There is a problem here as to whether that information has to be a trade secret or be merely confidential in order to attract the courts' protection. As was seen in chapter 1, in *Faccenda Chicken Ltd* v *Fowler* [1987] Ch 117 the Court of Appeal seemed to indicate that only a trade secret (or information akin to a trade secret) could form the basis for a restraint clause to be effective.

Faccenda, it will be remembered was, however, a case concerned only with the effect of confidentiality clauses. Any comments as to the effectiveness of restraint clauses must therefore be treated with caution as *obiter dicta*.

The formulation of what is or is not a trade secret is fraught with difficulties. Neill LJ's assessment of what constitutes a trade secret has been applied by later courts. However, the restricted interpretation in *Faccenda* of the viability of express confidentiality restraints has been doubted forcefully by Scott J in *Balston Ltd* v *Headline Filters Ltd* [1987] FSR 330 and by Harman J in *Systems Reliability Holdings plc* v *Smith* [1990] IRLR 377. Without repeating the arguments advanced in chapter 1, it is respectfully suggested that these more liberal interpretations of the efficacy of express confidentiality clauses are correct.

But if we assume that Neill LJ was correct, then the only other device capable of affording protection to information which falls short of a trade secret would be a restraint of trade clause. Given the present case law it would seem advisable that employers should seek to rely on restraint clauses relating to confidential information *as well* as inserting express confidentiality clauses. This did not seem to be common practice in the ILU survey.

With regard to restraint of trade, the consequences of Neill LJ's reasoning seem to be that it is more likely that those restraint clauses which are justified on the grounds of protecting confidential information are also limited to the protection of trade secrets or highly confidential information. This is because, given that restraint clauses are more onerous than simple confidential information clauses it seems fair to argue that the more restrictive restraint clause cannot be justified on lesser grounds than the narrower confidentiality clause.

The case law on restraint of trade, however, is not clear on this point and Harman J's decision in *Systems Reliability Holdings plc* v *Smith* would not admit such a distinction. The earlier House of Lords cases which dealt with the protection of confidential information (such as *Mason* v *Provident Clothing and Supply Co. Ltd* [1913] AC 724 and *Herbert Morris Ltd* v *Saxelby* [1916] AC 688 — see below) make the point that only 'trade secrets' are capable of attracting protection. In later restraint cases, the courts have tended not to address the question specifically whether the information must be a trade secret or merely confidential. The validity of these clauses has been examined simply on the basis of whether or not there is a legitimate interest founded on confidentiality in need of protection. Some more recent cases have, however, relied upon dicta in the original House of Lords authorities to limit protection to trade secrets or information akin to trade secrets.

As we noted in chapter 1, it is not obvious what information will fall into the category of a trade secret, or highly confidential information, or confidential information not protected under the *Faccenda* test, or even mere trivia. Furthermore, as we noted in chapter 1, in both *Mason* v *Provident Clothing and Supplies Co. Ltd* and *Herbert Morris Ltd* v *Saxelby*, the term 'trade secret' was used to distinguish particular information from the employee's general skill and knowledge — not to distinguish classes of information *inter se* (see recently *Ixora Trading Inc.* v *Jones* [1990] FSR 251 to the same effect). That distinction is still valid: the employee's skill and knowledge remain the property of the employee and cannot be subjected to a restraint clause. It is, however, unsafe to take this point too far by saying that these authorities are conclusive proof that only trade secrets can be protected under a restraint clause.

We would argue that, if there is a distinction to be made in the analysis of confidentiality and restraint clauses, it seems more logical to argue that express confidentiality clauses can protect ordinary confidential information, but that the restraint clauses, being more Draconian in effect, should be justified by reference to trade secrets only. It is, however, by no means clear whether such a distinction should be made.

What we can say is that the information under scrutiny in the restraint clause must at least be confidential; this is the baseline. The test for confidentiality will be the same as detailed in *Thomas Marshall (Exports) Ltd v Guinle* [1979] Ch 227, discussed in chapter 1. It is worth commenting in this context that the definition of 'trade secrets' is not an exact science and the categories of trade secrets appear to be somewhat chameleon and expanding (see *Lansing Linde Ltd v Kerr* [1991] 1 WLR 251).

Two final points deserve mention. First, where the employee has deliberately copied or memorised information before leaving, the courts will tend to treat this as a continuing breach of the fidelity owed during employment. As such, questions of classification of that information as trade secrets or not can be dispensed with; the breach attracts no judicial sympathy (see *Robb v Green* [1895] 2 QB 315). Secondly, in the case of confidentiality restraints, the rights of third parties may be affected to the extent that recipients of confidential information can find themselves bound by an injunction in the same way as the employee who disclosed the information.

2.2.2 Legitimate interest: preventing the employee dealing with the employer's trade connections and competitors

The second legitimate interest capable of attracting protection is that of protecting customer contacts and goodwill (what has been termed 'trade connections'). There are a number of aspects hidden in the term 'trade connections'.

There are categories to which the term clearly applies, namely:

(a) the employer's customers and clients;
(b) the employer's goodwill;
(c) the employer's suppliers.

There are categories where the application is likely to be made, namely, existing company employees.

And there are categories where the application is more debatable, namely:

(a) customers who no longer deal with the employer;
(b) future potential customers.

These more debatable categories will be discussed separately. Equally, there are different forms of restraint concerned with trade connections and competitors, namely:

(a) *non-competition restraints* (i.e., preventing the employee working in that industry as a whole, or at least with named competitors);
(b) *non-dealing restraints* (i.e. preventing employees accepting business from or conducting business with former clients);
(c) *non-solicitation restraints* (i.e., preventing employees actually initiating contact with former clients).

The ILU survey revealed that fewer contracts contained a restraint clause than contained a confidentiality clause. Where restraint clauses did appear they tended to relate to matters of non-solicitation rather than non-dealing or non-competition.

For reasons of convenience, the following analysis is aimed mainly at 'non-dealing' and 'non-competition' clauses. Restraints aimed at preventing the soliciting of connections are dealt with later as a separate topic. Non-solicitation clauses are usually less dramatic in their effect and, in many cases, procure a more sympathetic reception from the courts (see 2.2.5).

As with confidentiality restraints, 'non-dealing and non-competition' restraints may affect third party rights. Even where that third-party is the trade connection who wishes to follow the employee to the new job rather than continue dealing with the employer, any action by the employee may still constitute a breach of contract (see *John Michael Design plc* v *Cooke* [1987] ICR 445), and the third party may also have wandered into the tort of inducing breach of contract. The 'injured' employer may be able to obtain an injunction and recover damages against the new employer. If the clause only relates to non-solicitation, this will not affect third parties in terms of liability for inducement.

The duty of fidelity owed by the employee prevents the employee, during the currency of the contract, from competing with the employer or causing harm to the employer by working for a rival. It may also prevent the employee laying the foundations for future commercial dealings whilst still in the company's employ; though this is by no means a universal protection (see *Laughton* v *Bapp Industrial Supplies Ltd* [1986] ICR 634 and *Marshall Industrial Systems and Control Ltd* [1992] IRLR 294). Once the contract has been terminated, however, that duty of fidelity perishes; and no equitable duty will come to the employer's aid to prevent competition. The employer cannot be protected from competition *per se*, only from unfair competition. The restraint must also reflect reality. Thus in *Spencer* v *Marchington* [1988] IRLR 392, the geographical restraint was one of a 25-mile radius and related to an employment agency. All but one of the employer's customers were located within a 20-mile radius of the employer's business; and the rival agency was also located within this area. Nevertheless the clause failed. In effect, the excess of a five-mile radius in the clause was not protecting anything; the clause was drawn too widely.

The connections which are claimed to be in need of protection do not have to be exclusive to the employer, nor does the protection apply only to long-standing connections. The employer will be seeking to show that the customer and trade contacts made by the employee are such that personal influence could be brought to bear by that employee to induce away the employer's business. There may well be an overlap here with confidential information, e.g. the employee possessing knowledge of customers' credit, business preferences, suppliers' credit arrangements and so on. In such cases there is no bar on arguing both grounds of legitimate interest.

2.2.2.1 What level of contact is required?

The long-standing approach to this question has been to assess the degree of *influence* that could be exerted by the employee (see *Herbert Morris Ltd* v *Saxelby* [1916] 1 AC 688). The degree of influence is paramount. The argument runs: it is not just customer *contact* that matters — for many employees come into contact with customers without exerting influence — it is influence which counts. Obviously, the more a trade connection deals with a particular employee the more likely it is that influence will arise. But even when influence is present, one has to judge the significance and commercial reality of that influence: what advantage accrues to the employee from the contact? As the American judge, Hoover J, once indicated, it is quite possible that an employee can exert influence over connections but equally there is such a thing as 'an employer's hold' over customers (where the customer does business with the company and not because of the presence of the individual employee). The customer may also discontinue placing business with any former employee simply because of sheer inconvenience. In analysing the degree of influence, the court must set the employer's hold against the type of contact the customer has with the employee (the level of reliance), the seniority of the employee, the nature of the goods or services, and the frequency of contact.

Consider, for instance, a hairdresser's business. The receptionist, the apprentice or the person making the coffee and sweeping up may well have as much contact with a customer as the person cutting or styling hair. The receptionist, for example, will come into contact with all customers but the degree of influence is infinitely less than is likely with the particular stylist and, though a restraint might prove to be effective, the argument favours the employee. But if we move to the stylist there appears far greater justification for the imposition of a restraint clause. So now, if that stylist sets up in business a short distance away it is arguable that some customers may well follow (see *Marion White Ltd* v *Francis* [1972] 1 WLR 1423). However, it is equally arguable that the customers' allegiance is to the employer-hairdresser because of reputation, level of service, the inconvenience of change or whatever. If *influence* is missing the clause is less justifiable, unless there are other factors present such as deceit (*East* v *Maurer* [1991] 1 WLR 461). Again, when having a car serviced at a garage, it is likely that one's allegiance is owed to the garage, not to the individual mechanics (even if they are known to you).

The manager of the garage might present us with more difficulties. Where the manager is detached from customer contact, as in *S.W. Strange Ltd* v

Mann [1965] 1 WLR 629 (manager of a bookmaking business rarely dealing face to face with customers), any restraint is unlikely to be upheld. Repeated contact, however, can change the analysis. Managers of butchers' shops, solicitors' clerks, milk roundsmen who are known to the customers, tailors and others who procure business have been set in this category. This is because the frequency, coupled with some degree of attachment, can generate reliance and influence; even more so with doctors, dentists, vets or accountants. The closer the contact, the more tied to the employee the customer or supplier is, the more justifiable the restraint. As Salmon LJ stated in *Scorer v Seymour-Johns* [1966] 1 WLR 1419, the question is whether the trade connections rely on the employee to the extent that they regard themselves as effectively doing business with the employee rather than the employer.

What this reveals is that it is the *quality* of contact, not the quantity, that matters. It is probably more likely that senior employees will have the potential to exert more influence over trade connections. Clearly, however, there must be some contact, some opportunity to draw connections away when the employee leaves; and that 'draw' must be generated by more than the employee's pleasant personality. Middle management with customer contact should be treated differently from, say, factory-bound line managers.

It must be noted that some authorities do not support this analysis, producing instead a much looser test of what constitutes a legitimate interest. This looser test originates from cases such as *Gilford Motor Co. Ltd v Horne* [1933] Ch 935 and *G.W. Plowman and Son Ltd v Ash* [1964] 1 WLR 568. In this latter case the Court of Appeal was prepared to say that any contacts of the employer in existence during the time the employee worked for the employer constituted a legitimate interest to protect. These cases tended to ignore numerous contrary dicta of the House of Lords in *Herbert Morris Ltd v Saxelby* [1916] 1 AC 688 and in *Mason v Provident Clothing and Supply Co. Ltd* [1913] AC 724.

This looser test was noted in *Marley Tile Co. Ltd v Johnson* [1982] IRLR 75 where Lord Denning MR limited its relevance to situations in which the connections were small in number so that one employee might have had more general influence by simply working for the employer. Templeman LJ commented that, 'In the absence of any evidence that the defendant had a substantial influence over this massive 2,500 customers' there was no justification for the clause. The looser test was taken again, rather cursorily, by Millett J in *Business Seating (Renovations) Ltd v Broad* [1989] ICR 729. But a return to the more traditional approach was signalled in *Hinton and Higgs (UK) Ltd v Murphy* [1989] IRLR 519 when the Court of Session (Outer House) refused to uphold a restraint which referred to 'any previous or present clients'. Again, in *Office Angels Ltd v Rainer-Thomas* [1991] IRLR 214 the Court of Appeal adopted the traditional approach and limited the restraint to some form of contact.

We would respectfully submit that the 'traditional' analysis is the correct method of defining the employer's trade connections, with the proviso that in small businesses an employee's 'influence' might correlate to mere contact. Indeed, in the decisions of the House of Lords early in the 20th century, protection was given to prevent the gaining of what was termed 'special advantage', and personal knowledge of the customers played as much a part in that as actual 'influence'. It would at least be unsafe for an employer to believe that *any* customer-contact could be included in a restraint.

This brings us to a related point: to what extent can an employee's *reputation* be considered as a trade connection? Cases earlier in the 20th century indicate that actors or musicians might be legitimate subjects for restraint because of their ability to attract audiences. Whether this would apply to, say, a senior financial adviser in a modern company, where there might exist reputation without contact, is a matter for speculation. Clients might come to the company because of the reputation of certain key employees. Thus, the employee in question clearly possesses the potential for drawing away the employer's clients; at the same time the element of contact, of direct influence, is missing.

Certainly, reputation founded only on personal attributes such as honesty and speed of work was seen to be unprotectable in *Cantor Fitzgerald (UK) Ltd v Wallace* [1992] IRLR 215. There 'inter-dealer brokers', whose work amounted to acting as go-betweens with clients, were not caught by an elaborate restraint clause. Their work was found to involve minimal technical skill, they took no financial decisons, so that their competence rested on their personality and character. On these facts Judge Prosser's decision in the High Court is in keeping with earlier decisions. The learned judge's comment that the company did not actually have *clients* (and so no proprietary interest) 'because in the market every day is a new day and every deal a new deal' is, with respect, to over-simplify the question of influence and trade connections.

It is suggested that, if any form of restraint is permissible, it is most likely to be that of preventing solicitation of existing clients, rather than a general ban on acting within the general field of financial services. It is in this way that the decision in *G.W. Plowman and Son Ltd v Ash* can be best seen to operate.

There are two final issues to be considered in this area.

2.2.2.2 Poaching existing employees
The first concerns the position where the former employee might seek to draw away existing employees. Recruiting another employer's employees is not unlawful provided the poaching employer does not induce the employee to breach the existing contract. Equally, there seems to be no particular reason why an employer should not regard existing employees as 'legitimate interests' capable of being covered by a restraint. Thus a clause which seeks to prevent the non-solicitation of employees should stand or fall on the same tests as apply to any other trade connection or (and probably more justifiably) the protection of trade secrets.

This line of reasoning has been seen in *Kores Manufacturing Co. Ltd v Kolok Manufacturing Co. Ltd* [1959] Ch 108. Here, two companies entered into agreement not to employ each other's former employees for a period of five years following termination of the relevant contract of employment. As well as this restraint being rejected on grounds of public policy, the clause also fell foul of the reasonableness test in relation to the employees affected. The five-year restraint was held to be too long, especially in relation to manual workers. Thus, if the clause was unreasonable as regards those directly affected, it could not be deemed reasonable simply because it was concluded by the two companies.

Covenants restraining the recruitment or poaching of employees did appear with reasonable frequency in the ILU survey. Some clauses sought to prevent enticement both during as well as after employment, which, if competition is feared seems an eminently sensible approach. The usual time limitation for post-termination covenants was one year, though one did extend to three years — which, even in relation to senior employees must be counted as open to challenge. The clause in question in fact applied to all 'staff' employees and is therefore in an even more dangerous position.

2.2.2.3 The employee's client base

The employee may have legitimately brought to the business useful connections which he or she now wishes to carry forward to the next employment. To what extent have these connections become the 'property' of the employer? This matter was addressed in *M and S Drapers* v *Reynolds* [1957] 1 WLR 9, which concerned a salesman. The Court of Appeal viewed such contacts as belonging to the employee. As Denning LJ stated: 'His goodwill with those customers belonged to him and cannot reasonably be taken from him by a covenant of this kind'. The legitimacy of inserting an express clause in the contract to counter such possibilities, akin to partnership agreements, does not appear to have been reviewed by the courts.

Once the presence of a legitimate interest has been shown the question of reasonableness has to be tackled. The traditional dimensions to be measured in restraint cases have been those of time and area. We shall examine these in the next two sections. Although the unreasonableness of either factor by itself may invalidate the restraint, the factors do overlap a great deal. As Lord Shaw of Dunfermline said in *Herbert Morris Ltd* v *Saxelby* [1916] 1 AC 688: '. . . as the time of restriction lengthens, or the space of its operation extends, the weight of that onus [on the covenantee] grows'. The converse can also prove true: thus a restraint that is too wide in geographical terms will generally fail, but it may be saved if the time limitation is short. Likewise a lengthy restraint may be valid especially where the geographical limitation is not extensive.

In the text below we have analysed the concept of 'reasonableness' in relation to the headings of the market setting, time and area. Under the headings of 'time' and 'area' we have applied 'reasonableness' to each of the accepted legitimate interests, viz., protection of confidential information and trade connections. Specific case examples are referred to, but it should be stressed that this is an area of shifting sands, even without the introduction of public policy concepts. What we can say, however, is that the same general test applies to both trade secrets and connections: are the employer's interests in such jeopardy or open to exploitation because of the potential competition from the employee that the restraint can be justified?

In point 2.2.7 we shall consider the more nebulous aspect of public policy and the perceived needs of society.

2.2.3 Width of the clause: reasonableness in terms of the 'market' in which the parties are operating and the appropriateness in relation to that employee

In 2.2.4, 2.2.5 and 2.2.6 below we will address the issues of 'reasonable time' and 'reasonable area'. However, as a preliminary point it has to be stressed that in every case the court has to relate the restraint to the market setting of the company and the individual in question. Thus we need to find out what both the employer and employee were concerned with: what is the scope of the employer's activities and what was the employee employed to do? However reasonable the clause itself may look, however much it might fit a desirable precedent, if the clause does not relate to the employer's business or the employee's activities then it will be doomed. It is not reasonableness as an abstract concept that matters but rather reasonableness in relation to the *particular* contract of employment.

2.2.3.1 Scope of the employer's business
The term 'scope' here might first be applied to the geographical area that could be called the employer's area of operations. The nature of the employer's business has a significant bearing on the width of the geographical restraint; anything from a part of a city to the world as a whole. The term will also apply to the range of products or services in which the employer deals and even the siting of competitors. Thus, in what is perhaps the *fons et origo* of the modern doctrine, *Nordenfelt v Maxim Nordenfelt Guns and Ammunition Co. Ltd* [1894] AC 535, a worldwide restriction of 25 years' duration was held valid (though this was a commercial, rather than an employment, restraint) because that was the extent of the munitions operations in the business in question.

Consider, for instance, a somewhat simplified clause that reads:

> the employee will not engage directly or indirectly in any business carried on by the employer . . . for a period of six months within a radius of 20 miles from the company's premises from the date of termination of the contract.

The time-limit and area covered appear reasonable (provided there is a legitimate interest to protect in the first place). Equally, it seems reasonable to restrain the employee from competing with the employer. But what is the employer's business? The effects of a standard clause must be different, for instance, when dealing with a butcher's business, a finance company, an estate agency, or a national frozen foods company. What if a range of products are made and the employee was only ever concerned with one? For instance, in *Marley Tile Co. Ltd v Johnson* [1982] IRLR 75 the clause in question sought to restrain the employee from soliciting, canvassing or dealing with customers of the employer for a period of one year. The restraint related to customers falling within any area in which the employee had worked during the year prior to leaving. In that year the employee had worked mainly in Devon, but for several months before leaving he had worked in Cornwall. This meant that the possible number of customers covered by the clause was in the region of 2,500. The restraint was held to be void because of the size of the area covered, the number of customers covered, and the range of the class of products produced by the employer.

Again, in *Commercial Plastics Ltd* v *Vincent* [1965] 1 QB 623 the clause in question read: 'In view of the highly technical and confidential nature of this appointment you have agreed not to seek employment with any of our competitors in the PVC calendering field for at least one year after leaving our employ'. The clause was limited to competitors but still failed. It failed because, on the facts, the only matters that needed protection were those relating to the narrow field of PVC sheeting for adhesive tape, not the wider protection stated in the clause. The market in which the employer operated was the worldwide market for PVC sheeting production, but the clause (justified on confidential information grounds) went too far in relation to the particular product in question.

Returning to our example of a simplified clause: if the business is fashion design, how far should the word 'indirectly' be read? It is arguable that the word 'indirectly' draws the boundaries too widely — working on a market stall could theoretically be covered. Whilst this is an argument in theory, in practice, if the rest of the clause is reasonable the courts have the power to interpret the wording more narrowly and phrase any injunction accordingly. However, it should be clear from the clause (and the point should be defensible) whether the restraint is meant, for instance, to apply to wholesale as well as retail dealings. It is common to find the word 'indirectly' in restraint clauses, but for safety the nature of the interest being protected should be made clear in the clause.

One question charged with danger here is: would it make a difference if the business was located in the centre of London as opposed to a provincial town such as Taunton? In both instances a two-mile restraint might, in the abstract, appear reasonable. But those two miles may well cover many more customers in the heart of London than in Taunton. Paradoxically, the whole market for the service might be wiped out in Taunton whilst not significantly affected in London; more so if the business is that of selling farming equipment. Thus, the question only begs further investigation of the employer's business interests and how realistic the restraint is in relation to those interests.

Business methods have changed substantially from the 19th century, in which the conventional analysis of restraint clauses originated. More and more, the notion of preventing the maintenance of direct physical contact through a restraint clause represents only a preliminary stage of the analysis. For continued contact and influence may be exerted by means of telephone, advertisement, FAX or letter as well as by personal proximity. One can be situated in London and still *deal* with customers in Bristol, for instance. The courts therefore have to examine other factors in the arguments relating to the width of geographical boundaries.

It becomes open to the courts to say, as regards many modern businesses, that a United Kingdom, European Community, or even worldwide ban could be appropriate or, in the alternative, that a defined restraint of say 10 miles (other than perhaps a non-solicitation restraint) would in fact be pointless. In *S.W. Strange Ltd* v *Mann* [1965] 1 WLR 629, for instance, one of the reasons the clause failed was that a 12-mile-radius restraint was an irrelevancy where most of the employee's contact with customers, and so much of the employer's business, was conducted over the telephone. The same reasoning was utilised in *Office Angels Ltd* v *Rainer-Thomas* [1991] IRLR 214 regarding an employment agency and a clause which sought to prevent the employee engaging in or undertaking the trade or business of an employment agency within an area of 1.2 square miles from the relevant branch. The clause did not seem over-demanding but, again, client contact was generally made by telephone. The actual siting of any rival office was largely irrelevant.

The employer must therefore be able to show a functional correspondence between the area circumscribed by the restriction and the area particularly associated with the employee's former place of work. As seen in *Spencer* v *Marchington* [1988] IRLR 392, the geographical restraint must genuinely seek to protect something; its presence must make sense and the trade connections in question must relate to the area defined in the restraint clause. It may very well often be the case, for instance, that a non-solicitation clause, which is narrower in its effect than a non-dealing clause, would be the proper form of protection to be sought. It is for this reason that the courts have increasingly turned towards examining whether a non-solicitation clause would represent the minimum needed to protect the employer's interests. If such a clause will achieve the employer's objectives then any wider 'non-dealing clause' is likely to be held unreasonable.

Thus the smaller local business must guard against making the restraint unrealistically wide whereas employers with interests further afield may more easily justify wider areas of restraint. But these employers will also have to show that a narrowly constructed clause (which initially appears a safer bet) still has some commercial point behind it — that it has relevance to the protection of trade connections and is justifiable in the context of the market in which they operate.

When dealing with geographical restraints therefore the courts are not necessarily averse to imposing wide-ranging geographical bans in order to protect trade connections. They will do this where the nature of the industry and the terms of the particular employment call for it. So even if the business has a wide field of activity but the employee (e.g., a salesman) acted only within a small locality it is probably unreasonable to prevent his working outside that field (as seen in *Marley Tile Co. Ltd* v *Johnson* [1982] IRLR 75). If the restraint clause centres on the protection of confidential information then it is quite arguable that a worldwide restraint is necessary.

2.2.3.2 The status of the employee

M and S Drapers v *Reynolds* [1957] 1 WLR 9 illustrates the general point here. The restraint concerned a salesman and collector in the drapery trade and was a non-solicitation clause set to last for five years and applicable to the employer's connections who had been customers during the three years prior to termination. The Court of Appeal refused the restraint, partly on the grounds that the employee did not hold a position which warranted such a restriction. Junior employees are likely to get more gentle treatment from the courts than their seniors. In *Spafax Ltd* v *Harrison* [1980] IRLR 442, however, a branch manager/salesman was held bound to observe a two-year restraint when consideration was given to the seniority of his position. The covenant sought to restrain the employees from soliciting orders in relation to goods which they had dealt with on behalf of the employer or similar goods from anyone with whom they had dealt in the year prior to termination. The case is also of interest in that it focused on the effect of the clause in relation to the employee by looking at what the clause allowed the employee to continue doing rather than concentrating on what was forbidden. In other words, the court considered whether the clause acted to prevent unfair competition or sterilise activities. Thus care should be taken when dealing with employees who have gained expertise in a particular field to the exclusion of all else. If the restraint effectively prevents them working within that field it is likely to fall foul of the test for reasonableness: see *Commercial Plastics Ltd* v *Vincent* [1965] 1 QB 623.

Systems Reliability Holdings plc v *Smith* [1990] IRLR 377 provides an interesting example both as to the courts' attitude to employment restraints (as opposed to commercial restraints) and also the question of geographical restrictions. Smith was employed by ECS as a computer engineer. In 1989 he was dismissed for misconduct. He owned 1.6 per cent of the company's shares. When ECS was bought out by Systems Reliability Holdings the employee received £247,000 for the shares from the purchaser. The share sale agreement contained a restrictive covenant running for 17 months which prevented the employee being 'engaged or interested . . . in any business which competes with any business carried on at the date of the agreement' by the company or its subsidiaries. There were further restrictions on non-solicitation and on the use of confidential information. Smith then set up a rival business supplying computer services and approached former customers.

In the High Court action a number of points emerged. The first was whether this case should be treated as an employer–employee case (with its stringent tests of reasonableness) or as a vendor–purchaser case (with its more liberal test). This point is likely to be of increasing importance with the development of employee share option schemes in many companies. How is the employee to be treated when covered by a restraint clause: as employee or vendor? Harman J stated his reluctance to categorise other than for reasons of convenience (although he appears to have classified the case as vendor–purchaser dealings). Instead he emphasised that the court always 'has got to sit down and say: What is reasonable in this particular deal?' Nevertheless, the comment that, in the case of employee-shareholders, it would be 'most undesirable for the courts to say that such persons cannot be bound as vendors of the goodwill of a business' is worth noting.

The second point of interest was that Harman J upheld the worldwide ban because that is where the company's business lay and a computer engineer could work in Tokyo, Seoul, Paris or many cities in the United States. The ban reflected modern business conditions. Thirdly, the fact that some of the shareholders had no direct interest in the company's activities and so would not have been covered by any restraint did not invalidate the restraint against those who had been involved.

Thus at its simplest level this question asks: does the position held by the employee warrant the imposition of a restraint? There we have the contrast between the senior computer engineer and the labourer, or the employee who might or might not exert influence over the connections. But the question has further complications. As seen in *Marley Tile Co. Ltd* v *Johnson* [1982] IRLR 75, even if the employee's job is of the type meriting a restraint clause, the clause must reflect what the employee did in relation to the employer's business.

2.2.4 Width of the clause: reasonableness in terms of time

2.2.4.1 Time in relation to confidential information
The aspect of 'time' is of vital importance in relation to the protection of confidential information. The restraint can last no longer than the projected useful life of that information. There is therefore an obvious difference between the considerations to be applied to ex-employees of organisations famed for their 'secret recipes' and those, say, in the fashion industry, where the secrecy of next season's designs has a limited life span. The question posed by the courts is: What is necessary to protect the information? It may be reasonable in the former case to impose a lifetime ban; in the latter case, probably no more than six months to a year.

It must also be the case that different employees, or at least groups of employees, will have access to varying levels and types of confidential information. Thus, a restraint clause applied without variation to all employees is likely to fall foul of the reasonableness test because a one-year restraint, whilst reasonable in relation to the head of computer design, may be too great when applied even to a computer programmer or technician.

There is no minimum period which can be classified as safe, nor any fixed point at which the risk of unenforceability begins. The ILU survey showed that a one-year restraint is not an uncommon period to find in contracts, but this may be more relevant to non-solicitation rather than the protection of information. The determination of reasonableness rests mainly on whether the court can be convinced that the restraint does not go beyond the life span of the information.

Highly technical information will probably have a short life span, both because of the speed at which technology changes and also the fact that an employee could not retain enough detail of the information for too long. This second point will be of no significance, of course, if the employee has copied or specifically memorised data. On the other hand 'secret recipes' might well justify lifetime bans, even though it was established early this century that life-long restrictions are most likely void (*Attwood* v *Lamont* [1920] 3 KB 571).

The designer of a new compact disc player, for instance, is an ideal target for poaching by rival firms; but the confidentiality of the information may have a life span of only six months. A one-year restraint would have no more chance of survival than a one-year confidentiality clause. But taking our other example, the confidentiality of a low-technology 'secret recipe' may last for ever. The nature of the product, or at least its reputation, means that the secret cannot be revealed and does not fall into desuetude. We are ignoring for these purposes any other intellectual property rights the employer possesses, e.g., design rights or patent protection. These will have given the employer *specific* property rights in any intellectual property. What cannot be protected is the general skill and know-how that the employee has acquired whilst in employment. The distinction between confidential information and know-how is the same as detailed in chapter 1.

2.2.4.2 Time in relation to trade connections
A more relaxed attitude to lengthy or unlimited restraints has been taken by the courts in relation to trade connections. Thus in *Fitch* v *Dewes* [1921] 2 AC 158, where the employee (a solicitor's managing clerk) interviewed about half of the firm's clients, a clause preventing him from practising within seven miles of Tamworth Town Hall was upheld, even though the time-limit was unrestricted. But this does not set a general pattern. In reality, the usefulness of the trade connections will have a life span just as much as confidential information. The purpose of the restraint is not the maintenance of a competitive edge but the realistic prevention of unjustified soliciting.

Thus, even at the same time as *Fitch* v *Dewes* was being decided we have seen that, in *Attwood* v *Lamont* [1920] 3 KB 571, the courts were voicing their opposition to lifetime bans; in this case, relating to a tailor who was subject to an unlimited restraint not to carry on any similar business (as a tailor, dressmaker, general draper, milliner, hatter, haberdasher . . .) within 10 miles of Kidderminster.

It is obvious that as a restraint runs its course any advantage gained by the former employee will begin to fade. Knowledge of the market will become out of date and, more importantly, connections will be lost. With this in mind, Jessel MR suggested in *Middleton* v *Brown* (1878) 47 LJ Ch 411 at p. 413 that the duration of the restraint should be limited to the time it takes for a replacement employee to demonstrate his effectiveness to customers. In truth this does nothing more than give effect to the adage 'out of sight out of mind'. How soon will any hold that the employee had over trade connections cease or at least be weakened sufficiently? This suggestion seems eminently sensible, for after the restraint has ceased to be effective there is an open market in which the employee can compete.

2.2.5 Non-solicitation covenants and trade connections

The general rules described above apply equally to non-solicitation covenants as to non-dealing and non-competition clauses. We have separated out this area only because it brings with it some extra matters for consideration. As a matter of drafting practice it is advisable to separate out such clauses too. These clauses are narrower in scope and effect than other restraints, and, as we discuss below, isolating the various forms of restraint increases the chance of one aspect succeeding even when all others are falling by the wayside. Further, there seems to be a developing trend for courts to determine the reasonableness of, say, a geographical restraint by asking whether a non-solicitation clause could have served the purpose just as well. If it is found that the lesser clause could have safeguarded the legitimate interests then the wider clause will be held unreasonable. This form of approach was seen most recently in *Office Angels Ltd* v *Rainer-Thomas* [1991] IRLR 214.

Non-solicitation clauses relate to the protection of trade connections and goodwill. The time qualification in the restraint will therefore be germane, though the question of the area covered is usually irrelevant (see *G.W. Plowman and Son Ltd* v *Ash* [1964] 1 WLR 568).

One of the most straightforward clauses found in the ILU survey was:

> *The Employee shall not at any time during or within 12 months from the cessation of his employment solicit or endeavour to entice away from the Company any person firm or company who at any time during his employment shall have been a customer or employee of the Company.*

Some of the factors one has to consider here are: Is the time restraint justifiable? To what extent is it permissible to prevent the enticement of employees as opposed to trade connections? To what extent can the restraint be placed on *any* customer when the employee may not have had contact with them? This clause related to both senior staff and more junior staff. But, as has been noted above, such 'blanket' provisions are not advisable for, because of their lack of selectivity, the appropriateness to an individual employee is made more difficult to discern.

2.2.5.1 What constitutes solicitation?

Solicitation involves action by the employee: the enticing or active attraction of connections away from the former employer. Being approached by a former customer of the employer is not solicitation; and to prevent this activity the employer will need to insert a non-dealing clause. It may well be that this additional protection is not necessary in the circumstances relating either to the company's business or the type of employee involved. In the ILU survey it was found that few of the companies which had a specific restraint clause inserted both non-solicitation as well as non-dealing and non-competition clauses. The most favoured clause appearing in isolation was that of non-solicitation.

Apart from the more obvious act of contacting connections directly and overtly it is also probable that indirect approaches such as advertising in newspapers and trade journals will constitute solicitation. If the solicitation clause has a geographical limit the issue of advertising could become a problem. An employee would clearly be able to solicit custom outside that area, but what if the advertisement covered the area defined in the clause as well, e.g., as with national or trade advertising? There appears to be no direct case law on this point, though in *Cullard* v *Taylor* (1887) 3 TLR 698 a solicitor restrained from operating within a particular area who sent letters to clients residing in the area was held to be in breach of the restraint; and New Zealand authority (*Sweeney* v *Astle* (1923) 42 NZLR 1198) indicates that advertising which 'spills over' into the protected area so that customers become aware of the employee's position will be outlawed. If such is the position then the question of time constraint becomes particularly important if the clause is to be seen as reasonable rather than punitive.

In one company's very detailed restraint clause (one which was divided into numerous independent but related subclauses) non-solicitation was 'defined' by reference to activities such as:

> *Canvass solicit or approach or cause to be canvassed . . . [etc] Interfere or seek to interfere or take steps as may interfere with the continuance of supplies . . .*
>
> *Solicit or entice or endeavour to solicit or entice away from the Company or offer or cause to be offered any employment to any person employed by the Company.*

Another common term found for describing non-solicitation was to refer to a duty not to 'procure or seek to procure' custom, employees etc. away.

2.2.5.2 Which connections are covered?

These need to be capable of identification. The conclusive justification factor will then be whether the clause is protecting against influence being exerted by the former employee. Thus in *Gledhow Autoparts Ltd* v *Delaney* [1965] 1 WLR 1366 the clause sought to restrict the activities of a salesman. The clause prohibited solicitation 'within the districts in which the traveller operated'. Many of the customers had had no contact with the employee. The clause was therefore wider than necessary and void.

The same principle can be seen at work in *Marley Tile Co. Ltd* v *Johnson* [1982] IRLR 75. The covenant here failed because, *inter alia*, the relationship of the restraint to the range of customers covered was unreasonable, even though limited to a specific area.

In *G.W. Plowman and Son Ltd* v *Ash* [1964] 1 WLR 568 it was held that a restraint could extend to connections who were customers at the beginning of the employee's employment but who had ceased to be so before the employee left. Given our previously noted doubts about this case, we would suggest that this is treated with some caution. Indeed, in *Hinton and Higgs (UK) Ltd* v *Murphy* [1989] IRLR 519 a clause attempting to restrain contact with the employer's 'previous or present' connections was declared unreasonable (though Lord Dervaird did not rule unreasonable as such any restraint relating to customers with whom there had been no contact). An employer cannot, however, guard against the employee's contact with potential future customers of the employer (*Konski* v *Peet* [1915] 1 Ch 530). In *Gledhow Autoparts Ltd* v *Delaney* this was confirmed but with the possible proviso that the clause may be justified where the departing employee has made some initial contact with the customer before leaving. In dealing with a question of severance in *Rex Stewart Jeffries Parker Ginsberg Ltd* v *Parker* [1988] IRLR 483 the Court of Appeal also took objection to restraints which referred to customers arising after the employee had left. The clause in question there sought to prevent soliciting of 'the custom or business of any person, concern, firm or company who to your knowledge is or has been during the period of your employment a customer' The words 'is or' were severed as being unreasonable.

We have already noted that if a clause is otherwise reasonable it will not be deemed unreasonable simply because the employer's connections state they are unlikely to do business with the employer anyway: see *John Michael Design plc v Cooke* [1987] ICR 445.

2.2.6 Width of the clause: reasonableness in terms of area covered

The key point here is that the size of the area is related more to density of population than mere acreage. It is thus an oversimplification to state that the wider the area the more likely it will be unreasonable; although it is a convenient rule of thumb.

The first covenant unrestricted in terms of place was enforced in 1880, though there was a time limitation of 10 years. Equally, UK-wide bans have succeeded. In *Forster and Sons Ltd v Suggett* (1918) 35 TLR 87 the restraint was on an engineer and lasted for five years. In the more controversial case of *Littlewoods Organisation Ltd v Harris* [1976] ICR 516 a director concerned with mail order catalogues was restrained from employment within the UK for one year. Occasionally worldwide bans have been permitted by the courts (see *Under Water Welders and Repairers Ltd v Street* [1968] RPC 498, concerning a diver under a three-year restraint), but these examples should be treated with some caution.

With the increase in national and multinational companies the problems as to which area is to be covered by the restraint will be ever-increasing.

2.2.6.1 Area in relation to confidential information
Where the justification for a restraint rests on the protection of information, its geographical ambit may have to be very wide. After all, information knows no real boundaries. A piece of information may be just as useful to an employer in Aberdeen as in Penzance, whereas, as we shall see, trade connections may be more geographically limited.

For instance, let us say that the industry involved is that of computer development. Now, the disclosure of information to someone in the catering trade might be annoying to the employer, but is unlikely to be harmful. If the employer wishes to protect this form of disclosure there should be a pure confidentiality clause in the contract. But the restraint of trade clause is aimed at disarming competition. Thus, the general 'market' in which the employer operates is a justifiable 'area'; and that area might these days be the UK, Europe, or even worldwide. The maintenance of secrecy within a 10-mile radius, but no further, is probably pointless in this example. And once again, it is easier to police the non-disclosure of information if there is a restraint clause rather than a mere non-disclosure clause.

The restraint based on protecting confidential information is most likely to be aimed at preventing competitors from benefiting from the employee's expertise. Whilst, as we have said, neither pure competition nor the employee's skill and knowledge are valid justifications for restraints to operate, it is permissible to limit a restraint to named competitors or competitors within a defined area.

Perhaps the most notable example is that of *Littlewoods Organisation Ltd v Harris* [1976] ICR 516. The restraint was designed to protect business secrets, those being the fashion designs for the following year's mail order catalogue. Harris was in a senior position and had access to confidential information. The restraint was for one year. The clause was drafted to prevent Harris working for Littlewoods' major rival, Great Universal Stores (GUS). Harris left Littlewoods and went to work for GUS. The clause (which was effectively world-wide in its scope) was construed as applying only to the UK (because that was the only place where Littlewoods and GUS were rivals) and only to the type of business in which GUS competed with Littlewoods. With these limitations the clause was held to be enforceable. *Littlewoods Organisation Ltd v Harris* is often cited as the prime example of the courts adopting a more lenient view to restraint clauses. It is submitted that this is to overstate the position. Instead, it is submitted that the case simply recognises the form of restraint needed to protect confidential information; albeit with a court prepared to adopt an extremely liberal method of interpretation. A similar approach had already been witnessed in *Home Counties Dairies Ltd v Skilton* [1970] 1 WLR 526 where a widely drafted clause was confined in its effect to the actual work of the employee as a milkman.

2.2.6.2 *Area in relation to trade connections*

The reasonableness of geographical restraints in relation to trade connections is more problematic. Non-dealing or non-competition clauses are crude devices. And, as we have discussed, the justification for the protection of trade connections is based on the fact that employees can exert influence over these connections. In time, that influence will wane; but how far should the geographical restraint extend in the meantime?

To answer this the courts must do two things: first, they must survey the actual width of the employer's operations; secondly, they must determine whether the restriction effectively negates the former employee's potential *influence* over the company's connections. On the first point, for instance, if a company operates only in Coventry, a restraint extending to Newcastle would go beyond what is necessary. A lesser clause would serve to protect equally as well. Thus the extended area should be deemed unreasonable. This form of analysis works very well with local businesses such as shopkeepers, hairdressers, small firms of solicitors and accountants, or local tradesmen. The emphasis is on preventing the maintenance of physical contact and thus the perpetuation of influence.

When the employer's business is less localised the definition of a reasonable area has to rest on the factual point of understanding the employer's business and the appropriateness to the employee. It can no longer be the case that merely because the employer operates across the whole UK, the restraint should also cover such an area. The clause should at least relate to the siting of the employer's competitors and/or the employee's activities — and even then there may be problems as with *Marley Tile Co. Ltd* v *Johnson* [1982] IRLR 75 or *Office Angels Ltd* v *Rainer-Thomas* [1991] IRLR 214.

The ILU survey revealed a number of variations in relation to area covered. One such clause stated:

> *I undertake that I will not, without the consent of the Company,* anywhere in the United Kingdom *within 12 months after the termination of my engagement with the Company, however caused, either alone or jointly with or as employee of or as consultant or agent for any person, firm or company, directly or indirectly, carry on or be engaged in any business or be concerned in the affairs of any business which is competing or about to compete with any business of the Company carried on at the date of such termination, provided that such latter business is one in which I shall have been employed or engaged or with which I shall have been substantially connected within 12 months prior to such termination.*

An additional clause replaced the highlighted words with 'anywhere in the world outside the United Kingdom' but was otherwise identical. The clause is a non-competition clause and has a preliminary justification clause which refers to the particular employee having substantial contact with customers and/or being in possession of confidential information. The clause bears some resemblance to that which occurred in *Marley Tile Co. Ltd* v *Johnson,* but the last subclause seeks to limit the effect of the restraint to the actual activities of the employee and thus moves more towards reasonableness. The UK (or the alternative worldwide) restraint will be prima facie justifiable if that is where the company's business and the employee's activities lie. There is, however, a long list of forbidden activities and the word 'indirectly' appears again. It would be a question of fact whether any particular employee would be affected to the point that this clause would act to sterilise rather than protect.

Another such clause ran:

> *The employee agrees that he shall not . . . for a period of one year following termination, either on his own account or for any other person, firm or company engage in or be concerned with, directly or indirectly, any business carried on by this company as at the date of that termination of this contract.*

This clause has obvious weaknesses. First there is the issue that any business carried on by the company is supposedly covered by the clause. Unless the business has a narrow range of activities, or perhaps the employee is engaged in a wide overviewing role, the clause will encounter difficulties. More apposite to this section, the geographical limits of the clause are not mentioned. In general the courts will therefore view this as a worldwide restraint (thereby severely limiting its chances); at best the courts will relate the clause to competitors. In either case the clause is unlikely to prove successful.

In the final example, the contract separated out the non-competition and non-solicitation clauses. Subclauses then dealt with particular employments (e.g., technical or sales) and referred to a 'prohibited area'. The definition of prohibited area was contained in a separate clause, left blank in the model draft contract provided in the survey, presumably to be completed as appropriate for the particular employment. Assuming that each employee or grade of employee was subject to a distinct form of wording, this flexibility should prove extremely useful. The common wording in each subclause was to prohibit being:

> *directly or indirectly engaged concerned or interested . . . in any other business which is wholly or partly in competition with any business carried on by the Company.*

2.2.7 Width of the clause: public policy considerations

Strictly speaking, the whole doctrine of restraint of trade is based on the concept of public interest; the balancing of an individual's liberty with principles of freedom of contract (*Mason v Provident Clothing and Supply Co. Ltd* [1913] AC 724). Courts can therefore 'fall back' on pronouncements of public interest or public policy in order to strike out clauses which, though reasonable perhaps as between the parties, offend some vague judgment as to what is acceptable. The explanations for invoking public policy considerations have ranged from matters such as sanctity of contract, economic ideas of inequality of bargaining power, the requirement that society should not be deprived of particular skills, through to 'public pleasure' in relation to watching cricketers play!

One thing which is certain about public policy is that it is not immutable. The perceived needs of society vary from decade to decade so that no firm rules can be laid down. As Lord Wilberforce stated in *Esso Petroleum Co. Ltd v Harper's Garage (Stourport) Ltd* [1968] AC 269, there can be no 'absolute exemption for any restriction or regulation'. Nothing that has been said in this chapter, therefore, can guarantee that a specific form of wording carries with it magical qualities of immunity. We have accordingly mentioned a few points below which have occupied the courts' attentions; but these should not be taken as indicating clear-cut judicial approaches.

If the restraint has passed the tests of legitimate interest as well as temporal and spatial reasonableness it will fall on the employee to prove that it is nevertheless contrary to public policy (*Herbert Morris Ltd v Saxelby* [1916] 1 AC 688). It will not be contrary to public policy simply on the grounds that the employee's interests are more adversely affected than the employer's interests are protected. Except in the extreme case, where the employee is prevented from working at all, the effect on the employee is not really a consideration addressed by the courts. The test is not based on the *balancing* of interests (*Allied Dunbar (Frank Weisinger) Ltd v Weisinger* [1988] IRLR 60).

It was suggested in *Faccenda Chicken Ltd v Fowler* [1987] Ch 117 that the use to which an employee puts confidential information may have an effect on the court's approach to the protection sought. Neill LJ raised the idea that where the employee is not seeking to earn his or her living by making use of the information, but merely sells that information, the court will feel less fettered in assessing reasonableness. Such an approach is initially attractive, but, except on the general grounds of public policy, it is not that easy to defend.

Other examples of 'public policy' may be found, though no discernible general principles are obvious. In *Bull* v *Pitney-Bowes Ltd* [1967] 1 WLR 273 a pension scheme contained a clause to the effect that if the retired employee entered into any form of competition with the employer that employee's pension rights would be affected. This was held to be contrary to the public interest. And in *Kores Manufacturing Co. Ltd* v *Kolok Manufacturing Co. Ltd* [1959] Ch 108 two companies entered into an agreement that neither would, without the consent of the other, employ anyone who had been an employee of the other company during the previous five years. In an industry of high competition, and because of the proximity of the factories, this was seen to protect both their interests. The defendants broke the agreement to take on a research chemist. In the ensuing proceedings the court held that the restraint was void, *inter alia*, because it was objectionable 'from the standpoint of the public interest' (although no specific ruling was made on this point).

But public policy does not always damn restraint clauses. Thus in *Bridge* v *Deacons* [1984] AC 705 the Privy Council perceived the value of restraint clauses as providing a means whereby the young can replace the old. And in *Kerr* v *Morris* [1987] Ch 90 the Court of Appeal did not agree that doctors in general practice formed a special class exempt from the applications of restraint of trade clauses.

In the end, public policy may be seen simply as an adjunct to reasonableness. Throughout the history of this area public policy has proved to be an underlying and unpredictable factor of the 'I'll know it when I see it' kind. Ultimately, however, if the test of reasonableness has been satisfied it will be rare for the courts to find alternative grounds for not enforcing the covenant (a view recently re-inforced by the Court of Appeal in *Co-operative Retail, Services Ltd* v *Earl* (*t/a Nelson Dairy*) (1991) (LEXIS transcript).

2.3 DRAFTING AND INTERPRETATION

2.3.1 The problems in giving meaning to the clause

Given the courts' general opposition to restraint clauses it might be thought that an extremely literal interpretation would be applied to the wording of such clauses. This is the safest assumption to make, but the courts' position is, in fact, far less predictable than this. Thus the meaning of any clause should be made as clear as possible. In *Business Seating (Renovations) Ltd* v *Broad* [1989] ICR 729, for instance, the restraint sought to prevent soliciting of the 'business of any customers or clients of the [employer]'. The clause did not say what the 'business' was. The court interpreted the clause by reference to other clauses in the contract to define the business as that of the repair and renovation of office furniture; but the court could simply have struck out the clause for ambiguity.

As was also noted in *Office Angels Ltd* v *Rainer-Thomas* [1991] IRLR 214, phrases such as 'engage' or 'undertake' or 'carry on a business' are somewhat flexible expressions which may bear different meanings according to the nature of the business involved. The particular wording will therefore be subjected to close scrutiny, but equally some form of common sense is allowed to prevail.

A classic form in which this appears is to limit the application of any restraint, however widely worded, to the employer's actual business interests. *Home Counties Dairies Ltd* v *Skilton* [1970] 1 WLR 526 illustrates this point. The clause in question prohibited the employee-milkman from serving or selling 'milk or dairy produce' to any customers of his former employer. It was argued that this was so widely drawn that it would prevent such activities as the employee selling cheese in a grocer's shop. Perhaps it would, was the Court of Appeal's response, but clearly the clause was aimed only at 'the same type of business as the employer's'. Fanciful interpretations should not determine the general reasonableness of the clause. The clause was therefore valid inasmuch as it sought to protect real trade connections. The outcome, of course, might well have been different if the dairy's connections also extended to grocers' shops. The trade connections would have been present, but there would also be the danger that the employee was prevented from working in the industry at all.

It is therefore a logical question to ask: Should the employer make clear the interests for which protection is sought? Such interests could be spelled out in an introductory section, for instance. Indeed, in some of the contracts in the ILU survey, this practice was adopted. One such clause ran:

> *I acknowledge that my engagement with the Company may give rise to substantial connection with customers and will involve my acquiring and/ or generating information which is secret, confidential and proprietary to the Company, and of great value to it.*

At first sight this appears to be good drafting practice. However, the drafter may be caught on the horns of a dilemma. In *Office Angels Ltd* v *Rainer-Thomas* [1991] IRLR 214 the Court of Appeal provided some words of caution regarding the identification of a legitimate interest. Sir Christopher Slade indicated that where the restraint clause does not specifically state the interest which the covenant is intended to protect the court can look at the wording and the general circumstances to ascertain the parties' intentions. Where the covenant does state the interest the employer 'is not, in my opinion, entitled thereafter to seek to justify the covenant by reference to some separate and additional interest which has not been specified'. The introductory words in this case referred to the 'clients of the company' and safeguarding 'the company's goodwill'. The words did not preclude the employees from contacting the pool of temporary workers whom they had known in their work in the employment agency; the restraint could only apply to the employer-clients. Thus spelling out the legitimate interest gains the advantage of definition and certainty, but runs the risk of limitation.

Returning to the clause featured from the ILU survey, it is less likely that such a clause would suffer the same fate as the introductory words in *Office Angels*. It is worth noting, however, that the clause specifically relates to *customers*; on the *Office Angels* approach, suppliers, former employees and more remote connections might not be included. The ILU clause is useful inasmuch as it states a general purpose and warns employees of the purpose and importance of the agreement. It seems ironic that employers who make no attempt to indicate the legitimate interest being protected might be in a more advantageous position. Of course, even as regards the ILU clause, if the restraint was applied to employees who could not satisfy these conditions the sympathy of the court would be lost.

Clauses which are narrowly drafted will generally not be read as protecting wider interests. At its simplest, this will mean that a non-solicitation clause will fail to prevent employees dealing with customers who contact them. A corollary to this is that an employee who is subject to a non-dealing and non-competition clause will be able to write to clients in the restricted area. As regards the aversion to reading clauses too widely there are many examples. They obviously tend to come down to niceties of wording.

What the courts will not tolerate, however, are 'colourable evasions' — minor and meaningless alterations of status on the behalf of the employee (e.g., a change in job title) made simply to avoid the exact wording of the restraint. An employee who argues that acting as an assistant to, say, an architect, is not in breach of a restraint which forbids him 'carrying on that profession' will see little sympathy from the courts. Setting up a limited company under which to continue in the same trade will also count as a colourable evasion (*Gilford Motor Co. Ltd* v *Horne* [1933] Ch 935).

What must be stressed, however, is that if the contract is silent or ambiguous on a particular point it will most likely be construed against the employer. One of the most recent examples appeared in *WAC Ltd* v *Whillock* [1990] IRLR 23 where the clause in question prohibited a shareholder from carrying on a business in competition *personally* but was silent about taking on a directorship or becoming an employee of a competitor. The shareholder was therefore entitled to become a director.

On the other hand courts have shown some willingness to take a wide clause and restrict its meaning to a smaller geographical area: see *Littlewoods Organisation Ltd* v *Harris* [1976] ICR 516. Whether this is effectively rewriting a clause which was drafted too widely is a matter of opinion.

As a matter of drafting practice therefore it is imperative that any restraint clause actually reflects (without necessarily specifying) both a legitimate interest *and* the relevance of that clause to the employee's work. The easiest clauses to draft are those which prohibit actions on a sweeping basis. They are equally the most dangerous clauses because they cannot hope to cover all eventualities. Even an immaculately worded contract which contains only one general clause intended to cover the entire workforce will probably be drafted too widely to cover specific situations or will not be appropriate to some grades of employees.

In the ILU survey a number of companies therefore adopted a style of maintaining one general contract containing a large quantity of alternatives within clauses, or even of alternative clauses for each grade of employee. For example, one clause stated that the employee would not after termination (within defined times and area):

> *provide [technical] [commercial] [or professional] advice to any business.*

And another that the employee would not:

> *accept employment in any [executive] [technical] [sales] capacity with any business concern.*

The words in brackets indicate the types of employees affected. The inappropriate words would be struck out in the individual's contract.

2.3.2 Severance and 'blue-pencilling'

As hinted at above, the courts have no general power to rewrite a restraint to make it reasonable. We have seen that they may give some interpretation to the wording, but it is not the courts' function to make contracts. What they will do, however, is edit the clause — or apply the infamous blue pencil.

'Blue-pencilling' means that the courts may, within limitations, remove words or sentences which are felt to make the clause unreasonable. The remaining part of the clause is then allowed to stand and be effective. In truth this will occur most often when there are separate clauses: one clause may be struck out leaving the other (narrower) clause operative. Where the restraint stands as a single clause it is more difficult to sever parts so as to allow the remainder still to make sense gramatically and be considered reasonable. It is for these reasons that restraint clauses are sometimes structured so that wider clauses are accompanied by narrower *independent* promises — what has sometimes been called the 'shopping list' approach. The limitations in all cases are that the court cannot add words and the extant part of the clause must make grammatical and legal sense. Effectively, the promise requiring severing must be an independent promise in relation to the remainder of the restraint. As Lord Sterndale MR stated in *Attwood* v *Lamont* [1920] 3 KB 571 the contract is open to severance where 'the severed parts are independent from one another and can be severed without the severance affecting the meaning of the part remaining'.

A recent example is that of *Rex Stewart Jeffries Parker Ginsberg Ltd* v *Parker*

[1988] IRLR 483 which was noted above. There, various words were blue-pencilled such as the words 'is or' which had sought to restrain dealings with customers contracting with the employer *after* the employee had left, as well as references to associated companies. It is therefore a little surprising that few companies in the ILU survey adopted the approach of inserting separate, independent, but related clauses. Clauses which failed to adopt this approach run a major risk of being held unreasonable. The best 'shopping list' example ran to two pages of close type. Whilst we cannot reproduce the whole clause here, some indication of structure is noted below.

In order to protect information and connections one company inserted a clause which specifically limited the protection to the United Kingdom, including another clause (worded almost identically) which referred to anywhere in the world outside the United Kingdom. Indeed, there were separate clauses concerning the protection of information and the protection of connections. Distinctions were also drawn between non-solicitation and non-dealing covenants. A final clause then stated:

> *Each and every undertaking contained herein shall be read as a separate and distinct undertaking and the invalidity or unenforceability of any part of any of them shall not affect the validity or enforceability of the remainder. The employee agrees that the undertakings which have been given are reasonable for the protection of the legitimate interests of the Company.*

This is the kind of wording that would apparently have received approval in *Hinton and Higgs (UK) Ltd* v *Murphy* [1989] IRLR 519 had not the rest of the contract been unworkable because of its unreasonableness. In this case the wording ran: 'The restrictions contained in clause 14 are considered reasonable by the parties'. Lord Dervaird regarded this as an illegitimate attempt to oust the jurisdiction of the court — the same should be noted in the last part of the ILU clause. The *Hinton and Higgs* clause continued:

> . . . but in the event that any such restriction shall be found to be void would be valid [sic] if some part thereof were deleted or the period of application reduced such restrictions shall apply with such modifications as may be necessary to make them valid or effective.

Lord Dervaird had no objection to this provided this did not mean rewriting the contract but merely 'selecting that version of it which the parties have . . . made with each other'.

In *Sadler* v *Imperial Life Assurance Co. of Canada Ltd* [1988] IRLR 388 three conditions were stated as necessary for severance (or 'blue-pencilling') to occur:

(a) that the unenforceable provisions could be removed without the need to add to or modify the remaining part;
(b) the remaining terms continued to be supported by adequate consideration; and

(c) the removal of the words did not change the character of the clause, i.e., make the contract substantially different from that which was originally agreed. For instance, in *Attwood* v *Lamont* [1920] 3 KB 571 severance was refused on the grounds that, by excising the descriptions of the business which went too far, one would have to alter entirely the meaning of the covenant itself.

It is therefore impossible to rely on the notion of severance saving a bad clause. And although it has become common drafting practice of late to state specifically that the parties 'agree that the courts may sever any part of the clause and still give effect to it', this tactic does not always save the day either. What is not tolerated is a clause which states that it will be effective 'so far as the law allows' (*Davies* v *Davies* (1887) 36 ChD 359).

2.3.3 When is reasonableness determined?

The reasonableness of a clause is determined by looking at the point when it was entered into (*Gledhow Autoparts Ltd* v *Delaney* [1965] 1 WLR 1366). Promotions and changes in job titles, which effectively involve new contracts, could therefore have an effect on the reasonableness of any clause. The new contractual terms need to match the type of restraint required to the new status and responsibilities of the employee, e.g., as regards greater access to confidential information. It is common practice, therefore, to draft clauses which refer to events at the point of termination such as the prevention of solicitation of customers 'who have been customers of the employer during the last 12 months prior to termination'.

One worrying aspect of *Gledhow* does not seem to have been developed. In timing the assessment of reasonableness at the date of formation of contract the Court of Appeal also contrasted the length of notice due (two weeks) with the length of the restraint (three years). The court's view was that it was unreasonable that an employee of only a few weeks' standing could receive only two weeks' notice and yet be subject to a lengthy restraint. Whatever the validity of the reasoning in this case, if this was applied as a universal determinant of reasonableness it would mean that *nearly all* restraint clauses would be unreasonable.

2.4 IMPLIED AND INDIRECT RESTRAINTS

Stenhouse Australia Ltd v *Phillips* [1974] AC 391 provides a good example of such terms. The clause required the employee to pay to his former employer, for five years, half the commission emanating from deals struck with any of the former employer's customers. By another name this was a restraint clause.

The same reasoning can be seen on different facts in *Bull* v *Pitney-Bowes Ltd* [1967] 1 WLR 273. In *Sadler* v *Imperial Life Assurance Co. of Canada Ltd* [1988] IRLR 388 the employee was entitled under the contract to receive commission on life policies even after ceasing employment. However, the contract also stated that if he entered into competition with his former employer in a way defined in the contract by reference to competition *during* employment then this commission would cease to be payable. He entered into such competition and the employers refused to pay the commission. The clause was held to be an indirect restraint of trade clause and it was void as being drawn too widely.

Thus it is open to the courts to deem any clause which is considered seriously to affect an employee's chances of gaining employment as being in restraint of trade. Such might be the case even with confidentiality clauses if the prevention of disclosure relates to such a narrow market that the maintenance of secrecy itself means that the employee is prevented from working.

2.5 RESTRAINTS DURING EMPLOYMENT

In this section we deal with the question: When will an employee be prevented from competing with the employer's business? As an aspect of the duty of fidelity (or good faith) an employee must clearly not use the employer's time to compete with the employer. The employee should not put himself in a position which will generate a conflict of interest (*Thomas Marshall (Exports) Ltd* v *Guinle* [1979] Ch 227 — a case concerning a managing director, but the principles will apply equally to all employees).

The law of contract has always struggled with the notion of freedom of contract as set against morally untenable clauses. For the most part the contract is sacrosanct so that oppressive or unduly burdensome terms cannot be overturned merely because of perceived unfairness or injustice; and yet the cases sometimes reveal how the courts may unexpectedly put the brakes on such *laissez-faire* attitudes. The contract of employment has not escaped from this dilemma. However, inequality of bargaining power has never found a place in the analysis of contracts of employment, nor has the Unfair Contract Terms Act 1977 any part to play in determining the ambit of an employee's duties.

As we saw in the introduction there are a number of statutory imposed terms, e.g., relating to discrimination, but the common law has taken a more minor role and more circuitous route in placing constraints on employers' and employees' actions. Thus throughout the 19th century we see the introduction of some elements of good faith dealing, usually implanted in the contract by the means of implied terms such as mutual trust or fidelity. These notions have taken root and been nurtured by more modern forms of actions, especially in relation to constructive dismissal claims.

The history of employment contracts does reveal, however, that the courts have always taken a dim view of terms in a contract which could be classified as 'servile incidents' — unjustified restrictions on individuals' actions, notably in the employees' spare time. It may once have been the employer's prerogative to order the servant's life in a very general and authoritarian manner; but today's test for determining what constitutes a 'lawful order' is narrower.

That test centres on whether the order has any contractual force; and even express terms which are not aimed at service but have the feel of servitude behind them may be deemed unenforceable.

There is, of course, a close affinity between servile incidents and restraints of trade. Traditionally one would apply a test of 'servile incident' to clauses which operated during the currency of the contract (e.g., the width of a 'whole time and attention' clause) whilst reserving the application of restraint of trade doctrine to actions occurring *after* the termination of the contract. Following cases such as *A. Schroeder Music Publishing Co. Ltd* v *Macaulay* [1974] 1 WLR 1308 and *Clifford Davis Management Ltd* v *WEA Records Ltd* [1975] 1 WLR 61, however, there has developed a thesis that one should apply the restraint of trade doctrine to terms relevant to the currency of the employment contract (see *Electrolux Ltd* v *Hudson* [1977] FSR 312). This is despite the fact that all the leading cases positing this approach have not been concerned with employment law at all, but rather with commercial contracts (and most recently relating to exclusive contracts for 'exploited' songwriter-performers).

It might be thought that, to a large extent, this classification is an academic point — in either instance the court is effectively assessing the reasonableness of the term. But there are important distinctions to be drawn. First, courts are reluctant even today to upset express terms relating to the operation of the contract, e.g., terms relating to hours, pay etc. The courts display a far more protective attitude to the employer's interests during the currency of the contract. At the same time, courts have always subjected restraint clauses to a detailed and rigorous analysis. Secondly, an express term relating to the currency of the contract is presumed valid unless shown otherwise; restraint clauses are presumed to be void.

If, for instance, we analyse a 'whole time and attention' clause it will be seen that the initial classification plays a major role in the analysis. These clauses can often take the form of simply relating the employee's duties to apply himself or herself to the job, e.g., 'The employee will give his whole time and attention during the term of his employment exclusively to the duties of the job and the business of the employer'. It is more common, however, to find such a term related more specifically to the prohibition of competing with the employer.

Take the following clauses which appeared in the ILU survey:

It is a condition of your employment that during your employment you do not, without the Company's written consent, at any time, directly or indirectly, carry on or be engaged in any other business.

You will not engage in other employment or activity in any way which impinges, or is likely to impinge upon, any of the company's business activities without prior consent from the Company.

From a 'servile incidents' angle we need to judge the relevance of these clauses to the contracts taken as a whole; taking account of matters such as the financial incentives, the balance between other terms and conditions etc. The presumption is that the clauses are valid and the analysis of why they may be invalid is loose: that they overstep the bounds of acceptable industrial practice; that no harm to the employer's business would be evident if the clauses were removed (other ILU survey clauses related the duty more specifically to causing harm to the company); or that there is a breach of good faith. In the end the analysis tends to proceed on a rather impressionistic basis.

If the same clauses were to be judged under the restraint of trade doctrine, the most obvious difference is that they are presumed void. Further, there are specific tests as to legitimate interests, time and geography that must be met. Thus both restraint of trade and servile incidents may be based upon the same *common rule* of preventing undue restrictions on personal liberty, but one should be clear about which is being used. For instance, in chapter 4 one problem we will pose, in relation to ownership of copyright, is whether an express clause can redefine whether a particular, or every, act is 'within the course of [an employee's] employment'. Clearly a contractual term can set some legitimate limits on defining the course of employment, but what if the clause is drawn very widely, effectively saying that anything done at any time is within the course of employment so that the copyright in anything produced will belong to the employer? Should such a term be analysed along: (a) 'freedom of contract' lines; (b) servile incidents; or (c) restraint of trade? We would suggest one of the first two choices, though one can find authority to indicate the use of all three.

What is clear is that restrictions can be placed on the employee's activities during employment. As we stated in the introduction, there may also be *positive* duties incumbent on the employee (falling under a general conceptual umbrella of commitment to the enterprise) but normally these terms are restrictive in nature. Thus, in various circumstances, one has to examine the potential impact of a duty not to compete and a duty not to disclose confidential information. This latter point was dealt with in the previous chapter, so we will concentrate here on the duty regarding competition.

Without further agreement to the contrary employees are free to take on work in their spare time. The 18th century and early 19th century cases which tied the employee to the employer's needs for 24 hours a day have long since ceased to be operative. And this approach applies equally to full-time as to part-time workers. In order to analyse the rights and duties in this area we need to examine the roles of express and implied terms.

2.5.1 Express terms

These are the 'whole time and attention' clauses noted above. Frequently they state as their justification the prevention of competition during the currency of the contract. In most cases in the ILU survey the clauses sought to prevent competition occurring outside the hours of the contract as well as in company time. An express term can indeed limit the activities of employees undertaken in their spare time. Any restriction the employer imposes on the employee will not deprive the employee of earning any livelihood and therefore will most likely be tolerated by the courts. At least this should hold true with full-time workers; contracts with part-time workers or consultants may well be viewed in a different light — the light of servile incidents or restraint of trade. If the approach in *A. Schroeder Music Publishing Co. Ltd* v *Macaulay* [1974] 1 WLR 1308 has a part to play in employment law, it is most likely to be applicable as regards these employees.

In the ILU survey some clauses took a more direct line; these tended to be labelled 'conflict of interest' clauses. One contract sought to explain what was meant by a conflict of interest:

> *A conflict of interest exists when an employee's loyalties are divided between the Company's interests and the employee's own interests, those of the employee's family, or those of a customer, supplier or competitor. All the Company's employees are expected to avoid both the fact and the appearance of conflicts of interest.*

The clause then went on to detail and outlaw specific breaches such as those relating to speculative investment, employment, directorships, the receiving of gifts, personal loans and confidential information.

Another contract adopted the stance of outlawing direct or indirect concern or engagement in any other business; which activity was then defined as that of competing businesses, suppliers or customers of the employer.

As we noted above, there will be few restrictions placed on the employer's right to protect business interests, at least during the currency of the contract. Employment law has never really addressed the efficacy of such clauses. A serious breach of such a valid express term will allow the employer to dismiss summarily the employee or to claim for damages: see *Rely-A-Bell Burglar and Fire Alarm Co. Ltd* v *Eisler* [1926] Ch 609.

2.5.2 Implied terms

In the absence of an express term the employee will still be bound under the duty of fidelity to use the employer's time for the employer's purposes, i.e., not to pursue other activities during working hours. It is irrelevant here whether those activities might cause harm to the employer or not.

Nor does the absence of such a clause mean that the employee is generally free to pursue any outside activities. As seen in the introduction, an employee owes a duty to further the employer's interests. At its most basic level this will mean that the employee cannot:

(a) *compete with* the employer directly or indirectly;

(b) *cause harm to the employer's interests*, e.g., by divulging (or having the potential to divulge) confidential information (see *Hivac Ltd* v *Park Royal Scientific Instruments Ltd* [1946] Ch 169); or

(c) *cause harm to the relationship* (e.g., by undertaking work which adversely affects the proper fulfilment of the employment contract). The more senior the employee's status the greater this duty becomes.

It follows that some low-ranking staff will have greater freedom as to the use of their spare time and cannot be so easily limited (*Nova Plastics Ltd v Froggatt* [1982] IRLR 146, odd-job man not in breach when working for a competitor in his spare time). Proof of real or potential harm to the employer would be necessary for any restriction to have effect in the case of low-ranking staff.

2.6 PREPARATORY ACTIONS

If an employee is planning to terminate the contract and set up in business he or she will have to make some preparations. Any business venture will need some planning. If the employee uses the employer's time and facilities to do this then this action will constitute a breach of contract. In *Wessex Dairies Ltd* v *Smith* [1935] 2 KB 80 the employee milkman set about informing customers of his plans to set up in business on his own account. He did this on the last day of employment with Wessex Dairies. The Court of Appeal found this to be a breach of the employee's duty of fidelity and awarded damages accordingly.

More recently, adjustments have been made to the latitude allowed to enterprising employees. In *Laughton* v *Bapp Industrial Supplies Ltd* [1986] ICR 634 the two employees wrote to their employer's customers informing them of their intention to set up in business on their own account and asking for product lists, price lists and general terms. They were summarily dismissed when this was discovered by the employer. The EAT held that their actions did not amount to a breach of fidelity; their actions were merely preparatory. The position would have been different if they had used the employer's time and equipment; or even if there had been express terms forbidding such action. Again, in *Balston Ltd* v *Headline Filters Ltd* [1987] FSR 330 a director's intentions to set up in a competing business were held not to be a breach of fiduciary duty or breach of fidelity; nor were his actions which were undertaken during his notice period but at a time when he had been released from his duties.

These cases tended to focus on acts of preparation as distinct from substantive actions. What has not been entirely clear, however, is whether potentially harmful acts such as soliciting customers, suppliers or even fellow employees, pursued in the employees' own time will constitute a breach of fidelity. There are indications (see *Thomas Marshall (Exports) Ltd* v *Guinle* [1978] ICR 905 at p. 925 and *Hivac* v *Park Royal Scientific Instruments Ltd* [1946] Ch 169 at p. 178) that the answer would be that a breach has occurred. Certainly this should be the case where the contract contains a 'dedication to enterprise clause'. But even in the absence of such a clause the recent case of *Marshall* v *Industrial Systems & Control Ltd* [1992] IRLR 294 has limited the effects of *Laughton* v *Bapp*. The facts in *Marshall* were similar to *Laughton* v *Bapp* except that in *Marshall* the employee had formed concrete plans with a fellow employee to steal away the business of his employer's best client, and had tried to induce yet another employee to join him. These actions were found to go beyond the 'mere intention' identified in *Laughton* v *Bapp*.

If the employee is simply planning to leave the company to join another it follows from the above discussion that this will not constitute any breach of fidelity. As seen in chapter 1, however, care must be taken here to distinguish preparatory acts, such as attending interviews, from acts such as copying confidential information or memorising data (see *Robb* v *Green* [1895] 2 QB 315 and comments in *Laughton* v *Bapp Industrial Supplies Ltd*) and undertaking private work for one of the employer's customers. In *Sanders* v *Parry* [1967] 1 WLR 753, for instance, an assistant solicitor agreed with one of his principal's clients to resign and set up in business, in premises provided by the client, taking with him the client's business. Havers J commented that the employee was 'knowingly, deliberately and secretly acting, setting out to do something which would inevitably inflict great harm on his principal'. Thus, such actions will constitute a breach of contract and may render the employee subject to an injunction.

2.7 ASSOCIATED COMPANIES

If the employee works only for a particular business and has no contact with associated or subsidiary companies any restraint which seeks to cover these businesses will be unenforceable. In *Stenhouse Australia Ltd* v *Phillips* [1974] AC 391 it was, however, seen that the position may be different where the employee's business transactions overlapped with these other companies, e.g., where the subsidiary provided the installation service for the main company.

Some 'subsidiary' restraints did surface in the ILU survey. In one the restraint sought to prevent dealing with:

> *any business concern which is wholly or partly in competition with any business carried on by the Company or any of its subsidiaries.*

In a similar vein one company utilised the following wording to restrain solicitation of:

> *any person firm or company who at any time during the employee's service with the Company or the Associated Companies was an employee or customer of or in the habit of dealing with those parts of the business of the Company or the Associated Companies in which he was involved whilst in the employment of the Company or the Associated Companies.*

Another adopted a more complicated structure: the main clauses referred to the company itself, but a later clause allowed for the substitution of:

> *the Company or any company whose ultimate holding company, as that expression is defined in section 736 of the Companies Act 1985, is the Company.*

The idea of the whole family of companies being protected by such a clause would probably be unreasonable in itself. However, the main clause did limit the restraint to the actual work of the employee, i.e., to some direct involvement on the employee's behalf. To this extent the element of reasonableness is again established, at least as regards the legitimate interest of protecting confidential information. The question of protecting trade connections is more debatable. Where the clause relates to the supply of goods or services one would need to know the status of the employee and the frequency of contact in order to establish some form of influence. Of more concern are the words in one clause directing a restraint where the employee has been:

directly responsible or responsible through the sales, marketing, technical or support activities of any subordinates within the 12 months prior to such termination.

The inclusion of 'subordinates' in this clause is questionable, though there should be no reason why an employee in charge of a team (especially if 'fronting' the sales promotion in terms of initial contacts or formal presentations) should not be covered by such a restraint.

One slight variation on the theme made reference to associate companies of trade connections. The clause sought to impose restraints on dealing with companies:

to whom or to which (or to any associate company of which) during the last 12 months prior to such termination the employee shall have supplied goods or services on behalf of the Company.

The inclusion of the associated or subsidiary companies of a trade connection would normally be difficult to defend. In *Business Seating (Renovations) Ltd v Broad* [1989] ICR 729 Millett J, it will be remembered, followed *G.W. Plowman and Son Ltd v Ash* [1964] 1 WLR 568 and adopted a very loose test as to the need to correlate real contact by the employee with trade connections. But even here the learned judge felt unable to extend the protection to customers of a company associated with the employer. The same was seen in *Hinton and Higgs (UK) Ltd v Murphy* [1989] IRLR 519 whilst in *Rex Stewart Jeffries Parker Ginsberg Ltd v Parker* [1988] IRLR 483, the clauses relating to associated companies were severed from the contract. If there is no common interest between the various businesses in the group a restraint clause extending to other companies would have little chance of success.

As the ILU survey clause above relates the restraint to the work actually undertaken by the employee, it has a better chance of survival. In some contracts in the ILU survey we found clauses which stated that the restraint did not apply where the employee's involvement in the associated or subsidiary businesses was merely incidental to that employee's main duties. We would suggest that this is a safer line to take.

2.8 THE EFFECT OF DISMISSAL

2.8.1 Wrongful dismissal

As we noted in the introduction, at common law an employer can terminate the contract for any reason provided the proper notice is given. In such a case there is no breach of contract and the restraint clause will survive the termination of the relationship. However, if the dismissal constitutes a wrongful dismissal this will amount to a repudiation by the employer and all contractual duties will cease. This will mean that the employer cannot rely on any post-termination covenants. This principle, as applied to restraint clauses, was established by the House of Lords in *General Billposting Co. Ltd* v *Atkinson* [1909] AC 118. It has a major impact on all we have discussed.

As we noted in the introduction, there is little penalty imposed on the employer who fails to give proper notice under the contract. Damages will be assessed according to the notice due, i.e., the amount that should have been paid or worked in the first place. However, if restraint clauses fall by reason of the wrongful dismissal then all protection against 'competition' has gone. There is no authority on whether *General Billposting Co. Ltd* v *Atkinson* applies to the type of express confidentiality clauses covered in chapter 1. It is submitted that the principle in the case will apply to such clauses.

Over the last few years it has been common drafting practice to include in restraint covenants a statement that the clause would be effective no matter how the contract came to an end. A number of such clauses appeared in the ILU survey. These clauses recounted the restraint and added that it would be binding:

> *after termination of the employment* however that comes about and whether lawful or not *(emphasis added)*

or:

> *notwithstanding the manner in which or the lawfulness of any dismissal*

or:

> *following termination for whatever reason.*

For some time it was unclear whether such clauses could effectively sidestep the decision in *General Billposting Co. Ltd* v *Atkinson*. In *Briggs* v *Oates* [1990] ICR 473 the *General Billposting* point was taken as applying to contracts even when clauses like those noted above were included. The position is not finally resolved, however, as *Briggs* v *Oates* is only a High Court decision.

The principles of *General Billposting Co. Ltd* v *Atkinson* do not apply to unfair dismissals; only to wrongful dismissal or wrongful repudiation cases. Whether they might apply to a finding by a tribunal that an employee was constructively dismissed and that dismissal was also unfair is open to question.

We would suggest that, owing to the contractual nature of constructive dismissal claims, the principles should be applicable.

2.8.2 Justifiable dismissal

A dismissal without notice or with inadequate notice may still be a lawful dismissal if there is a contractually justifiable reason (known at the date of dismissal or discovered later: *Boston Deep Sea Fishing and Ice Co.* v *Ansell* (1888) 39 ChD 339). The breach by the employee must have been so serious that further continuance of the relationship would prove impossible, such as fraud: see *Sinclair* v *Neighbour* [1967] 2 QB 279. A justifiable dismissal represents the employer accepting the repudiation of the contract by the employee. The employer is still able to rely on the restraint covenants.

2.8.3 Resignation by the employee

If the employee resigns without giving notice, in the face of repudiatory conduct by the employer, he or she will have accepted the repudiation so that the restraint clause will cease to have any effect, as with a wrongful dismissal. If the employee gives notice, however, it seems that this will preserve the restraint clause (*Normalec Ltd* v *Britton* [1983] FSR 318).

2.8.4 Dismissal with payment in lieu of notice

In *Rex Stewart Jeffries Parker Ginsberg Ltd* v *Parker* [1988] IRLR 483 the Court of Appeal dealt with the situation where the contract of employment contained a non-solicitation clause of 18 months' duration. The employee was dismissed with six months' wages in lieu of notice. He then acted in breach of the non-solicitation clause. The employer sought to enforce the clause. The court held that the principle of *General Billposting Co. Ltd* v *Atkinson* [1909] AC 118 did not apply here because the contract specifically allowed for payment in lieu of notice. It would seem to follow then that if the contract does not allow for payment in lieu such a method of terminating the contract (whilst making any wrongful dismissal claim somewhat pointless) may have the side-effect of invalidating any restraint clause.

2.9 GARDEN LEAVE

The rather graphic term 'garden leave' refers to attempts to hold the employee (who wishes to terminate the contract) to his or her notice period. The idea is that the employee will not be forced to work during that notice period but may stay at home (in the garden!) and still be paid. If successful, the effect of such a clause is that it operates as some form of restraint because the employee cannot work for any competitor during this time owing to the employee's duty of fidelity. Contacts and confidential information thus become less and less useful. Injunctions have been granted to this effect. Such relief is discretionary.

The most well-known instance arose in *Evening Standard Co. Ltd* v *Henderson* [1987] ICR 588. Henderson was the production manager for an evening newspaper. His notice period was 12 months. He sought to leave to work for a rival newspaper, giving only two months' notice. The employer sought to hold him to the full notice period. As noted in the introduction, courts do not grant injunctions to compel specific performance of the contract; an employee cannot be forced to work for an employer, nor can an employer be forced to employ someone. Nevertheless in this case an injunction was granted because the company were not seeking to compel Henderson to continue working as such, nor was the company refusing him the right to work, nor would they be seeking damages from him for not working.

In *Provident Financial Group plc* v *Hayward* [1989] ICR 160, the employee (the financial director) gave six months notice as required by the contract. After working for two months he agreed to take four months' pay on the understanding that: (a) he did not work elsewhere during this time (i.e., he took garden leave); and (b) he maintained confidentiality for a period of two years. He sought work with another estate agent and his ex-employer sought an injunction to prevent him doing so. The Court of Appeal held that the injunction should be refused. The key point in granting an injunction is whether breaching an 'anti-competition' clause materially and adversely affects the employer. Here, on the facts, it was found that the employer's position would not be seriously affected by Hayward taking up the new contract.

2.10 CHECKLIST

What does the law require from an employer who wishes to protect against competition from former employees? The text above clearly demonstrates that competition itself cannot be restrained. Nor can an employee be prevented from continuing to earn a living by use of acquired skill and knowledge. Thus employers must be aware *what* they are protecting, *why* it is deserving of protection, and how the *form* of protection can be justified. The following points should therefore be borne in mind.

Any restraint clause requires justification. An employer can only seek to protect a legitimate interest. The traditonal legitimate interests are those of business secrets and trade connections, though the list is not closed. An employer must, however, be clear about the basis for any restraint and the reasoning must be defensible.

Restraint clauses require a written contract. Strictly, this has never been expressed to be mandatory. It is difficult, though, to see how else the clause would be effective. What should be avoided is reliance on s. 1 Employment Protection (Consolidation) Act 1978 written statements to effect restraints. Written statements are not contracts of employment. The restraint clause may be inserted in the contract at any time from initial employment through to

agreement on determination of the contract. However, any *unilateral* variation
of the contract carries with it risks of breach of contract.

The clause itself must be drafted so as to be reasonable. Reasonableness
is determined at the time of making the contract. Whenever the employee
changes job during his or her career the restraint clause should be updated
and, if necessary, redrafted. Alternatively, clauses which refer to activities
in a period just prior to termination can make the clause continually operative.
'Catch-all' terms may have the psychological effect of deterring employees;
but it is unlikely that this type of generalisation will withstand the rigours
of judicial analysis.

Reasonableness will depend upon:

(a)   The appropriateness of the clause to the employer's activities.
(b)   The appropriateness of the clause to the employee's role within the
enterprise.
(c)   The time element.
(d)   The area (if any) covered.
(e)   The public interest.

It is far more sensible to draft a conservative clause that has a reasonable
chance of success than a wider restraint, the more extravagent parts of which
might jeopardise the enforceability of the whole clause.

The clause can only extend to what is adequate to protect the interest. It
must fit the legitimate interest exactly. Where a clause of lesser effect could
have served the purpose just as well (e.g., a non-solicitation clause) this will
make any wider restraint unreasonable. Employers need to assess the minimum
level of restraint necessary to protect their interests.

The clause will generally be interpreted in the employee's favour. An employer
must begin with this premise. Thus it is imperative that definitions and terms
used in the covenant are clear and reflect the realities of the business operation.
General trade usage will not excuse an otherwise unreasonable clause.

Subdivisions are advisable. Clauses should be drafted in the form of
interrelated but independent provisions and promises. The most common
method of achieving this is with the use of a 'parent' clause accompanied
by subclauses. As severance is discretionary it will not be used where the
remainder of the clause ceases to reflect the original agreement.

References to associated companies should be treated with care. We have
seen that it may be possible to protect competition relating to the activities
of associated companies, but this will only apply (if at all) where the employee
clearly had connections with the activities of that associate.

Care needs to be taken with summary dismissals. If the employer breaches
the contract, e.g., by wrongfully dismissing the employee or wrongfully
repudiating the contract, the restraint clause (however reasonable) becomes
inoperative. Dismissal with payment in lieu of notice will have the same effect
unless this action is allowed for in the contract. An employer's enthusiasm
to rid himself of an employee should therefore be tempered by the long-
term consequences.

Once a breach has been detected action should be taken swiftly.

2.11 BIBLIOGRAPHY

2.11.1 Books

Anderman, S.D. (1992), *Labour Law: Management Decisions and Workers' Rights* (London: Butterworths).

Bean, D. (1991), *Injunctions*, 5th edn (Longman Practitioner Series) (Harlow: Longman).

Bowers, J. (1990), *Employment Law* (London: Blackstone Press).

Chitty, J. (1989), *Chitty on Contracts*, 26th edn by A.G. Guest (London: Sweet & Maxwell).

Harvey, R.J. (ed.) (1984), *Industrial Relations and Employment Law* (London: Butterworths).

Heydon, J.D. (1971), *The Restraint of Trade Doctrine* (London: Butterworths).

Mehigan, S. and Griffiths, D. (1991), *Restraint of Trade and Business Secrets*, 2nd edn (London: Longman).

Smith, I.T. and Wood, Sir John C. (1989), *Industrial Law*, 4th edn (London: Butterworths).

Upex, R. (general ed.) (1992), *Sweet and Maxwell's Encyclopedia of Employment Law* (London: Sweet & Maxwell).

PART II

INTELLECTUAL PROPERTY RIGHTS: OWNERSHIP AND COMPENSATION

Intellectual property is a generic title which covers, in its widest sense, legal rights safeguarding the various products of human intellectual pursuit. It includes, amongst other things, patents, copyright, trade marks, and design rights. The common denominator is that each right to some extent prevents any member of the public from reproducing or imitating the particular subject-matter, be it an invention, a literary work, a drawing or catchy marketing phrase, without the prior approval of the owner. The protection afforded is not uniform. Thus, whereas copyright would protect literary works for the lifetime of an author plus 50 years, patents for inventions last for 20 years, whilst the new 'registered design' right normally extends for only 10 years from first marketing.

In a commercial sense, the value of these rights depends upon the enhanced competitive edge that they provide for their owners. For instance, one effect of trade marks is that they encourage product differentiation, enticing the public to pay more for goods associated with a mark which has the reputation of quality. If this quality is absent then a trade mark owner will receive very little return on his advertising budget. Equally, an employer who obtains patent protection for an employee's invention will normally only derive a financial benefit if it leads to a marketable product whose sales outstrip initial capital expenditure.

The purpose of this section is to consider the legal position of employees whose innovative, novel and inventive work generates enforceable property rights which contribute to the profitability of their employers' businesses. It has been estimated that upwards of 80 per cent of all inventions are arrived at by salaried employees and yet, whatever benefits employers derive from their successful exploitation, there is rarely any corresponding right for the employee to receive compensation. This position was somewhat changed by the Patents Act 1977 which introduced a limited scheme of compensation for employees who produce patentable inventions.

The first chapter in this part will focus upon employees' patentable inventions and their rights to compensation. The second chapter will consider other forms of intellectual property, such as copyright and design rights, all of which might cover employees' work. Questions will also be asked about whether any recent statutory amendments have extended the patent compensation scheme to these latter rights.

3 Employees' Patentable Inventions

The Swan committee of 1964 recognised that the availability of patent protection stimulated technical progress in four ways:

(a) encouraging research and invention,
(b) inducing disclosure,
(c) offering a reward for developmental expenditure,
(d) inducing entrepreneurial capital investment in new lines of production

Nowadays this approach is received with rather more scepticism. Apart from the pharmaceutical and heavy engineering industries there is little evidence that companies would stop inventing if patent protection was abolished; producing new innovative ideas is vital to maintaining a competitive edge. What is not in issue, however, is the potential profit that a patent owner can derive from exploiting the right. The first scientist (probably an employee) who finds a cure for Aids will transform the earnings capability of his employer — assuming that other companies cannot produce the same result without infringing the patent. Similar benefits, albeit on a reduced scale, can be obtained by a company whose research staff invent a completely new product (e.g., the sailboard, the compact disc player, the video recorder). Should these employees have a right to share, financially, in their employers' success?

In this chapter we shall adopt the following approach:

3.1 Introduction to the patent system.
3.2 History.
3.3 The Patents Act 1977: the structure.
3.4 Proof of inventorship under the Patents Act 1977.
3.5 Ownership of inventions under the Patents Act 1977.
3.6 Pre-assignment clauses.
3.7 Ownership of inventions: miscellaneous matters.
3.8 Conditions for compensation.
3.9 Calculating the compensatory award.
3.10 Contracting out of the compensation provisions.
3.11 Checklist.
3.12 Bibliography.

3.1 INTRODUCTION TO THE PATENT SYSTEM

A patent is a grant of a monopoly by the State for a limited period of time (currently 20 years) which provides the owner of an invention with an exclusive right of exploitation. A patent protects the physical embodiment of an invention which is:

(a) novel;
(b) inventive (i.e., not obvious);
(c) capable of industrial application;
(d) not excluded from patentability by other sections in the Patents Act 1977.

3.1.1 Novelty

The Patents Act 1977 introduces what is commonly known as the 'absolute novelty test'. Basically, one cannot claim patent protection for any information disclosed in a patent application which has already been made available to the public, in any way, anywhere in the world. Thus, prior public disclosure destroys novelty. The disclosure in question may be by way of written or oral description and will include, amongst other things, information contained in previously published patent applications, published books, conference papers, television programmes, exhibitions, or even casual conversations — although one would expect a UK court to impose a heavy burden of proof in the last situation where, for instance, the conversation took place on a remote island in the Pacific!

In *Asahi Kasei Kogyo KK's Application* [1991] RPC 485 the House of Lords made it plain that an invention was not made available to the public merely by a published statement of its existence unless the method of its working was so self-evident as to require no explanation. Thus, if a company demonstrates one of its new inventions in a public setting, prior to applying for a patent, then novelty will only be destroyed to the extent that any member of the audience can deduce from visual inspection (and physical handling if permitted) the actual workings of that invention.

In the employment sphere, employers generally ensure that their employees are properly notified of the need to maintain secrecy at all times. Under the Patents Act 1977 an accidental disclosure can destroy the novelty of a patentable invention, although by s. 2(4), where information is leaked in breach of confidence (a duty readily implied into contracts of employment), a subsequent patent application will be allowed to proceed provided it is made within six months of the unauthorised disclosure.

At present, apart from the *Asahi* decision, there are only a few indications on how the word 'published' in s. 2 Patents Act 1977 will be interpreted, so existing precedents under previous statutes, insofar as they relate to the concept of novelty and publication, may continue to offer valuable assistance to the courts. For instance, publication has always been difficult to establish where employees within a company talk with one another on the current stage of their research, or members of a project team cooperate with each other on the writing up of a report for head office. In either situation, the confidant employees are not treated as members of the public, nor does the public have a right of access to that information unless, for instance, the employer actively encourages employees to publish their findings. In similar vein, information contained in company libraries, in which employees may browse freely, would not be considered available to the public provided outside access was appropriately restricted; unless, of course, the information was available through the normal inter-library loan facilities.

Most companies in the ILU survey had an established vetting procedure which ensured that employees did not divulge company information without prior authorisation. For example, in one contract the following clause was inserted:

> *The employee shall not during the continuance of his employment hereunder (except in the proper course of his duties as aforesaid) deliver any public lecture or offer for publication or allow the publication of any article or communication on a matter directly or indirectly connected with the activities of the company or affecting its external relations in any way without the prior approval of the company in writing in each individual case.*

It is perhaps advisable for an employer to demonstrate the importance of such a clause by adding that any contravention will lead to immediate disciplinary hearings and possible suspension or termination of employment.

3.1.2 Inventive step

Section 3 Patents Act 1977 states that a patentable invention must involve an 'inventive step' which will be established only 'if it is not obvious to a person skilled in the art, having regard to any matter which forms part of the state of the art'. Thus obviousness is judged by a person skilled in the relevant field. This person will be acquainted with normal workshop techniques, will be experienced in the tricks of the trade, and will be imbued with all the information disclosed during the novelty search (i.e., s. 2(2) Patents Act 1977). However, such persons do not possess any imagination or inventive ability (cf. *Genentech Inc.'s Patent* [1989] RPC 147 & 203) and have, therefore, been described as dull albeit competent plodders. The object of the exercise is for the patent applicant to convince the Patent Office examiner that the claimed invention incorporates some spark of imagination, some degree of originality (or scintilla of invention), which the skilled reader would have been incapable of achieving.

Interestingly, the hypothetical addressee need not constitute just one individual. In *Valensi* v *British Radio Corporation* [1973] RPC 337, concerning research into colour television in the late 1930s, the Court of Appeal decided that between the leading experts and the manual workers who were constructing the experimental sets, there must have been skilled technicians from whom a *team* could be drawn. Team members would have possessed the common knowledge of those in the relevant art but without any capacity to make elaborate additions to or modifications of the discoveries disclosed in the relevant patent applications. On the basis that such a team comprises lower grades of research staff one must conclude that the average employee (i.e., not a leading expert) who comes up with a supposedly 'bright idea' may find that the 'invention' is considered obvious when judged by the skilled reader who, in many instances, would be the employee's hypothetical colleague or research associate.

Finally, an 'inventive step' often refers to an invention at an early stage of development which needs to be converted from drawing-board theory into marketable reality. Companies, therefore, may hold back for months or even years before filing a patent application in order to give staff an opportunity of refining an invention. Nor should one forget the length of time which was required to arrive at the invention in the first place. The problem is that research staff will be coming and going during this extended period. Ideas germinated in one environment may be nurtured in another. As the act of invention is often cerebral in nature it becomes difficult to pinpoint the moment when an inventive idea was conceived. For this reason a few companies in the ILU survey incorporated the following type of clause into their research staff contracts:

> *If any application for any UK or foreign patent related to or useful in the business of the company [X] . . . shall be filed by an employee during the period of one year after the termination of his or her employment, the subject-matter covered thereby shall be presumed to have been conceived during that person's employment with the company [X].*

Whether such a clause would be construed as being in restraint of trade is an arguable point, although the use of the word 'presumed' would suggest that it is not. Notwithstanding this, an employer who suspects unauthorised use of confidential information by an ex-employee would be entitled to seek an injunction to prevent further use of the information and, possibly, even seek an *Anton Piller* order in relation to any documents that may have been taken (for a fuller discussion see 0.7).

Two other practical safeguards could be adopted by an employer in this situation: (a) explain the problem to each departing employee, discussing their current research work and warning them against use of any of the employer's proprietary information in their new employment, and (b) the new employer could be informed, in broad terms, of the type of work which the employee was doing for the previous employer, thereby placing a marker for future litigation if new products of the new employer, over the next two to three years, suggest misuse of confidential information by that employee.

3.1.3 Capable of Industrial Application

Under s. 4 Patents Act 1977 an invention is capable of industrial application if it can be 'made or used in any kind of industry, including agriculture'. As Pearson and Miller point out (1990, p. 49):

... an inventive product, method or process must have some useful application or advantage in a practical sense and result in a changed physical state of affairs (rather than a change in a purely intellectual sense).

Section 1(2) Patents Act 1977, offers a list of inventions which are presumptively unpatentable. The list includes, amongst other things, a discovery, scientific theory, literary work, a method of doing business, a computer program, and the presentation of information. In many ways these examples, as they stand, are incapable of industrial application. But s. 1 adds that it prevents such examples from being treated as patentable inventions 'only to the extent that' a patent or patent application relates to these things 'as such'. Thus, find a practical industrial application for them and patent protection may be forthcoming. For instance, a discovery that a particular known material is able to withstand mechanical shock would not be patentable 'as such', but a railway sleeper made from that material could well be patentable; a computer program is not per se patentable, but a program which controls a new form of digital image processing as applied to television manufacture might be; a physical theory of semiconductivity is not patentable, but new semiconductor devices incorporating this theory may be.

In Re Gale's Application [1991] RPC 305, Browne-Wilkinson V-C concluded that any matter excluded from being an invention by s. 1(2) Patents Act 1977 could not qualify as being patentable simply by being incorporated 'in a product or process unless such product or process is either itself novel or produces a technical effect which is novel'.

A further list is given in s. 4(2), excluding 'as such' any method of treatment of the human or animal body by surgery or therapy or of diagnosis practised on the human or animal body. The word 'method' does not include instruments, such as surgical appliances, which will be employed in the particular treatment — although with the advent of the EMI bodyscanner it becomes harder to discern the difference between an instrument used in the treatment and the treatment itself. In addition, s. 4(3) states that any product consisting of a substance or composition (e.g., a prescribed drug or medicine) used in the method of treatment may still be patentable.

3.1.4 Exclusions

Section 1(3)(a) Patents Act 1977 automatically excludes from patentability any invention which is likely to encourage offensive, immoral or antisocial behaviour. Paragraph (b) provides the same for new varieties of animals or plant (capable of protection under the Plant Varieties and Seeds Act 1964), or any 'essentially biological' process for the production of animals or plants not being a microbiological process or the product of such a process. Thus, unlike in the USA, one cannot patent a new genetically engineered strain of mouse or a new genetic mutation of an existing species.

3.1.5 Employee compensation: why pay more?

In the 1970s, when Parliament addressed the issue of employee compensation, a variety of conflicting interests quickly became apparent. Employers argued that they took considerable risks when investing in new products — less than one-third of patented inventions are ever worked in the UK with many proving to be expensive flops either at the drawing-board or marketing stage. This risk was counterbalanced by the right to unfettered exploitation of their employees' inventions. Employees' organisations, on the other hand, maintained that their members should receive appropriate stimulus to make and even disclose their inventions, even if they were paid to invent.

Superimposing itself upon these arguments was the public interest in rewarding inventors, through the grant of a patent monopoly, for the valuable contribution they made to society whilst safeguarding the interests of business people who wished to market their new products on a commercial scale.

The Patents Act 1977 offers a compromise position between all these conflicting notions. However, by looking at the pre-1977 position we can at least get some idea of how the rights to compensation of employee inventors have been fundamentally altered.

3.2 HISTORY

The question whether an employee or employer owns the rights to a particular invention has received very different responses since 1700. The reason that we need to discuss this, however, lies in the present. For inventions made before 1 June 1978 are not encompassed by the Patents Act 1977 and as the lifetime of a patent is 20 years, the old case law will have effect as regards these inventions until 1999. Equally, the Patents Act 1977 does not apply to directors or consultants who are not also employees, nor to employees who work mainly abroad. Finally, it is likely that many of the concepts developed under the old law may yet be called upon in interpreting the Patents Act 1977.

Somewhat surprisingly, perhaps, between 1700 and 1890 an employee had full rights to the exploitation of his invention. From 1890 the emphasis changed. At that time the responsibilities owed by companies to their shareholders was perceived as overriding the rights of employees. This did not mean (though it was commonly believed) that all inventions made by an employee belonged to the employer. What it did mean is that various methods of analysis were used to explain the new relationship between employer and employee.

The invention could thus be said to belong to the employer on the following grounds:

(a) because the contract of employment contained an express pre-assignment clause; or

(b) because, whatever the specific terms of the contract, every contract of employment carried with it an implied term that anything the employee produced was the property of the employer so that the employee could be said to be a trustee of his or her invention resulting from performance of contractual duties or special responsibilities.

3.2.1 Pre-assignment clauses

The nature of such a clause is that the employee has agreed to assign to his employer rights in inventions which lie in the future. An express clause of this nature would be almost conclusive of the rights relating to the invention. Such clauses therefore occurred frequently where there was any suggestion that an invention might arise from performance of the employee's duties. Some agreements provided for the sharing of rights and benefits between employer and employee. In reality, if such standard terms were concluded at the start of the employment relationship there was little practical room for the employee to bargain or negotiate the point anyway.

Until the case of *Electrolux Ltd* v *Hudson* [1977] FSR 312 it had been assumed that there was complete freedom of contract on this matter (certainly with regard to full-time employees) and that the courts would not question the employer's rights under the clause. In the *Electrolux* case Whitford J analysed a pre-assignment clause as being in restraint of trade and unenforceable. The reasoning employed by the court, however, is questionable. In orthodox terminology, the 'restraint of trade doctrine' has always pertained to constraints placed on an employee once the employment relationship has ended and only at that stage. In *Electrolux* the employee was a storekeeper who, in his own time, invented a new bagging system for vacuum cleaners. While the employee was still working for Electrolux the employer claimed ownership of the invention based on an express pre-assignment clause in the contract of employment. Whitford J refused the company's claim, classifying the clause as unenforceable because it was in restraint of trade.

This analysis appears to stretch the restraint of trade doctrine too far. There are indeed cases where the analysis has been applied to continuing contracts (e.g., *A. Schroeder Music Publishing Co. Ltd* v *Macaulay* [1974] 1 WLR 1308) but these examples arise either in commercial contracts or contracts *for* services (see chapter 2). If the pre-assignment clause in *Electrolux* was a restrictive covenant it should have been analysed as a fidelity clause or 'whole time and attention' clause and so subjected to the normal rules of contractual analysis. This would have meant that the chances of it being classified as unenforceable would have been more remote, though not inconceivable. Thus, on the facts of *Electrolux* the court might well have been entitled to strike down the clause on the grounds of public policy as the clause extended far beyond the protection of the employer's legitimate business interests.

The more well-defined limitation on the freedom of contract principle therefore occurred where employers sought to extend the continuing effectiveness of pre-assignment clauses to inventions made *after* the employment relationship had ended. Such clauses were traditionally presumed to be void, as being in restraint of trade, and will fall under the same analysis in consequence of the Patents Act 1977. The same was true where the employer sought to bind the employee to secrecy over matters which could not be classed as confidential information. But both presumptions could be overridden if the clause could be proved to be necessary to protect the employer's business.

3.2.2 The implied term of the employer's property rights

In the absence of express terms, or where the express term had been declared void, the law presumed that any invention belonged to the employer provided it was made in the course of the employee's employment. The difficulty therefore lay in deciding whether an employee was acting in the 'course of employment' when the invention was made. The practical effect of so doing was that if the invention was made in the course of employment the employee would either be forced to assign the rights over to the employer or, if the patent was already in the employee's name, hold the patent on trust for the employer. Subject to the employee's expenses the employer would therefore hold all the beneficial interests in the patent.

This implied term might arise in two ways: first, because the invention had arisen from the employee's contractual duties as with the straightforward examples of research workers (as in *Triplex Safety Glass Co.* v *Scorah* [1938] Ch 211) or designers (as in *Sterling Engineering Co. Ltd* v *Patchett* [1955] AC 534); secondly, where the employee held such a high position in the company that the trust arose from the duty of fidelity or good faith owed to the company (see *Worthington Pumping Engine Co.* v *Moore* (1903) 20 RPC 41).

In *Worthington Pumping Engine Co.* v *Moore*, Moore was a general manager for an American business. His position of trust was such that he was described as the *alter ego* of the American company; almost equivalent to a partner. He was highly paid. The litigation centred on patents he had taken out which were improvements to the plaintiff's pumps. Byrne J decided that Moore held the patents as trustee for the company. It was pointed out, however, that this was not simply because Moore had used company time, materials and money to develop these inventions. These were relevant but not determining factors. The key point was that Moore's position was 'inconsistent with an observance of that good faith which ought properly to be inferred or implied as an obligation arising from his contract'. Thus the employee's status had an effect on ownership of patents, and that level of 'good faith' (and thereby the question of ownership) would vary according to that status: a point noted again in, amongst other cases, *Vokes Ltd* v *Heather* (1945) 62 RPC 135.

The mere existence of the employment relationship did not automatically provide the employer with rights to the patent; although the twofold test was expansive. One can, for instance, find cases where the employee retained the rights to the invention, e.g., *Charles Selz Ltd's Application* (1954) 71 RPC 158. Here, the company made lampshades. The manager of a company, whose job involved design work as well as general management, invented a spray plastic for use in display signs. The spray could also have been used on lampshades, but the invention was held to be outside his course of employment.

However, the House of Lords decision in *Sterling Engineering Co. Ltd* v *Patchett* [1955] AC 534 altered the perspective on these earlier cases. The case concerned s. 56(2) Patents Act 1949. This subsection dealt with the problem that, unless the employee owned the invention outright, the employer would be under no legal duty to provide the employee with any compensation for the work done. Section 56(2) stated that:

unless satisfied that one or other of the parties is entitled, to the exclusion of the other, to the benefit of any invention made by the employee . . . [the court could] . . . provide for the apportionment between them of the benefit of the invention.

In *Sterling Engineering Co. Ltd* v *Patchett*, Patchett made a number of inventions in respect of which patents were applied for in the joint names of the employee and employer. Patchett received no compensation from the company. He claimed that either the inventions belonged to him or that, if jointly owned, s. 56(2) entitled him to compensation. On the first point the House of Lords decided that, as Patchett was the chief designer, the inventions belonged to the company because they had come about in the course of Patchett's employment. This followed the traditional pattern outlined above.

Nevertheless, Patchett claimed there had been an 'understanding' to the effect that the rights of the employer were subject to some royalty payments. This rather vague 'understanding' was held to be insufficient to displace the ordinary position that the employer was entitled to the benefits of the inventions. However, of particular interest are general *obiter* comments, by Lord Reid and Viscount Simonds, that the duty of good faith noted above did not vary with the employee's status — it applied universally, irrespective of position. Thus any employee, whether employed to invent or not, might have no rights to the invention.

On the second point the House of Lords drove a coach and horses through s. 56(2). Section 56(2) was held inapplicable to the case because compensation could only be given where neither party was 'entitled' to the invention. This was held to mean 'legally entitled', not 'justly entitled'. For the reasons recounted above the employer was held to be 'legally entitled' to the invention; as, it would seem, would be the case in any employment relationship which did not have an express 'joint ownership' clause. Thus in one fell swoop s. 56(2) had ceased to be of any practical effect. Once the question of 'course of employment' or 'fidelity' had been decided in favour of the employer, the employer would nearly always own the invention and would not have to pay compensation to the employee.

Consequently, under s. 56(2) Patents Act 1949, the employer is only bound to pay compensation to the employee in rare circumstances. Further, the section only applies to employees, not to directors who are not also employees nor to independent contractors.

In summary, therefore, where the 1977 Act does not apply (i.e., the invention was made before 1 January 1978) we must revert to the old case law and the 1949 Act, the employer establishing ownership over an invention where:

(a)   an express pre-assignment clause states this; or
(b)   it comes about as part of the employee's duties; or
(c)   where the employee's status means that the duty of fidelity entitles the employer to the invention (on the strength of the *obiter* comments in *Sterling Engineering Co. Ltd* v *Patchett*, this applies to *any* employee).

3.3 THE PATENTS ACT 1977: THE STRUCTURE

The Patents Act 1977 introduces a completely new framework for dealing with ownership and compensation disputes. Sections 39 to 42 (with additional points provided under s. 43) embrace four basic objectives:

(a)   to enact a statutory test for determining the ownership of all employees' inventions (s. 39),
(b)   to offer employee inventors a limited opportunity for claiming compensation for their inventions where ownership of the inventions resides with their employers, and more limited opportunities where ownership initially resides with the employee (s. 40),
(c)   to establish criteria by which an award of compensation can be fairly judged (s. 41), and
(d)   to reinforce these rights by declaring any contractual provisions unenforceable to the extent that they diminish employees' rights under the Patents Act 1977 (s. 42).

3.4 PROOF OF INVENTORSHIP UNDER THE PATENTS ACT 1977

Before any right of ownership can arise, a court must first determine who made the invention. Only if an employee can prove that he or she made the invention will the employee possess any possible right to ownership and/ or compensation.

3.4.1 Has an invention been made?

The Patents Act 1977 does not provide a complete definition of an 'invention' although it would appear to encompass anything 'come upon' (from the Latin *invenire*) or 'devised' by the inventor (s. 7 Patents Act 1977). More specifically, one should think of patentable inventions as new ideas with useful practical applications in manufacturing processes or as self-standing products or, in rather more vague terms, as anything 'capable of industrial application' (s. 1(1)(c) and s. 4(1) Patents Act 1977). So patent law is set apart from the aesthetic fine arts, or the realms of pure scientific theory, where copyright might be the more appropriate medium for legal protection.

However, there is nothing to suggest that in dealing with s. 39 Patents Act 1977 and the ownership of employees' inventions the word 'invention' refers only to something which is patentable, or, more to the point, something for which patent protection has been successfully obtained. There are two reasons for this. First, for the purposes of s. 39 Patents Act 1977, which determines ownership of all employees' inventions, it is immaterial whether a patent application has been filed or not. In particular, the section regulates ownership of inventions for the purposes of Patents Act 1977 and 'all other purposes', thereby including non-patentable subject-matter. This point was reinforced by the decision in *Kokta's Applications* SRIS 0/16/90 which excluded questions of patent validity in determining entitlement to a patent application.

Secondly, in *Viziball Ltd's Application* [1988] RPC 213 it was held that, in the context of s. 8 Patents Act 1977 (which concerns applications for proprietorship of pending patent applications), the word 'invention' does indeed embrace unpatentable subject-matter whether because the information has already been disclosed (i.e., lacks novelty) or because it is expressly excluded from the ambit of the Patents Act 1977 (e.g., s. 1(1) and (2) Patents Act 1977). In the subsequent decision in *Norris's Patent* [1988] RPC 159 all aspects of the invention were considered including any details which played 'a significant part in the viability' of the invention and were used to perform the invention (p. 164). This wider reasoning was adopted in *Rawlplug Co. Ltd* SRIS O/145/88.

If the above interpretation is followed by the courts then s. 39 Patents Act 1977 will apply equally to unpatentable inventions such as suggestions submitted by employees under a company suggestion scheme. Employers will need to take care that any rules of such schemes which purport to regulate ownership of the submitted suggestions are in harmony with the provisions of s. 39 Patents Act 1977. However, if the *compensation* provisions of the Patents Act 1977 only apply to patented inventions or those upon which patent applications have been submitted (see later) then, as two companies in the ILU survey recognised, it is perhaps worth inserting a clause into staff contracts along the following lines:

> *In respect of any of your inventions . . . which are not patentable or which, being patentable, are not patented and which belong to the company under the provisions of the Patents Act 1977 or which you have assigned to the company, the company shall reward you to such extent if any as the company in its sole discretion considers to be fair and reasonable.*

In the next chapter we will be considering the possibility that employees' rights under the Patents Act 1977 have been extended to other forms of intellectual property such as copyright and designs, again placing a burden upon employers to ensure conformity with the provisions of the Act.

3.4.2 Who made the invention?

Once it has been established that an invention has been made the next question will be: Who actually made the invention? Particular problems will arise in research teams where several members will be claiming joint inventorship. Section 7(3) of the Patents Act 1977 provides:

In this Act 'inventor' in relation to an invention means the actual deviser of the invention and 'joint inventor' shall be construed accordingly.

Little light is thrown upon the meaning of 'actual deviser'. Section 43(3) emphasises that a person who merely contributes 'advice or other assistance in the making of the invention' will not be considered to be the inventor or a joint inventor. Beyond this we must assume that the person who supplies the 'inventive step' will be regarded as the inventor. The following extracts may be considered declaratory of the existing law:

There were, undoubtedly, different persons discussing the subject, and they were all trying to contribute to the solution of the question which was before them; but I certainly think that Mr Homan is the person who is entitled *to claim originality* in this matter. (*Re Homan's Patent* (1889) 6 RPC 104.)

. . . if a person has discovered an improved principle, and employs engineers, or agents, or other persons, to assist him in carrying out that principle, and they, in the course of the experiments arising from that employment, make valuable discoveries *accessory to the main principle*, and tending to carry that out in a better manner, such improvements are the property of the inventor of the original improved principle, and may be embodied in his patent. (*Allen* v *Rawson* (1845) 1 CB 551.)

. . . but where the employer has conceived the plan of an invention and is engaged in experiments to perfect it, no suggestions from an employee, *not amounting to a new method or arrangement, which, in itself is a complete invention*, is sufficient to deprive the employer of the exclusive property in the perfected improvement. (*Agawen Woolen Co.* v *Jordan* (1868) 74 US (7 Wall) 583. This case relied upon the English authority of *Allen* v *Rawson* (1841) 1 CB 551.)

These extracts are taken from 19th century cases simply because the growth of pre-assignment clauses in contracts of employment in the 20th century, as well as the emerging use of the trust concept, rendered an investigation into who had actually made the invention (as between employer and employee) rather pointless before 1977. In particular, inventions made in the course of employment or by employees occupying important managerial posts inevitably belonged to the employer with no applicable scheme of compensation.

Under the Patents Act 1977 procedure, the above cases will provide the most useful guidance on employer–employee proprietorship disputes. On a more substantive point of law, the emphasised aspects in the above citations will help to clarify s. 43(3); that is, it is the person or persons who contribute the protectable originality in a patent application who are entitled to claim inventorship. For this reason, s. 36 Patents Act 1977 provides for the possibility of joint inventorship.

If an employer establishes inventorship, then employees will have no right

to compensation under the Patents Act 1977, however useful their assistance
was to the making of the invention (see s. 43(3)).

3.5 OWNERSHIP OF INVENTIONS UNDER THE PATENTS ACT 1977

3.5.1 Introduction

Under s. 39(1) Patents Act 1977, an invention made by an employee will belong
to his employer 'for the purposes of this Act and for all other purposes'
if:

> (a) *it was made in the course of the normal duties of the employee or
> in the course of duties falling outside his normal duties, but specifically assigned
> to him, and the circumstances in either case were such that an invention
> might reasonably be expected to result from the carrying out of his duties;
> or*
> (b) *the invention was made in the course of the duties of the employee
> and, at the time of making the invention, because of the nature of his duties
> and the particular responsibilities arising from the nature of his duties he
> had a special obligation to further the interests of the employer's undertaking.*

Section 39(2) adds that any other invention made by an employee shall,
as between employee and employer, belong to the employee. In many ways
the effects of subsections (1) and (2) are not dissimilar to the pre-1977 position.
Subsection (1)(a) would have been achieved through the normal contractual
pre-assignment of employees' inventions, or by identifying a trust which arose
in favour of the employer, whilst para. (b) is most clearly illustrated by the
decision in *Worthington Pumping Engine Co.* v *Moore* (1903) 20 RPC 41. In
this context, s. 39(2) merely represents a residual category where ownership
cannot be affirmatively proved by the employer. However, although s. 39
offers a statutory formulation for determining ownership predicated, at least
to some extent, upon the old common law rules, it expressly states that the
new test will apply 'notwithstanding anything in any rule of law'; a clear
indication that the old case law may influence but will not determine its
application.

3.5.1.1 Joint ownership?

It is probable that a finding of joint ownership, as opposed to joint inventorship,
between employer and employee is not available under s. 39. Logically, as
subsections (1) and (2) are mutually exclusive, the Comptroller should have
no right to use his discretionary powers under other sections in the Patents
Act 1977 to grant a patent to joint proprietors. This would confirm the position
in *Sterling Engineering Co. Ltd* v *Patchett* [1955] AC 534. However, although
no reported court decision has yet emerged on this point, in *Szucs* SRIS 0/
27/88 the Comptroller awarded a free licence to the employer who was claiming
proprietary rights of entitlement over his employee's invention under s. 37

(which determines entitlement rights after a patent has been granted). It is arguable whether this effectively amounts to a recognition of joint proprietorship.

3.5.1.2 The position of non-employees

Section 39 has no application to inventors who are non-employees, and so does not apply, for example, to research work commissioned from an independent consultant. Ownership of any patent rights derived from the ensuing research project will be determined by the existing agreement and common law principles, or, where copyright or design rights have arisen, will be regulated by the Copyright, Designs and Patents Act 1988. In practice, the commissioning body, which has paid for this work will have a vested interest in ensuring the automatic transfer of all proprietary rights in the end-product of that research. However, if the research work is carried out by an employee within the independent consultancy, and an invention results, then no agreement between the principal parties regarding disposition of those rights can affect the operation of s. 39 and the employee's possible right of ownership under s. 39(2).

3.5.1.3 Directors and partners

If a director is also an employee of a company then ss. 39 to 43 Patents Act 1977 will apply. As the introduction emphasised, a contract of employment is a contract of service. However, special considerations apply when determining whether a director is an employee. For example, the 'control' criterion is not especially apposite. Rather, it will be the actions of the parties, the contents of the articles of association and the general resolutions passed by the company. Attention will be focused particularly upon (a) whether the director receives a salary or draws income from company dividends — the former implying a contract of employment, (b) whether there is a written service contract in existence — if not, a contract will need to be implied at law (s. 318 Companies Act 1985 requires a company to keep a copy of every written contract of service and a written memorandum of every oral contract of service).

There is nothing untoward in a person acting in a dual capacity; for example, a director acting as an agent of a company in negotiating a contract of service as between himself and the company (*Lee* v *Lee's Air Farming Ltd* [1961] AC 12). The words of Cohen J provide the most instructive judicial attitude:

> When I find a man who is bound to devote his whole time to the affairs of the company, to do all in his power to develop and extend the business of the company, not to engage in any other business and who is engaged on terms that his employment may be determined by the company by notice in writing, I find it impossible to say that he is not employed by the company. (*Trussed Steel Concrete Co. Ltd* v *Green* [1946] Ch 115 at p. 121.)

If the director is not an employee, ownership of any invention will be determined by existing common law principles, that is, the fiduciary obligations owed by the director and any express contract terms. Naturally, a director may have a better opportunity of negotiating a contract which vests ownership of certain inventions in himself (see *Charles Selz Ltd's Appn* [1954] 71 RPC 158). However, if the invention relates to the director's employment any contract provisions contrary to the common law may be considered to be inconsistent with the observance of good faith (*Worthington Pumping Engine Co.* v *Moore* [1903] 20 RPC 41). Moreover, there is authority for suggesting that an agreement whereby an employee director receives extra payment for an invention, held in trust for his employer, will be unenforceable for want of consideration (see generally *Barnet Instruments Ltd* v *Overton* (1949) 66 RPC 315).

Partners are not employees of a firm, even if they do not share in the profits, so the normal common law rules will apply on ownership of inventions (see generally, *Palumbo* v *Stylianou* (1966) 1 ITR 407). As for 'salaried' or 'junior' partners, if such persons share in the profits of the firm, or personally accept liability for the firm's debts, generally they will not be considered employees. Although a partnership contract is of the 'utmost good faith', it is submitted that *any* invention made by a partner which is unconnected with the firm's business, and which does not have the potential to compete with the firm's existing products is presumptively owned by the partner (see *Coffey's Registered Designs* [1982] FSR 227).

3.5.1.4 Overseas employees

Section 43(2) of the Patents Act 1977 states that the ownership and compensation provisions will only apply to an employee inventor who, at the time he made the invention, was either 'mainly employed in the United Kingdom' or, if the place of employment was indeterminate, the employer had a 'place of business in the United Kingdom to which the employee was attached, whether or not he was also attached elsewhere'. This formula clearly echoes the wording of s. 141 of the Employment Protection (Consolidation) Act 1978 which adopts a 'base of operations' test in order to determine the place of employment. In applying s. 141 Employment Protection (Consolidation) Act 1978, courts have taken account of the currency in which the employee is paid, the expected place of residence, and any reference within the contract of employment to the location of the employer's headquarters (see also 0.6.1). Peculiarly, whereas the Copyright, Designs and Patents Act 1988 defines an employee as a person employed 'under a contract of service or of apprenticeship' (s. 263(1) Copyright, Designs and Patents Act 1988), s. 130(1) Patents Act 1977 makes no reference to apprenticeship contracts thereby raising doubts as to the applicability of s. 39 to such people.

3.5.1.5 Onus of proof under section 39

Regarding proof of ownership under s. 39, it would appear more appropriate if the burden was placed on the employer to show that the facts corresponded to one of the situations in s. 39(1) — one possible interpretation of the decision in *Harris's Patent* [1985] RPC 19 (discussed later). However, it should be noted that, in parallel proceedings under ss. 8, 12, 37 or 82 (regulating ownership of inventions in normal entitlement proceedings), the Comptroller of the Patent Office (to whom ownership disputes will generally be referred) has always assumed that the onus is upon the party referring the matter to the court or tribunal.

3.5.2 Section 39(1)(a) — duties: normal or specifically assigned

It is arguable that an employee's 'normal duties' are all those mentioned in the contract of employment. These duties are derived from a number of sources including, *inter alia*, the original job advertisement to which the employee replied, any letter of appointment, the written particulars of the job as stipulated by s. 1 Employment Protection (Consolidation) Act 1978, any other individual agreement, plus any collective agreement to which the employee was subject. However, if this is the case, then the term 'specifically assigned' would be rendered almost completely redundant. It would only refer to those duties which had been unilaterally imposed by the employer and, even here, any subsequent consent of the employee, express or implied, would automatically incorporate such duties within the existing contract of employment (i.e., they would become normal duties).

It is probable, therefore, that 'normal duties' refer to those duties commonly performed by the employee (i.e., standard, everyday duties). This would place greater emphasis on a 'functional' test rather than a somewhat abstract all-embracing 'contractual' test, thereby avoiding many of the problems encountered in defining 'work of a particular kind' in redundancy situations. Duties which are 'specifically assigned' would then refer to:

(a)   other duties within the employee's contract of employment which the employer may wish the employee to perform on an ad hoc basis (see *Secretary of State for Defence* (1989) IPD 13063), and
(b)   duties which fall outside the employee's contract of employment at the time of their assignment (see below).

Examples of (a) might include a temporary reassignment to another research team within the same department where, for instance, leaves of absence have left the remaining staff short-handed. In these situations it would be preferable for the employer to state in writing the purpose of the reassignment, its nature and likely duration, and the duties (if different from the present position) which the employee would be expected to perform.

As for (b), if the employee accepts these duties they would become part of the contract (e.g., if the change was permanent then the duties might be designated 'normal'), or form part of a separate contract to perform that particular task. The same would apply if the employee carried out those duties on a 'without prejudice' basis and a court, subsequently, decided that the duties did form part of the employment contract.

What if the employee rejects these newly assigned tasks? If no task is performed then no invention should arise. It becomes merely a matter for the employer to decide what action would be appropriate in the circumstances (i.e., dismissal, suspension, other disciplinary action, or acquiescence). But if an invention arose in the interim (i.e., while negotiations were proceeding), a court might be faced with an extremely delicate issue: should an employer be entitled to claim ownership over an employee's invention which arose out of duties specifically assigned yet unlawfully demanded? An affirmative answer would be an endorsement of unlawful behaviour.

3.5.2.1 Relevance of implied duties

Superimposed upon this structure are a number of 'implied duties' which common law courts have automatically implied into all contracts of employment. For example, the duty of fidelity would require employees to perform their tasks with honesty, avoiding situations where their financial interests conflicted with those of their employers. Other examples include the duty of obedience, demonstrating a willingness to carry out all lawful and reasonable orders of the employer properly and without undue delay. In *Harris's Patent* [1985] RPC 19 these duties were held to be coextensive with and did not go beyond the express contractual duties. Thus it would be preferable to regard them as 'normal duties' as an employee would be subject to them whatever the duties being performed; but these implied terms would reflect more 'how' the job was to be done rather than 'what' the job is.

3.5.2.2 Job description and written particulars

The above analysis clearly emphasises the importance of the employee's job description and the written particulars embodied in the s. 1 Employment Protection (Consolidation) Act 1978 notice. In fact, some academics have advocated as wide a definition of duties as possible in order to ensure that the employer can establish ownership over any inventions arrived at by his employees. It is submitted that such an approach is misconceived for, apart from the possible prohibition of s. 42 of the Patents Act 1977, which will be discussed later, one cannot view inventions in isolation. First, a wide job description reduces an employer's flexibility to declare employees redundant where 'work of a particular kind' is expected to diminish, as there will be more chance that other work 'for which the employee is employed to work' is still available (see s. 81(2)(b) Employment Protection (Consolidation) Act 1978); in particular, it would be more difficult for an employer to argue that there was not some other 'suitable alternative work' to which the employee could be deployed rather than being made redundant (e.g., *Vokes Ltd* v *Bear* [1973] 1RLR 363).

Secondly, in the only reported decision on s. 39 (*Harris's Patent*) the court was not unduly influenced by job titles but preferred to 'lift the veil' to establish detailed facts. The facts of the case are as follows. Harris's primary duty was to sell valves and use his specialist knowledge to deal with problems experienced by customers of his employer (R). He had no research laboratory, and never undertook creative design activity. Nor did he attend board meetings even when, as manager, his department was under discussion. Whenever major design problems arose they were referred to S, licensors of R. It was held that as R never took it upon themselves to solve design problems in the valves, it could not have been part of H's *normal* duties to provide solutions to these problems.

Seen in this light, it is doubtful whether a clause in H's contract stating that it was his duty to 'provide innovative and inventive solutions to resolve customers' problems' would have unduly influenced the court. Unless, of course, separate research facilities had been provided for H and, as manager, he had been appointed to take overall responsibility for major design difficulties being experienced by customers.

Previous common law precedents may also be of help here. The doctrine of restraint of trade has been used in pre-1977 cases to avoid pre-assignment clauses which were not confined to those employee inventions that flowed naturally from the performance of their duties (see, for example, *Electrolux Ltd* v *Hudson* [1977] FSR 312. In the post-1977 era it is possible that any attempt to extend the job description of an employee, merely for the purposes of asserting ownership over all his inventions, would fail on the parallel grounds of being unrelated to current employment duties.

3.5.2.3 Inventions made outside normal working hours
How will the courts view a technician who arrives at an invention whilst tinkering away in his small workshop at home, or the researcher who has a spark of genius whilst sunbathing on some exotic beach? In *Peart and Co. Ltd* (1987) SRIS O/209/87 the Comptroller did not accept the argument that an invention outside working hours automatically fell outside the scope of an employee's duties. Perhaps the courts will assume that for the purposes of s. 39(1)(a) of the Patents Act 1977 any invention connected with the employee's duties is presumptively made in the course of those duties unless the employee can show otherwise, with the reverse presumption operating where no connection exists. Beyond this, there are clearly other facts which may be of assistance:

(a)   Is the employee paid an hourly rate or in receipt of a monthly salary?
(b)   Is the employee expected to complete any outstanding work at home?
(c)   Has the employer paid for any facilities which the employee uses at home?
(d)   Can the employee claim overtime payment whilst working at home?

An affirmative answer to the last three points is more likely to suggest that any invention made at home belonged to the employer — subject to the above presumption. Put another way, the more flexible the working arrangement the more disadvantageous it may be for the employee. This might be reinforced by a clause in the contract claiming ownership over inventions made in the course of employment, whether on company premises, at home or elsewhere.

3.5.3 Reasonable expectation of invention under section 39(1)(a)

Under s. 39(1)(a) of the Patents act 1977, an employer must also show that an invention was 'reasonably . . . expected to result' from the performance of the employee's duties. The condition itself prompts three questions:

(a) Whose expectations will the court consider?
(b) At what point in time will those expectations be established? and
(c) What factors will be taken into account?

3.5.3.1 Whose expectations?

Undoubtedly the test is objective but the section remains silent on whether it is the employee, or employer, or the reasonable person, who ascertains inventive expectation. It has been argued that it would be fairer, and less partisan, if the views of a non-litigant were to be consulted. Perhaps use could be made of the 'skilled technician', the standard by which all patent lawyers will examine the potential originality of an invention. But, ironically, one of the primary attributes of such a technician is his inability to invent, rendering him rather unsuitable to pass judgment on this issue.

As yet, there are no definitive statements on this point, but it is submitted that a court, acting as a reasonable person, will place greater emphasis on the role of the employer. As employers allocate the duties their *apparent* motivation must be of paramount importance: it would not rank highly on the scales of justice for employers to obtain ownership of an invention which they never expected to result from the performance of duties which they allocated for different purposes altogether. This may well have been the approach adopted in *Harris's Patent* [1985] RPC 19 where Falconer J, referring to this condition, commented that it must be:

> . . . an invention which achieves, or contributes to achieving, whatever was the aim or object to which the employee's efforts in carrying out those duties were directed.

As the aim or object of any employee's endeavours must be to perform his or her duties properly, rather than to disobey them and concentrate on other non-essential, non-designated tasks, it would seem that the employer's original motivation and continuing instructions and supervision are pivotal in determining the question of expectability.

3.5.3.2 Timing of expectation

Should this expectation of invention be present:

(a) at the time of entering the contract, or,
(b) at the time when the duties, the performance of which led to the invention, were allocated, or,
(c) at a time immediately prior to the invention being made?

The first possibility appears superficially attractive. In particular, in *Harris's Patent* [1985] RPC 19, the question posed was not whether the *particular* invention was expected but rather whether *some* sort of invention was contemplated. If an invention results soon after engagement then the initial job description and express terms might seem relevant; moreover, if any subsequent promotion involved a new formulation of the contract then expectations would start from then. However, the longer the time lapse between the contract date and the act of invention the more difficult it becomes to sustain this thesis. For instance, at the time of an employee's engagement it may be difficult to establish what the normal duties will be until a few months have elapsed — the training, aptitude and development of the employee will all be relevant considerations for an employer when choosing the appropriate employee for the appropriate task.

Test (a) also assumes that one can predict, with confidence, how those duties will change as experience is gained. Cases in employment law have established that the contract of employment is not immutable and that, as an implied term, an employee is expected to be flexible and adapt to changing circumstances (see *Cresswell* v *Board of Inland Revenue* [1984] ICR 508). Thus, for example, where duties are specifically assigned, or new duties are assimilated into the employment contract, it is by no means clear that a new contract will be created. This undoubtedly restricts the ambit of (a).

Regarding (b), it is arguable that the word 'expected' in s. 39 implies a forward-looking approach in which expectation is examined at the time when the duties in question were placed upon the employee. Furthermore, it avoids the dangers of *ex post facto* analysis — just as any person will admit that given the answer to a nettlesome problem the solution is obvious, similarly once it is known that an employee has invented something in the course of his duties it becomes all too easy to believe that the invention was an expected consequence of performing those duties.

However, the difficulty with (b) is that the act of invention is not a predictable occurrence; thus, at the time when the duties were allocated the foreseeability of them resulting in an invention will often be too conjectural. The process of invention is often preceded by, if not integrally involved with, painstaking and lengthy experimentation. As the research evolves, especially in a team, an employee's abilities and skills may develop rapidly, rendering any expectations at the inception of the project somewhat misinformed.

Option (c) accommodates these problems. If one considers an employee's duties to be reaffirmed each day that he or she comes to work, a court will presumably place itself in the position immediately preceding the step which led to the invention and then gauge its *general* expectability. This would, for example, resolve the problem of an employee being transferred to another department where there was no duty to invent, nor any expectation that an invention would occur from the performance of the duties. The approach in (b) would only seem appropriate where no clearly defined step could be identified in the whole research process as supplying the 'inventive step', thereby requiring a prospective examination of whether an invention was expected at the time when those duties were initially allocated to the employee.

3.5.3.3 Factors to take into account
Three factors are worth considering here:

(a)   the employee's expertise *vis-à-vis* the technical difficulty of the invention,
(b)   the terms of the employment contract,

(c)   the connection between the invention and the employee's duties.

Expertise of employee   Presumably, the more senior the employee and the more his or her duties are research-orientated, the more likely that an invention will be expected to result from performance of those duties; the more junior an employee and the more mechanical or non-technical the duties, the less likely an invention will be expected. Clearly there will be many exceptions. The chief accountant in a firm will not be expected to invent a new calculating machine. Conversely, a junior laboratory technician, employed on random testing of new pharmaceutical compounds and their suitability in current projects specified by senior research personnel, may offer the potential for making patentable inventions.

Reid (1979, p. 351) adopts an interesting test related to the scale of scientific difficulty which an invention demonstrates *vis-à-vis* the expected abilities of the employee. He refers to a number of older cases involving engineering inventions made by draftsmen (e.g., *Adamson* v *Kenworthy* (1932) 49 RPC 57) where, because of the innate abilities of a person occupying such a position, the inventions invariably belonged to the employer. It might follow that the average factory-floor employee, such as a machine operative, although highly skilled in terms of his individual capacity, would be entitled to claim ownership over any of his or her inventions. If so, ownership would relate, in part, to the intrinsic creativity of the job and the skills of the person expected to perform the relevant tasks. An appropriate clause covering aspects of this issue might be:

> *Where the duties of the employee comprise the making of inventions, he/ she shall not be entitled to claim ownership over inventions made in the performance of those duties unless the degree of creative or inventive contribution exceeds that which is normally required of an employee having the said duties.*

A court would then be more likely to permit an employer to adduce evidence of other employees occupying similar positions who had also made inventions involving comparable standards of ingenuity as a means of showing that the said invention was expected.

Terms of the contract   As s. 39 envisages an independent assessment of whether inventions are 'reasonably expected to result' it is unlikely that an employer could circumvent this condition by incorporating a 'duty to invent' clause. This is clearly the implication one derives from a reading of *Harris's Patent* [1985] RPC 19, especially when dealing with relatively junior employees.

However, in other ways, an employer who spells out clearly the employee's actual duties may provide valuable assistance to a court in applying the expectation criterion. For example, if in *Harris's Patent* the contract had specified that the employee inventor's duties included solving customer's problems, and that proper facilities would be provided for the performance of this task, then the court might have concluded that the process of solution was expected to produce patentable inventions of the type under scrutiny. It is arguable that *such* duties should be spelt out in the contract of employment. Hoolahan (1979, p. 141) uses the example of technical sales representatives who are expected to have technical knowledge of the company's products and an ability to adapt them to suit customers' requirements. Inserting a clause that such employees are 'expected to innovate . . . [and that] patentable inventions may result' might benefit the employer, although a reading of *Harris's Patent* suggests otherwise.

As most writers have commented, particular difficulties will emerge with regard to lecturers in higher education who are employed to teach. For example, staff in science and engineering faculties are expected to pursue their own research interests, but often with no specific contractual duty to do so. Are the products of their research the property of their employer? An affirmative answer is more likely where there is a formalised system of timetable relief associated with a specific research project, as this may incorporate research as part of the normal duties, but in any situation where an opportunity is being given to research, and facilities and encouragement are forthcoming, one might argue that the ownership of research-related inventions would reside with the employer institution. This analysis is supported by the current university guidelines emanating from the Committee of Vice-Chancellors and Principals (CVCP) which recommend that all academic staff contracts include an express obligation to undertake research.

The real problem arises where, as is often the case, the research is not related to the lecturer's current teaching commitments, i.e., the *type* of invention is not reasonably expected. At present this point remains open although some establishments of higher education have shown an even-handed attitude to staff who find themselves in the above position (e.g., Sussex University compensation scheme cited in (1978) 114 IRLIB 4 at p. 5).

Connection Do the words 'an invention' in s. 39(1)(a) refer to *the* invention which is the subject of the dispute, a broader class of invention, or any expected invention? In *Harris's Patent* [1985] RPC 19 the court concluded that the first possibility was too narrow, whilst the third by-passed the connection between the invention and the performance of the employee's duties. Falconer J preferred the second alternative as it encompassed any invention:

> . . . which achieves, or contributes to achieving, whatever was the aim or object to which the employee's efforts in carrying out those duties were directed . . . that is to say, such an invention as that made though not necessarily the precise invention actually made and in question ([1985] RPC 19 at p. 29).

Therefore, there must be a logical connection between the invention and the performance of the contractual duties. For example: in *Charles Selz Ltd's Application* [1954] 71 RPC 158 the plaintiff was employed as a general manager, conversant with design production and the routine business of lampshade manufacture. He invented a new plastic coating for wires which could, amongst other things, be applied to lampshades. It was held that the invention belonged to the plaintiff as he had never been directed to apply his mind for the purposes of devising an invention.

In applying the Patents Act 1977 the courts are likely to conclude that the stronger the link between the invention and the employee's duties the more likely that that particular invention was expected.

3.5.4 Section 39(1)(b) — special obligations

Where the employee's status within his employer's business creates a special obligation to further the interests of the employer then the invention is more likely to belong to the employer. As yet there has been no need to define the term 'special obligation' although it will probably follow the tests expounded in *Worthington Pumping Engine Co.* v *Moore* (1903) 20 RPC 41 and *British Syphon Co. Ltd* v *Homewood* [1956] RPC 225 & 330. This obligation might arise where the employee represented the *alter ego* of his employer, occupied a position very high in the management structure, or was an employee-consultant being paid a high salary to invent.

Middle management will be exempt, normally, from the strictures of this subsection. Accordingly, as the employee in *Harris's Patent* [1985] RPC 19 was merely a departmental manager with no duty to attend board meetings the court concluded that no special obligation arose. Of greater interest is the growing inclusion of the following type of clause:

You agree that by virtue of the nature of your duties and the responsibilities arising from them that you have a special obligation to further the interests of [your employer].

It is highly questionable whether such a practice would stand up to judicial scrutiny. Apart from contravening the spirit of ss. 39 to 42 Patents Act 1977, s. 42(2) renders unenforceable any term in an employee's contract which 'diminishes his rights in an invention'. The above clause appears to do this in two ways:

(a)   It substitutes the much wider phrase 'in the course of duties' in s. 39(1)(b) for those duties which are termed 'normal' or 'specifically assigned' in s. 39(1)(a).

(b)   It imposes special obligations upon the employee not warranted by the status of the employee within the relevant establishment.

Perhaps one solution is to soften the wording of the above clause so that it gives the impression that the employee may have a special obligation in certain circumstances without in any way appearing prescriptive on this matter. For example, one company adopted the following clause:

As a result of your position within the company, and your associated duties and responsibilities, it is likely that any invention will become the property of the company.

This would clearly indicate to a court how the employer perceived the role of the employee within the organisation without specifically claiming ownership of every invention which resulted from the performance of the relevant duties.

In the course of duties Even where a special obligation is established the invention must still arise 'in the course of the duties of the employee'. This particular condition was not adopted in the pre-1977 decisions of *Worthington Pumping Engine Co.* v *Moore* (1903) 20 RPC 41 and *British Syphon Co. Ltd* v *Homewood* [1956] RPC 225 and 330. Such duties will include those designated as 'normal' or 'specially assigned' under s. 39(1)(a). They will also include any other duties which the employee has undertaken, whether specifically assigned or otherwise, provided they are consistent with the employee's position within the business. In *E. Peart and Co. Ltd* (1988) SRIS O/209/87, the Comptroller held that s. 39(1)(b) was potentially applicable even where the employee had maintained an involvement in research and development matters in direct contravention of his employer's explicit prohibition. The judgments in *British Reinforced Concrete Engineering Co.* v *Lind* (1917) 34 RPC 101 may provide useful assistance in determining the other types of duties which an employee with a high status within his employer's organisation may be expected to perform. However, in reported patent litigation the predictability of defining such duties, and applying them in varying factual situations, appears low (contrast *Charles Selz Ltd's Application* (1954) 71 RPC 158 and *Fine Industrial Commodities Ltd* v *Powling* (1954) 71 RPC 253).

3.5.5 Entitlement proceedings

Assuming that the employer or employee wrongly applies for a patent, the Patents Act 1977 provides the other party with certain rights to have patent proprietorship transferred to themselves. Other remedies may be available, such as seeking interlocutory relief in order to prevent further use of an invention. But the most practical course of action is to initiate entitlement proceedings because: the cost of appearing before the Comptroller is comparatively low; the procedure can be relatively fast; and, once ownership has been established the rights of exploitation are clarified for the purposes of subsequent infringement actions, claims for damages and the pursuit of a permanent injunction.

Pre-grant The employer or employee may question the ownership of any invention, even before a patent application has been filed, in entitlement proceedings before the Comptroller (s. 8 Patents Act 1977). The same applies to patent applications filed or to be filed in other countries, including international applications and applications for European patents (ss. 12 and 82 Patents Act 1977).

Post-grant After a patent has been granted, an employer or employee will have the right to question its ownership in entitlement proceedings before the Comptroller (ss. 37 and 39 Patents Act 1977). Equally, where the validity of the patent is in issue then the question of entitlement may arise under s. 74 Patents Act 1977.

3.6 PRE-ASSIGNMENT CLAUSES

Section 42(2) of the Patents Act 1977 provides:

> *Any term in a contract . . . which diminishes the employee's rights in inventions of any description made by him . . . shall be unenforceable against him to the extent that it diminishes his rights in an invention of that description so made, or in or under a patent for such an invention or an application for any such patent.*

This subsection applies to three different contracts:

(a) Agreements between the employer and employee.

(b) Agreements entered into by the employee with a third party, at the request of the employer.

(c) Agreements entered into by an employee with a third party, in pursuance of an existing contract of employment.

One must first distinguish a pre-assignment from a post-assignment clause. The former seeks to effect an automatic transfer of an employee's invention *before* that invention has been made, whereas the latter attempts to transfer ownership rights *after* the invention has been made. This second possibility will be dealt with later (see 3.10) as it involves the controversial practice of 'contracting out' of the statutory compensation provisions (ss. 40 and 41 Patents Act 1977).

The operative words in s. 42(2) are: 'to the extent that it diminishes his rights'. What sort of clauses will be considered to diminish an employee's rights and, if found, how will these clauses be excised from the contract of employment? Three clauses, in particular, are worth considering for their effect upon the employee's rights: notification clauses, disclaimers, and restraint of trade clauses.

3.6.1 Notification clauses

It is generally agreed that an employee's rights will not be diminished if there is a requirement to notify the employer of any invention made in the course of employment. But consider the following two ILU clauses which deal with this matter in a subtly different manner:

> *It is the duty of staff to make written reports to the Company of the results of their work, including inventions and technical and commercial developments related to the Company's business.*

You will promptly notify the Company of any invention you make or contribute to (even in your own time) during your employment with the Company.

There may be nothing objectionable in allowing an employer the opportunity of assessing whether the relevant invention falls within s. 39(1) or (2) provided, of course, there is a willingness to respect the statutory rights of the employee. However, whereas the first clause is only providing for this opportunity where the invention relates to the employer's business, the second is more open-ended.

It is clearly arguable that an employee's rights are being diminished where compulsory disclosure relates to an invention unrelated to the employer's business and not made in the course of duties. At the very least, the employer is increasing the possibilities of the employee's invention being leaked (i.e., novelty being destroyed) prior to applying for a patent. The importance of this latter point is more theoretical than practical as one would expect the employer to be bound by a duty of confidence not to disclose the details of any invention found to belong to the employee. Moreover, for the purposes of maintaining good industrial relations, the employer may consider undertaking an express obligation of confidentiality.

Notwithstanding the above, it is submitted that as one cannot always confidently expect an employee to apply the provisions of s. 39 Patents Act 1977 properly, it is preferable to adopt the first clause but with the following proviso: *any* patent application made by an employee, whether or not related to the employer's business, must be notified to the employer immediately. This would give the employer the opportunity of:

(a)   checking on any possible ownership dispute,

(b)   ensuring that the patent application is professionally drafted prior to its publication by the Patent Office if the invention is owned by the employer (amendment of an existing patent application is far easier at this stage),

(c)   withdrawing the patent application for commercial reasons, if ownership is established under s. 39(1) (the Patent Office has a duty not to disclose the contents of any application withdrawn before the publication date),

(d)   applying for an injunction in order to prevent the disclosure of any confidential information in the patent application (publication of an application normally takes place approximately 18 months after its submission).

And what happens if the employee refuses to sign such an undertaking? Attention should be drawn to certain restraint of trade cases where, in analogous situations, an employee's refusal to sign a new restraint clause warranted his dismissal (see *RS Components Ltd* v *Irwin* [1973] ICR 535 and Bowers 1990, p. 228). Whether this is a wider application of a common law duty of good faith is as yet unclear, but it does seem to provide a clear answer to the above question.

Finally there has been an increase in the use of 'notification and consent' clauses. Such clauses not only demand notification of all employees' inventions to the employer, they also require the employer's consent before employee inventors can exploit their *own* invention where competition with the employer's own products is likely. This appears to 'diminish' an employee's rights under s. 42(2). However, it is submitted that the subsection must be read in the light of the employee's other contractual duties, express and implied. In particular, courts have not been averse to implying a duty of fidelity which restricts an employee's ability to compete with his or her employer (*Hivac Ltd* v *Park Royal Scientific Instruments Ltd* [1946] Ch 169). Provided employers' use of 'consent' clauses is not at variance with the duty of fidelity it is unlikely that s. 42(2) will prove an obstacle.

3.6.2 Disclaimers

The practice most commonly advocated is to insert a blanket pre-assignment clause, especially in service contracts, with an appropriate caveat; that is:

All employee's inventions belong to your employer [*X company*], *subject to s. 39(1) of the Patents Act 1977.*

In terms of maintaining good employee relations, as the clause is meaningless to the average employee, possibly sowing seeds of mistrust and confusion, one would expect some further explanatory notes to be added. The merit of such a clause is that it catches all inventions which are not owned by the employee under s. 39(2).

But there are dangers. For example, what if the employee is transferred to an overseas office? This might entail complete forfeiture of any rights under s. 39 as the employee now falls outside its protection (see 3.5.1.4). The clause would then operate to transfer *all* the employee's inventions to the employer, irrespective of whether they were made in the course of employment or not. If the common law considered this clause to be too widely drawn for the protection of the employer's legitimate business interests the clause would be declared unenforceable in its entirety (see *Electrolux Ltd* v *Hudson* [1977] FSR 312).

It is preferable, therefore, for the contract of employment to spell out clearly the wording of s. 39, with appropriate modifications where the language of the Parliamentary draftsman is too obscure for a clear understanding by the average employee.

3.6.3 Restraint of trade clauses

The foregoing analysis raises a question of more general application. In particular, is it advisable to insert a clause which is known to be too widely drawn, in the expectation that s. 42 Patents Act 1977 will render it unenforceable *only to the extent* that it diminishes an employee's rights? One clause adopted by certain companies is:

Subject to the Patents Act 1977, any inventions, developments or modifications made by the employee shall be the sole property of the company and the employee will take all necessary steps to effect this, including the assignment of any patent rights.

In patent law, it is a common practice to insert into a patent application a blanket disclaimer to the effect that if the application is claiming protection for any information which has already been published (or not inventive, or has been claimed in previous patent applications, and so forth) that part should be deleted. But we are dealing here with employment matters, not issues of patent procedure.

It is certainly arguable that the normal rules applicable to restraint of trade are more appropriate here; in which case one must focus on the 'blue pencil' test. In simple terms this test prevents a court from simply adding to, altering or reframing a restraint clause in order to make it conform with existing public policy criteria. Rather, it must be possible to delete the offending words with a blue pencil and still retain the clause's grammatical sense. In a blanket disclaimer, stated to be subject to the provisions of the Patents Act 1977, it might be difficult to delete any word without making total nonsense of the remainder.

Finally, as noted in the historical discussion in 3.2, great care should be exercised in applying the principles of restraint of trade to the wider field of restrictive covenants. The blue pencil test is not a device for rewriting general terms in a contract; it is limited to restraint of trade clauses. General contract terms stand or fall in their totality in accordance with their wording, the arguments centring on their presumed meaning and common law public policy constraints. Until this issue is resolved by future litigation it is advisable for employment contracts to contain the following clause:

Should any portion of this Agreement be judicially held to be invalid, unenforceable or void, such holding shall not have the effect of invalidating or voiding the remainder of this Agreement not so declared or any part thereof . . . the offending portion shall be deemed amended or reduced in scope, otherwise to be stricken therefrom, only to the extent required for the purposes of conformity with section 39 of the Patents Act 1977.

3.7 OWNERSHIP OF INVENTIONS: MISCELLANEOUS MATTERS

3.7.1 Informal settlement of disputes

Settling disputes over inventorship will be considerably cheaper if achieved internally within the employer's organisation or by some other informal mechanism. Any non-judicial procedure must be fair to the employee, not unduly daunting, and comply with the rules of natural justice as operated within industry. As was stated in *Courtaulds Northern Textiles Ltd v Andrew* [1979] IRLR 84, all contracts of employment contain an implied term that employers should not 'without reasonable and proper cause conduct themselves in a manner calculated or likely to destroy or seriously damage the relationship of confidence and trust between the parties'.

Failure to abide by this implied term may entitle an employee, with a qualifying period of two years' service, to resign and claim compensation for unfair 'constructive' dismissal under s. 57(1)(c) Employment Protection (Consolidation) Act 1978 (see, generally, *Western Excavating (ECC) Ltd* v *Sharp* [1978] QB 761).

3.7.2 Constructive trusts

The possibility that an employee holds an invention on constructive trust for his employer is almost completely eliminated by s. 39 of the Patents Act 1977, unless the relevant contract of employment is not governed by UK law. But the converse is more likely (i.e., the employer holds on trust for his employee). As s. 39 will remain unpredictable in its effect until more reported decisions occur, there will be occasions where an employer, because of access to legal and business expertise, will wrongly persuade an employee that the latter's invention belongs to the employer. If this is the case, the employer will hold the patent on trust for the employee. However, the employee must take the liabilities of the resulting trust just as much as the benefits (e.g., *Triplex Safety Glass Co.* v *Scorah* [1938] Ch 211). For instance, the employer might be entitled to compensation for any expenditure that was incurred in protecting the invention, such as suing potential infringers. Conversely, if the employer solicited the services of the employee beyond the scope of his contractual duties, in order to apply for or retain patent protection, the employee might be entitled to the remedy of *quantum meruit* to recover the value of those services from the employer.

3.7.3 Ownership and infringement of ancillary rights

Paragraph 11 of sch. 5 to the Copyright, Designs and Patents Act 1988 deals with an anomaly whereby copyright in works produced in the course of employment will normally belong to the employer (see chapter 4) whereas that is not of itself sufficient for any associated patent to belong to the employer under s. 39 Patents Act 1977. A new subsection (3) was inserted into s. 39 to protect the employee (or those claiming under him) entitled to a patent under s. 39 from liability for infringement of design right or copyright belonging to the employer 'in any model or document relating to the invention'. Otherwise, an employer could use copyright or design rights to prevent an employee fully exploiting a patent which it is the policy of s. 39 to leave with the employee.

Note that s. 39(3) only applies to those rights enforceable as between employee and employer. If the employee (who owns the patent) operates within a research team, other employees may acquire copyright or design rights in documents relating to the invention, preventing the employee inventor from fully exploiting the invention without their permission, or, more likely, unless payment of an appropriate licence fee is forthcoming.

3.7.4 Clauses which require the cooperation of employee inventors

Assuming that the invention belongs to the employer there is still the problem of applying for patent protection. When applying for a patent in the UK it will be useful to produce a written, signed undertaking in which the employee inventor acknowledges that ownership of the invention resides with the employer. For example, a signed document showing that the provisions of the Patents Act 1977 have been explained to the employee, with a clause to the following effect:

> *I agree with the company and I hereby acknowledge that the said invention was made in circumstances falling within section 39(1) of the Patents Act 1977 and that accordingly as between me and the company the said invention and all United Kingdom and foreign rights therein including the right to apply for a patent and similar protection belong to the company by virtue of that subsection.*

This will reduce the chances of subsequent litigation by the employee in which ownership is called into question.

Equally, if the employer applies for protection elsewhere in the world there may even be a requirement that the employee inventor applies on behalf of the employer. Clearly the employer would rather not face a recalcitrant employee, refusing to sign appropriate authorisations and application forms! For this reason, the majority of firms in the ILU survey, although certainly not all, inserted a clause to cover this problem. For example:

> *I hereby undertake to execute and do at the company's request and expense all such documents, acts and things as may be required by the company for the purpose of applying for, prosecuting, obtaining and maintaining Letters Patent or similar protection throughout the world in respect of the said invention and for vesting the same when obtained in the company or the company's nominee absolutely.*

In order to prevent any undue anxiety or confusion it is advisable to add that:

(a)   The employer will pay the costs associated with such activities.

(b)   The employee should not disclose the invention, prior to its publication, during this international patenting phase.

(c)   The employee's duty to cooperate extends to other matters such as, for example, giving evidence in infringement or patent validity proceedings (whether orally or by sworn affidavit) and executing any necessary assignment of the rights to designated persons (providing a suitable indemnity in respect of all costs, claims and damages, incurred in connection with the discharge of those duties).

(d)   The employee's duty to cooperate will extend beyond the employee's termination of employment, with an appropriate level of compensation for any time actually spent by the employee at the employer's request on such assistance.

(e) If by virtue of any foreign law the employee nonetheless retains rights in the said invention, perhaps even the sole right to apply for a patent or similar protection, then the employee must acknowledge that such rights are held in trust for his or her employer.

3.7.5 Importance of good record-keeping

An employee inventor may apply for compensation under Patents Act 1977 at any time after the patent has been granted, but not later than one year after the patent has expired, or six months after refusal of any application for restoration of the patent caused by failure to pay renewal fees. Thus, it is essential that proper records are kept of all circumstances relevant at the time of the invention. In particular, the following points can be identified as meriting inclusion within a company's procedure for handling the ownership of employees' inventions under s. 39:

(a) Name of inventor.

(b) Nature of employment and grading details.

(c) Job description, original job advertisement and letter of appointment.

(d) Actual employment duties at time of invention.

(e) Any records of instructions given to employee.

(f) Any written explanation of why patentable inventions might result from performance of those duties.

(g) Restrictive covenants affecting the employee's right to disclose confidential information.

(h) Nature and date of invention.

(i) Any statement made by the employee (written and witnessed if possible) accepting that the invention was made in the course of his or her duties.

(j) A procedure for notifying the employee inventor when the patent expires or lapses from failure to pay renewal fees.

3.8 CONDITIONS FOR COMPENSATION

Section 40 Patents Act 1977 lays down certain conditions which must be met before an employee can claim compensation for an invention. These conditions vary depending upon whether the employer or the employee owns the invention under s. 39. Both possibilities will be looked at separately.

3.8.1 Employer owns the invention

Once it has been established that the employee made the invention but that it is owned by his employer, s. 40 imposes an extremely heavy burden on the employee inventor which must be discharged before any question of compensation arises.

> *Where it appears to the court or the comptroller . . . that the employee has made an invention belonging to the employer for which a patent has been granted, that the patent is (having regard among other things to the size and nature of the employer's undertaking) of outstanding benefit to the employer and by reason of those facts it is just that the employee should be awarded compensation to be paid by the employer, the court or the comptroller may award him such compensation of an amount determined under section 41 below.*

The section requires the fulfilment of three main conditions:

(a)   The invention must be patented.
(b)   The patent must be of outstanding benefit.
(c)   It is just that the employee obtain compensation from the employer.

3.8.1.1 Invention must be patented

Assuming, for the moment, that we are dealing exclusively with patent protection, one crucial question is surely: What happens if the employer deliberately chooses to suppress the invention, or for some other reason fails to gain available patent protection? As all patent applications are published, giving competitors the opportunity of 'inventing round' the patented invention, the employer may recognise that the invention is of more value if retained as a trade secret. The classic supposed case of an oil company suppressing petroleum substitutes might be an example here. Alternatively, the employer might not see that the benefits of patent protection outweigh the costs of application, especially when the additional burden of yearly renewal fees is also taken into account.

Subject to the possibility that the employee might apply for a patent secretly, s. 40 clearly establishes that it is the patent which gives rise to the possibility of an employee being compensated, not the invention itself. Thus, even if patent protection were successfully to be obtained by an employer, a subsequent revocation of the patent (e.g., on grounds of obviousness) would foreclose any consideration of further benefits derived by the employer from a continuing profitable use of the invention (although chapter 4 may show that the employer retains other ancillary rights after revocation for which the employee should be compensated).

Many companies in the ILU survey added a clause which gave some rights to an employee whose invention the employer did not wish to patent. For example:

> *If, following such a decision [i.e., not to patent] you wish to apply for a patent, either yourself or with another, you must first inform the company of your intention to do so. Within a reasonable time, following such notification, the company must tell you whether it would object to your proposed application. The sole ground for such objection is that the disclosure to third parties of trade secrets or other confidential information belonging to the company may damage the interests of the company.*

This type of clause accords with good industrial relations practice. There is no reason why an employer should frustrate the entrepreneurial instincts of an employee by refusing to exploit an invention or allowing the employee to do so, as it merely consigns the invention to the scrap heap for no purpose whatsoever.

3.8.1.2 Outstanding benefit

The word 'outstanding' is not defined in the Patents Act 1977. It has been variously described as denoting 'a humdinger of a winner'! (Lord Elwyn Jones) or, on a rather more basic level, as referring to inventions which are 'extraordinary', 'prominent', 'conspicuous' or which 'stand out'. The last attempt may well be the most accurate as s. 40(1) does indeed refer to assessing the benefit 'having regard among other things to the size and nature of the employer's undertaking'. This would appear to support employees in smaller firms where the contribution of one single invention may be far greater (i.e., stand out more) than one might expect in a larger firm. For example, in *British Steel Plc's Patent* [1992] RPC 117, the hearing officer pointed out that the employer's annual turnover exceeded £5 billion. Even if the yearly benefits derived from the employee's invention was £5 million this was hardly outstanding as it represented only 0.1% of turnover (see Chandler (1992), p. 600).

In particular, a monopoly business may derive little benefit from a brilliant invention if it merely represents a better version of the old but very popular one. In *GEC Avionics Ltd's Patent* (1989) IPD 12047 evidence was submitted by the employer, a medium-sized company, that although considerable benefit had been derived from the relevant patented invention, comparable benefits had been acquired from the sale of a similar, but unpatented, product. The Comptroller held that the employee had failed to discharge the burden of proving that the benefit from his patent had been 'outstanding'.

However, s. 43(4) ensures that foreign patent grants 'or other protection' covering the employee's invention will also be taken into account when evaluating the benefit derived by the employer (see *GEC Avionics Ltd's Patent* [1992] RPC 107, 112). The phrase covers benefits derived from employing patent-type rights in foreign jurisdictions (e.g., petty patents, utility models etc.). As it is more normal for the larger multinational companies to possess substantial foreign patent portfolios, employees within these firms may increase their chances of arguing that any benefit derived from their inventions is outstanding.

In s. 43(7) the word 'benefit' is defined as 'money or money's worth'. This means that the profit which an employer derives from use of the patented invention is not the sole criterion. 'Money's worth' will presumably include rather more intangible advantages. For instance, if an employer uses the patent to block the successful entry of other potential competitors into the market, or prevents the progress of existing competitors, then this might constitute a benefit (perhaps outstanding in its effect) irrespective of the revenues derived from marketing the patented product. Equally, the benefit obtained by an employer from the patent might also include such things as increased prestige or status amongst competitors or, more generally, within the employer's industry; for example, being awarded a Queen's Award for Technology, although a court will find considerable difficulty in assessing the actual benefit thereby secured. However, as has been pointed out, the court is assessing 'outstanding benefit not outstanding merit'.

In *Elliott Brothers* it was considered to be a rebuttable presumption that part of any benefit derived from a patented invention was the actual existence of the patent right (known as *GEC Avionics Ltd's Patent* [1992] RPC 107, 112). The converse therefore appears likely: not all of the benefit derived by the employer will necessarily result from the patent right. How courts will deal with this matter is as yet impossible to say.

On the one hand, in *British Steel Plc's Patent* [1992] RPC 117 the hearing officer recognised that if the employer was unable to demonstrate *prima facie* that he had derived no benefit from the patent 'then it is to be assumed that any benefit he derived from the invention is at least partly due to the existence of the patent' (at p. 122). Conversely, in *re Memco-Med Ltd* SRIS 0/106/91, Aldous J posed the question of when a patent has produced some benefit for the employer:

> *To assume that question it is likely to be useful to assume that the patent was never granted . . . . It will then be possible to ascertain the benefit from the patent by comparing the actual position of the employer with the position he would have been in if the patent had not been granted, bearing in mind the benefit must be in money or money's worth.*

On the facts, although the patented sales had represented over 80% of the employer's sales over four years, there was no proof of outstanding benefit. The reason was simple. The employer sold exclusively to one client who had encouraged and funded the development of the patented invention. All the evidence demonstrated that the existing business relationship would not have been jeopardised by the absence of patent protection as the client had continued to make the same level of purchases from the employer of second generation equipment which had superseded the patented invention.

Benefit to employer   Under s. 41 it is the 'employer' who must benefit, so if he is ill-equipped to make use of invention it seems compensation will not be forthcoming. Consider the following examples:

(a)   The employer assigns the invention for free to an associated employer.
(b)   The employer closes down the company and reopens under a new name.
(c)   The employer encounters a legal impediment to seeking a patent grant.

In the first example, company lawyers may regard the employer as a legal entity separate from that of its associated employers and that the employer has derived no benefit from the patent! It is true that s. 41(2) provides that the amount of any benefit derived by an employer from the assignment or grant of a patent to 'connected persons' will be that which could reasonably be expected to be so derived had no connection existed (the word 'connected' being defined in s. 838 of the Income and Corporation Taxes Act 1988). But s. 41 is headed 'Amount of Compensation' whereas s. 40 is laying down certain conditions precedent before any assessment of compensation can take place. It is questionable whether a court would allow an employee to establish 'outstanding benefit' by recourse to the provisions of s. 41 which themselves assume that s. 40 conditions have already been met (see *British Steel Plc's Patent* [1992] RPC 117).

Regarding the second example, s. 130(1) Patents Act 1977 defines 'employer' in relation to the employee inventor as 'the person by whom the employee is or was employed'. Unless the new company is considered to be 'connected' with the old company (see above) the employee may lose any right to compensation. The only other possibility is that the old company was transferred as a 'going concern' to the new company, in which case reg. 5 of the Transfer of Undertakings (Protection of Employment) Regulations 1981 (SI 1981 No. 1794) provides that all the transferor's duties and liabilities under the contracts of employment, of any person employed directly before the transfer by the transferor, will pass to the transferee. This would make the latter liable to pay compensation to the original employee inventor.

In the third example, the only benefit that an employer will gain will be from the invention, as patent protection will have failed to materialise.

3.8.1.3 Justice and fair dealing
This particular criterion is the most difficult to define. Should one ask whether it is *just* that the employee receive any compensation, or, as a lawyer versed in the traditions of equity would put it: has the employee come to the court with clean hands?

Consider the possibility of an employee intentionally going behind the employer's back and applying for a patent. Arguably, by applying without permission the employee will be in breach of the implied duty of fidelity. Perhaps interlocutory relief will be sought if the employer wishes the invention to remain a trade secret rather than be published in a patent specification. But will the relevant criteria be limited to a contractual analysis? The employee may have acted out of pure frustration, the employer being unable to see the benefits of patent protection. The employee may even openly admit this action once the application had been lodged with the Patent Office. Moreover, even if a patent has been wrongly granted to the employee, under s. 37 Patents Act 1977 the employer may apply to the Comptroller for appropriate rectification of the proprietorship register. In the following circumstances, it is submitted that a court might properly ignore the employee's actions provided it is confident of his or her subjective innocence:

(a) The employee applies for a patent honestly believing that he or she owns the invention.

(b) The employee informs the employer that he or she has applied for a patent in the employer's name.

(c) The employee applies for a patent in his or her own name when the employer states that the invention is going to be disclosed in a television programme at some later date (see 3.1.1).

In any of these situations the court, if it thinks fit, will always be entitled to deduct a specific sum from the employee's ultimate compensation award. For example, in the second situation, it might be reasonable for the employee to bear the costs of application. Conversely, all rights to compensation might be forfeited if the employee knowingly broke any duty of confidence to the employer, or applied for a patent in the knowledge that the employer would gain greater benefits if the invention remained a trade secret.

Whatever else, it is vital that when courts come to apply this 'just' criterion that they do not adopt an all-or-nothing approach. Any award is capable of infinite variation depending upon the conduct, honesty and fair dealings of the parties. For this reason, it is possible that all those factors in s. 41(4) (see later) which supposedly affect the quantum of compensation may also be used in this area, e.g., nature of benefits derived by the employee from the invention, extent of the employee's participation in the development of the invention, degree of skill exercised by the employee. For example, in *re Memco-Med Ltd* SRIS O/106/91 it was held that where the invention resulted from the performance of the employee's *paid* duties then any benefits derived from the patent should be exceptional before it would be 'just' that the employee inventor be further compensated.

3.8.1.4 Procedure for application

Under r. 59 Patents Rules 1990 the employee must make an application for compensation within one year after the patent has ceased to exist (e.g., expired or not renewed) or six months after any application for restoration has been refused. Chartered Institute of Patent Agents 1990, p. 315, makes some useful comments on the problem that will be encountered by many employees regarding the possible non-renewal of existing patent rights by employers, or their assignment, without any communication to the employee.

Under s. 40 applications can be made to the Comptroller (a more informal, cheaper procedure) or to the court, although the Comptroller is given the discretion to refuse any application if it 'involves matters which would more properly be determined by the court' (s. 40(5)). Any decision by the Comptroller is subject in the normal way to an appeal to the Patents Court and so forth.

Of note is the unreported decision in *Ibstock Building Products Ltd* (1988) SRIS O/1/89 where a request for a broad discovery of documents and financial data from the patentee was conceded. Although the whole process might be time-consuming, access to this information may be the only way of establishing that a particular patent has been of outstanding benefit. For further information on the conduct of proceedings see Chartered Institute of Patent Agents 1990, pp. 319 and 320.

3.8.2 Employee owns the invention

An employee can only claim ownership of an invention where it was:

(a)   not made in the course of normal duties or in the course of duties specifically assigned, and

(b)   if either condition is fulfilled, it was not reasonably expected that an invention would result from performance of those duties.

Even if these conditions are established, s. 40(2) still provides a limited opportunity for the employee to claim compensation. For this, the employee will be expected to establish that:

(b)   his rights in the invention . . . have since the appointed day [1 June 1978] been assigned to the employer or an exclusive licence under the patent or application has since the appointed day been granted to the employer;

(c)   the benefit derived by the employee from the contract of assignment, assignation or grant or any ancillary contract . . . is inadequate in relation to the benefit derived by the employer from the patent; and

(d)   by reason of those facts it is just that the employee should be awarded compensation to be paid by the employer in addition to the benefit derived from the relevant contract.

Section 40(2)(a) states that the right to compensation stems from the act of patenting. So an employee who is persuaded to assign the invention to the employer, *before* applying for the patent, and then finds that the invention is being suppressed by the employer (e.g., because the invention may offer greater rewards as a trade secret) may have no claim to compensation. However, any clause in the contract of employment which provides for the assignment or exclusive licence on an invention before it was made will be rendered unenforceable under s. 42(2) insofar as it diminishes the employee's rights.

3.8.2.1 Assigned or exclusively licensed

Section 130(1)(b) Patents Act 1977 defines an exclusive licence as one which confers on the licensee 'to the exclusion of all other persons (including the proprietor or applicant), any right in respect of the invention to which the patent or application relates'. If the employee retains the right to license the invention to other companies, subject to any possible breach of confidentiality, then no compensation will arise as the licence granted to the employer is merely non-exclusive. No definition of an assignment appears in the Patents Act 1977 although it should refer to any written, signed document transferring the proprietor's patent rights to another which conforms to the particulars in s. 30(6) Patents Act 1977.

At first glance, s. 40(2) appears to offer a perfect compromise: an employee can retain all rights to the invention and attempt to exploit it individually. If the licence is non-exclusive the employee, whatever the sum negotiated with his employer, will be able to maximise potential income from other sources. If the licence is exclusive (or the invention assigned) then the employer must pay a fair price to the employee or risk a claim for further compensation at a later date. In practice, s. 40(2) may be weighted in the employer's favour for a number of reasons. For example:

(a) An employee may be unable to exploit the invention elsewhere without breaking existing duties of confidentiality to his employer (the employer therefore gains from being a buyer in a buyer's market).

(b) An employer may agree only to a non-exclusive licence, knowing that the employee will be unable to license elsewhere, thereby eliminating any claim to compensation (this may be contrary to the spirit of the section although there is nothing in the Act to suggest that this is the case).

3.8.2.2 Inadequate value

In applying this factor, the court or Comptroller will assess the employee's benefit first. This will include the sum of money received under the assignment or licence agreement, and may include ancillary gains such as promotion or increased salary consequent upon the agreement, especially where a direct link between agreement and subsequent promotion is established. One then assesses the benefit derived by the employer from the patent.

It is at this point that problems emerge from the loose wording of the subsection. What do the words 'inadequate in relation to' actually mean? No formula for apportioning the benefits equitably is advanced. Should benefits be split equally or in some other way? Perhaps the subsection should have read 'inadequate . . . in relation to what an employee would have received if the patent had, from the outset, belonged to the employer'. A court would then have clearer guidance on what to do and how to go about it. The courts may still follow this path although it will involve retrospective and, to some extent, specious analysis. For instance, one would be forced to assume that compensation was payable, and assess its worth, before deciding whether the condition of 'inadequacy' was established — a condition which must be met before any right of compensation arises. Alternatively, a court could assess 'inadequacy' in terms of what a willing licensor, dealing at arm's length, would have expected a willing licensee to have paid for the patent.

No attempt is made in the subsection to define the constituents of inadequacy. Apart from any sums of money which have been transferred to the employee under the assignment or licence, what other factors will be relevant? Remembering that the word 'benefit' is defined as 'money or money's worth' one would expect a court to take account of other advantages derived by the employee, such as promotion within the employer's business, increased salary and more attractive productivity schemes, provided that these benefits were a direct result of the assignment or licence. Put together, the benefits received by an employee may not be inadequate. The only difficulty with this approach is that s. 41, which refers to factors which a court may take notice of in assessing the amount of compensation, already incorporates these points. So a court would be employing such data for two quite different purposes: to adjudicate on the issue of adequacy and, separately, to award compensation equivalent to the difference between the benefits received (inadequate) and the benefits which ought fairly to have been received (for a fuller discussion see 3.8.2.3).

Date for assessing adequacy Another controversial issue will be the point in time at which inadequacy is assessed. Consider the employee who receives a reasonable sum of money for the assignment of the rights in the invention. The employer's business is then taken over as a going concern by a multinational company which quadruples the profitability of the invention. At the time of the assignment the employee's compensation was not inadequate. Can this issue be reopened?

On the one hand, as we shall see below, there is a strong tendency amongst the courts to uphold existing contracts freely entered into by the parties. This is especially relevant in our context because the employer who pays too much to an employee for a patent assignment or licence (the invention subsequently turning out to be a flop) may be unable to claim reimbursement in a court (see, however, r. 61(1) Patents Rules 1978 and s. 41(8) Patents Act 1977 on the variation of existing awards). On the other hand, an employee who fails to obtain compensation is entitled to reapply at a later date (s. 40(7)).

It is submitted that the courts will probably adopt some form of compromise stance. The most likely test will be to consider adequacy at the date of assignment or licence, but allow the employee to pursue further claims where there has been a fundamental change in the profitability of the invention caused by events that were not reasonably foreseeable at the original date of contracting. In this regard one might distinguish the employee who receives royalties from the employer for the exclusive licence of the invention and the employee who receives an immediate lump-sum payment for assigning the invention. A court will look more favourably on the latter as compensation will not increase with sales. Moreover, during the assignment negotiations it would have been difficult to estimate the true earnings potential of the invention.

3.8.2.3 Is it 'just' that the employer pay compensation?

As mentioned earlier, the word 'just' might refer to the old equity maxim that one must 'come to court with clean hands'. An employer who has wilfully deceived an employee into parting with patent rights for an undervalue would not be viewed with favour. Equally, an employee who blithely enters into an agreement without checking the small print may be treated with similar disdain. Clearly, the word 'just' gives the Comptroller a broad discretion, but if the case is heard in a court other conflicting tensions come into play.

Specifically, the courts have always been reluctant to rewrite any contract freely entered into by the parties. For example, the principle of 'inequality of bargaining' which emerged in the 1960s has been roundly criticised for its vagueness and uncertainty by a series of more recent decisions (e.g., *Pao On* v *Lau Yiu Long* [1980] AC 614 and *National Westminster Bank plc* v *Morgan* [1985] AC 686). Nowadays, in arm's-length negotiations, this freedom of contract principle is rarely questioned unless the conduct of the parties provides evidence of some unconscionable or morally repugnant behaviour. In particular, the doctrine of economic duress in the UK requires two conditions to be met:

(a) Illegitimate pressure.
(b) Coercion of will.

The first term still awaits authoritative definition but is clearly more than just hard bargaining or some other form of normal everyday commercial pressure. The second term requires the victim of pressure to establish the lack of any practicable alternative course of action open to him at the time that the pressure was exerted other than submission to that pressure (see Chandler (1989), p. 275).

Consider how one would apply such broad concepts in a case where the employer forces the employee to assign the invention on pain of dismissal or implies that by adopting a more 'constructive' approach the employee will 'enhance' his or her prospects of promotion. As the court will assume that the employer and employee are dealing at arm's length it is doubtful that it would impose any duty upon the former to put the interests of the employee first. Equally, a court may recognise the weaker bargaining strength of the employee (e.g., lack of access to expert advice), but it is unlikely to adopt the position of an independent arbitrator. So, evidence of illegitimate pressure will be difficult to establish unless, for example, the employer wilfully concealed important information, or threatened the employee with physical violence!

As for 'coercion of will', a court might easily conclude that the employee should have resigned and then sued for unfair dismissal compensation whilst exploiting his or her invention freely (see generally *Hennessy* v *Craigmyle and Co. Ltd* [1986] ICR 461).

One should not ignore such issues especially if judges, faced with the skeletal provisions of ss. 39 to 43 Patents Act 1977, adopt the rich diversity of common law precedents dealing with matters of bargaining inequality and contract formation.

One alternative is that all those factors in s. 41(5) which supposedly affect the quantum of compensation may be used in this area. For example, can one assess the inadequacy of the employee's benefit in relation to the employer's without regard to the contribution made by the employer to the making, developing and working of the invention (s. 41(5)(c))? If the success of the employee's invention is due in whole to the risks which the employer is prepared to take in marketing and advertising the end-product then the ultimate benefits to each party must surely reflect this imbalance (see 3.9.1.3).

3.8.2.4 Costs of litigation

Whether the employee owns the invention or not, in any proceedings before a court involving s. 40 Patents Act 1977 there is a broad discretion to make special awards of costs taking account of the financial position of the parties and other relevant circumstances (see s. 106 Patents Act 1977). This ensures that an employee will not normally face heavy costs especially associated with contesting proceedings on appeal. As yet, there is no indication of whether legal aid will be available for actions before a court, although it is unlikely where the employee is attempting to secure a *personal benefit* from ownership of a patent (see generally *Halpern and Ward's Patent* [1974] FSR 242).

As for proceedings before the Comptroller, legal aid is not available (Legal Aid Act 1988 s. 14 and sch. 2, part 1) but may be available on appeal from the Comptroller (see *Tiefenbraun's Application* [1979] FSR 97). However, under s. 107(1) Patents Act 1977 the Comptroller may award to any party such costs as he may consider reasonable and direct how and by what parties they are to be paid.

3.9 CALCULATING THE COMPENSATORY AWARD

Subsections (6) to (8) of s. 41 of the Patents Act 1977 state that an award may be a single monetary sum or periodical payments. Awards may be varied, amended or discharged; failure to obtain an award does not prevent a further application for compensation. An application, under s. 41(8), to vary an existing award can be made to the Comptroller or court, with the specific procedures being laid down in r. 60 of the Patents Rules 1990.

We separate consideration of this topic into two, dealing first with the situation where ownership in the invention resides with the employer, and then where it resides with the employee.

3.9.1 Employer owns the invention: basis for compensation

Section 41(1) of the Patents Act 1977 provides:

> *An award of compensation . . . shall be such as will secure for the employee a fair share (having regard to all the circumstances) of the benefit which the employer has derived, or may reasonably be expected to derive, from the patent or from the assignment, assignation or grant to a person connected with the employer of the property or any right in the invention or the property in, or any right in or under, an application for that patent.*

The aim of this section is to secure for an employee a fair share of the employer's benefit or expected benefit derivable from the patented invention. This benefit may accrue from the employer's exploitation of the invention (e.g., manufacturing the patented product) or from licensing the patent (e.g., royalties) or from assignment of the rights to others (e.g., the price derived from an outright sale). The word 'benefit' has already been considered and includes not just money but other benefits of a more intangible nature.

3.9.1.1 Expected benefits
Section 41(1) also allows a court to take account of benefits which the employer might 'reasonably be expected to derive' from the patent. For example, if the employer purposely undersells, or even gives away, the patent rights in an employee's invention to a sister company or associated employer, the employee may claim that the employer's benefit is what the latter ought to have obtained if dealing at arm's length with an unrelated business concern rather than the sum which was actually received (see s. 41(2)). Applying this

type of objective test creates its own difficulties. An employer acting in good faith may make commercial decisions based on a number of commercial criteria unrelated to the maximisation of profit; for example, selling at a loss in order to break into a hitherto oligopolistic market. Should a court retrospectively punish the employer by assessing benefit on the basis of what 'could' have been acquired?

This particular problem will rarely arise if the employee has to demonstrate that the patent *is already* of 'outstanding benefit' before any right to compensation can arise: if an employer gives the patent away for a mere pittance to another associated employer then the benefit is not 'outstanding' under s. 40(1), ergo no compensation should arise under s. 41(1) (see generally *British Steel Plc's Patent* [1992] RPC 117). If this interpretation is followed then the criterion of 'reasonably expected' profit will normally only apply where an employee has sought compensation during the lifetime of a patent, has established outstanding benefit, and now seeks compensation for predicted profit during the remainder of the patent's lifetime in order to obviate the need for further litigation in the future.

The above analysis also highlights another problem, relevant to ss. 40(1) and 41(1): the practical difficulties of accurately assessing the benefits that the employer received from sales of the patented product. Not only will the employee have to show that the patent has been of outstanding benefit (s. 40) but in order to claim a fair share of the benefit (s. 41) this 'benefit' must be known. Will an employer voluntarily produce details of the benefits derived? It is more likely that an application for discovery will have to be made. This will be supported by the provisions of the Rules of the Supreme Court 1965, Ord. 104, rr. 8(2) and (3), which provide for the disclosure and proper validation of financial information and accounts by the employer (see Chartered Institute of Patent Agents 1990, pp. 324–5 for further details).

3.9.1.2 Special employers: Crown or research council
Section 41(3) covers situations where the employer is the Crown or a research council (as defined in s. 1 Science and Technology Act 1965) and the patent, or any right thereunder, is assigned to a body devoted to its exploitation. This might disadvantage the employee as the employer will often be more interested in the utilisation of a patent rather than its profitable marketing — the employer may even be the sole customer for the patent. Section 41(3), in part, redresses the balance by specifying that any benefit to such a body will be treated as a benefit obtained by the Crown or research council. Interestingly, this benefit may be solely derived from the invention rather than any ensuing patent or patent application.

3.9.1.3 Calculating the fair share
Section 41(4) of the Patents Act 1977 provides:

> *In determining the fair share . . . the court or the comptroller shall, among other things, take the following matters into account, that is to say —*
>   *(a) the nature of the employee's duties, his remuneration and the other*

advantages he derives or has derived from his employment or has derived in relation to the invention under this Act;

(b) *the effort and skill which the employee has devoted to making the invention;*

(c) *the effort and skill which any other person has devoted to making the invention jointly with the employee concerned, and the advice and other assistance contributed by any other employee who is not a joint inventor of the invention; and*

(d) *the contribution made by the employer to the making, developing and working of the invention by the provision of advice, facilities and other assistance, by the provision of opportunities and by his managerial and commercial skill and activities.*

. . . the nature of the employee's duties, his remuneration and the other advantages he derives or has derived from his employment or has derived in relation to the invention under his Act, (s. 41(4)(a)).

This provision contains three criteria:

(a) nature of the employee's duties,
(b) general remuneration derived from employment,
(c) specific remuneration derived from the invention.

The first criterion has been roundly criticised by some as s. 39 would have already ensured that the invention was made in the course of the employee's duties, or duties specially assigned to the employee. The argument is that although distinguishing between an employee who is paid to invent and one who is not is relatively simple, it is highly questionable whether this should affect the amount of compensation that each should receive.

Nevertheless, there may be two justifiable reasons. First, the word 'nature' in the subsection may encourage a court to distinguish between those employees who have a special obligation to further the interests of their employer and those who do not. Clearly the former may be treated less sympathetically by the courts as their employment will often be inextricably linked with the general running and welfare of the company. Secondly, one cannot view the first criterion in isolation. An employee who is expected to invent will not be a shopfloor mechanic or junior draughtsperson — one would expect any salary to mirror this higher status. Where a discrepancy exists (high pay but low expectation of invention) then s. 41(4)(a) allows a court to make a suitable adjustment. This reflects the reality that the fruits of research are what an employer is paying for.

Looking at general remuneration in isolation, this is another criterion with a suspect heritage. The level of an employee's salary will not detract from the intrinsic value of the benefit derived by the employer from the patent. One can only assume that where pay is high, and conditions of employment attractive, a court will downgrade the employee's 'fair share of the intended benefit'. In colloquial terms, an employee who has benefited from an employer's previous generosity, will have to take the rough with the smooth. It is debatable whether this means that the unfortunate employee whose employer acts in accordance with a Dickensian workhouse philosophy will actually gain from this interpretation. Regarding other benefits, presumably the ubiquitous productivity bonus will reduce the employee's compensation to the extent reflected by the invention itself.

The final reference is to any direct benefits which the employee secures as a result of making the invention. These will include: promotion, increased salary, direct one-off payments, enhanced status within the business, and the permission to exploit the invention (normally provided no competition between employer and employee arises). It might also include the legal right to be named as inventor in the patent specification, although whether a court would attempt to assess the resulting possibility of headhunting from competitor businesses is doubtful.

'. . . the effort and skill which the employee has devoted to making the invention' *(s. 41(4)(b))* Superficially, it is difficult to identify the relevance of this criterion. Patent protection often derives from a spark of imagination, the flash of inspiration which emerges after only a second's thought. Courts have never attempted to distinguish between arduous experimentation and sudden flashes of genius. But perhaps this criticism is misconceived. The purpose of ss. 39–43 Patents Act 1977 is to apportion the benefits of invention more equitably — whether an invention is patentable is dealt with by ss. 1 to 4 Patents Act 1977 which are of general application to all inventions. By analogy, the hotel porter who carries five suitcases up a flight of stairs deserves more of a tip than one who carries a briefcase. So, the employee who works long hours, perhaps at home over the weekend, the painstaking experimenter who refuses to give up the fight, the recalcitrant employee who perseveres in spite of express instructions to the contrary, all may be said to deserve a higher standard of compensation because the benefit derived by the employer owes more to the conscious will power of the employee, rather than to any unexpected fortuitous find.

One word of warning. Although this subsection may encourage a court to compensate the unskilled worker more highly than his or her skilled counterpart, there is a limit. For one thing, the patented invention will only belong to the employer if it was made in the course of the employee's duties and an invention was reasonably expected to result. If this condition is fulfilled (i.e., an invention was expected) it might appear contradictory for a court to value contributions on different levels as it would imply that there are differing *degrees* of expectancy of an invention arising which depended in part on the status and ability of the employee.

'. . . the effort and skill which any other person has devoted to making the invention jointly with the employee concerned, and the advice and other assistance contributed by any other employee who is not a joint inventor of the invention' *(s. 41(4)(c))* By way of explanation, s. 43(3) adds that where references are made to an employee making an invention, alone or jointly, such references

do not include the mere contribution of advice or other assistance. This subsection effectively minimises the problem of disputes arising between members of a research team. As has already been said (see 3.4) only those employees who supply the originality can be taken to have contributed to the inventive step incorporated within the patent specification. The effect of this subsection may be contrasted with the position in Germany where compensation is shared out amongst all the members of a research team who have made a 'creative contribution' — i.e., a contribution of a standard above that of a person skilled in the art.

Where joint inventorship has been established, the court will have the unenviable task of identifying whether each employee has, in comparative terms, made a greater or lesser contribution than others in the team. Moreover, difficulties will emerge where these employees occupy different positions within the employer's business. For example, there may only be two employees concerned, the first being a highly paid research designer and the other a low-paid technical innovator. If their contributions are of equal weight, will a court attempt to distinguish one from the other on grounds of employment status, and thereby accommodate such evident dissimilarities by awarding differing amounts of compensation? Perhaps the courts will adopt the reasoning of the Assistant Comptroller in *Florey's Patent* [1962] RPC 186.

> . . . whatever their several contributions may have been, the members of a team pursuing different aspects of a research project under the direction of a team leader should, in any event, be entitled to an equal share in any benefit resulting from what must inevitably be regarded as a joint effort. The fact that one member of the team was fortunate enough to be allotted a line of investigation which led eventually to an important discovery ought not, in my view, to entitle him to a bigger share in the proceeds than other members of the team whose contributions in other directions, however, ingenious, may not have been so fruitful.

Provided this approach is tempered by the condition that only members who actually contribute to the protectable originality in the patent application are entitled to compensation, it would seem eminently sensible.

Similar problems will arise where joint inventors belong to different employers within a joint venture. If employer A employs A1 and A2, and employer B employs B1 and B2, what happens if A1 and A2 contribute more than B1 and B2 but B derives a greater benefit from the patent than A? At present there is no answer although it is arguable that all four employees should receive an identical share in accordance with the reasoning in *Florey's Patent*.

Lastly, the above criterion appears to discriminate in favour of the employer. The employee inventor who only receives advice and assistance from other colleagues (i.e., no original contribution) may have his compensation reduced accordingly, thus securing for his employer a windfall benefit (see Phillips and Hoolahan 1982, p. 71) as these other employees will have no separate right to compensation under Patents Act 1977. One possible rejoinder is that the employer is already paying the salaries of these employees, but this is surely different from paying them compensation under Patents Act 1977.

'. . . *the contribution made by the employer to the making, developing and working of the invention by the provision of advice, facilities and other assistance, by the provision of opportunities and by his managerial and commercial skill and activities' (s. 41(4)(d))* As with s. 41(4)(c), one should differentiate between an employer as joint inventor, and a person who merely supplies assistance and advice. The problems remain equally complex as discussed below.

Compensating the employee where the employer is a joint inventor Two possibilities emerge: (a) assume the employer to be joint employee inventor — assess the totality of compensation that should be given to the 'employee element' and then subtract from that a sum of money equivalent to the value of the employer's inventive contribution, or (b) attempt to assess a 'fair share of the employer's benefit' in the context of the employer making a real contribution to the benefit received.

It is submitted that the first alternative should be preferred. The purpose of compensation is not to share out the benefits equally between employer and employee, but to divide them up fairly. The employer will always acquire a greater share in accordance with the increased financial responsibility of business ownership: the risk of bankruptcy, the costs of capital and research expenditure, the obligations to shareholders as well as employees and so forth. Within that context, compensation under s. 41 is really an assessment of the employee's special (the patent must be of outstanding benefit), almost unpredicted contribution to the success of the employer's business. Thus, an employer as joint inventor is, primarily, making a contribution to the inventive process and must therefore be accommodated on the employee's side of the equation.

Employer's advice or assistance which falls short of being inventive What type of contribution from an employer will persuade a court to reduce the employee's compensation? It is submitted that the normal, expected contribution of an employer is irrelevant here. An employee who performs the duties associated with his or her employment contract has no right to receive special compensation. If the employee produces inventions of a 'non-outstanding' nature the existing salary is viewed as payment enough. Equally, one would expect an employer to spend money on advertising a new product, to invest in new lines of manufacture as and when they come on stream, and spend money on reconfiguring existing plant and machinery to accommodate new products. Put simply: the Patents Act 1977 does not compensate an employee for normal patentable inventions, so why should an employee's compensation be reduced by an employer's normal contribution?

What is needed is something extra from the employer which transforms just another new product into an outstanding success. Put another way, a contribution which strengthens the employee's claim that the initial conditions for compensation (especially outstanding benefit) have been fulfilled. This might embrace the following examples:

(a) A new product which would have achieved little success, given a normal advertising budget — the employer takes the risk of a massive increase in advertising expenditure which eventually pays off (n.b. the invention rather than the patent may be 'outstanding').

(b) A totally new product which requires a purpose-built factory for its manufacture, not just an adaptation of existing plant and machinery.

(c) A product whose market potential and profitability is overseas — the employer is purely a domestic producer who now has to establish a complex network of overseas export contacts, dealers and agencies.

(d) A new product which can only be manufactured by a specialist, or completely retrained, staff of employees.

3.9.1.4 Post-invention record-keeping

Clearly in the light of the above and the possibility that an employer will be expected to reconstruct the history of the invention in order to establish the 'fair' benefit awardable to the employee, employers should ensure that the following information is properly recorded wherever possible:

(a) Inventors' contribution.
(b) Contributions of other employees.
(c) Outside costs (e.g., independent consultants).
(d) Research and development costs (including post-invention innovation costs).
(e) Pilot plant costs.
(f) Production, marketing and advertising costs.
(g) Use made of invention.
(h) Sales figures, profits and income from licensing.
(i) Estimated net profits after deduction of all the above costs.

3.9.2 Employee owns the invention: basis for compensation

Section 41(5) of the Patents Act 1977 deals with the factors regulating compensation. As in s. 40, the governing criterion for an award is that the employee should secure a 'fair share of the benefit', a notion that has already been discussed. The text of s. 41(5) is as follows:

In determining the fair share of the benefit to be secured for an employee in respect of a patent for an invention which originally belonged to him, the court or the comptroller shall, among other things, take the following matters into account, that is to say—

(a) any conditions in a licence or licences granted under this Act or otherwise in respect of the invention or the patent;

(b) the extent to which the invention was made jointly by the employee with any other person; and

(c) *the contribution made by the employer to the making, developing and working of the invention as mentioned in subsection (4)(d) above.*

'. . . any conditions in a licence or licences granted under under this Act or otherwise in respect of the invention or the patent' (s. 41(5)(a)) Subsection (a) refers to the possibility that an employee will be in a strong enough position to negotiate the insertion of some very beneficial licence conditions. For example, a grant-back provision whereby any patentable improvements made by the employer to the employee's original invention will belong to the employee (subject to the compendious laws of the EEC on this matter). Alternatively, the employee may agree to license only if his existing notice period of termination is extended or his existing salary is increased. In all these situations, the court must take account of such advantages in awarding any additional compensation. Note, however, that the employee must have already established that the exclusive licence afforded inadequate remuneration (s. 40(2)(c)) before the above mathematical variances can be taken into account.

The word 'licence' presumably includes a compulsory licence (provided exclusivity is awarded by the Comptroller under s. 49(3)(b) Patents Act 1977). Under s. 48 any person has a right to apply to the Comptroller to be awarded a compulsory licence where, *inter alia*, it can be shown that the demand for the patented invention is not being met in the UK or that the proprietor (i.e., employee in this case) is refusing to grant a licence on reasonable terms. Of course it may be difficult for the employee to argue that the royalties derived from the compulsory licence are 'inadequate' when the rate has been set by the Comptroller in accordance with existing practice. What is more likely, although, strictly speaking, not relevant here, is that the employer owns the patent and the employee applies for a compulsory licence on the basis that the patent is not being exploited fully by his employer — the employee may wish to resign and set up business on his own.

'. . . *the extent to which the invention was made jointly by the employee with any other person' (s. 41(5)(b)); and 'the contribution made by the employer to the making, developing and working of the invention as mentioned in subsection (4)(d)' (s. 41(5)(c))* These factors are almost identical to those which appear in s. 41(4) where compensation for an employer's patent is being considered. Reference should be made to previous discussions on these points (see 3.9.1.3).

Section 41(5) adds that the above factors are not exhaustive. Others, therefore, may be equally relevant:

(a) The employee may make an important contribution *after* the invention has been patented, providing innovative refinements to the invention during its conversion process from the drawing-board into a marketable commodity.

(b) The employee may refuse lucrative offers for an exclusive licence of his invention from competitors of his employer.

(c) The employee may spend a considerable portion of his spare time (unpaid) attempting to sell the invention to new customers or contributing in some other way to the increased marketing potential of the invention.

These points, and many others, will help a court to determine the employee's fair share of the benefits.

Exploiting an employee's patent and the duty of confidence   If the proprietary rights in an employee's invention are not transferred to the employer under s. 39(1)(a) or (b) then, in principle, the employee is free to exploit the patent freely without hindrance from the employer. However, in practice, the knowledge contained in a patent is only the tip of the iceberg. Manufacturing know-how and technical skills, often jealously guarded by a company, may be necessary to make the patented invention work properly. An employee must not breach his or her duty of confidentiality nor disclose any trade secrets or other classified information in attempting to exploit the invention. In practice, one would expect some sort of clause in the contract of employment to spell this out. For example, an employee might have agreed:

> *not to use for your own benefit or gain or divulge to any persons, firm, company or other organisations whatsoever any confidential information belonging to [employer] excluding that which has come into the public domain by authorised disclosure.*

This type of clause does not 'diminish the rights' of the employee as s. 42(3) provides that s. 42(2) will not operate to derogate from any duty of confidentiality which an employee may owe to his employer. For example, if the invention belongs to the employee there will be a right to apply for a patent, but care must be taken not to disclose in the application any information which is confidential to the employer's business. Any attempt to do so would be met, presumably, by an employer applying for an interlocutory injunction preventing disclosure (see 0.7).

3.10 CONTRACTING OUT OF THE COMPENSATION PROVISIONS

3.10.1 Employer owns the invention

From the employer's standpoint the compensation provisions may represent an unwanted obstacle to the full exploitation of an invention. Costly litigation may be required to ascertain whether the employee actually made the invention, whether it belongs to the employer, whether it has been of outstanding benefit, what proportion of the benefit should be shared with the employee, and so forth. Far better that an arrangement is entered into whereby the employee agrees to give up all rights of compensation in an *existing* invention for a sum of money. It is questionable whether such a contract would fall foul of the Patents Act 1977. Section 40(4) provides for ignoring any such agreement where the employee owns the patent rights but then negotiates a transfer to the employer. But the subsection does not concern itself with situations where the employer already owns the patent rights.

Section 42(2), on the other hand, might appear more relevant. Surely any such agreement 'diminishes the employee's rights' if the sum of money turns out to be rather less than a court would have awarded as compensation in those circumstances? Here is the rub. At the time of contracting an employee may recognise the risk of the invention being of only marginal, not outstanding benefit, to the employer (i.e., no right to any compensation), or that it will take many years before it moves from the drawing-board or prototype stage to its eventual commercial marketing (i.e., a long delay before compensation) and, even then, that other competitors may have developed equally good substitutes that will dampen projected profits (i.e., reduce possible compensation). Faced with the reality of everyday business, the employee may willingly agree to such a contract — a bird in the hand is worth two in a bush. Assuming that the negotiations are fairly conducted, all factors are fully disclosed by both sides, that there is no evidence of untoward pressure (see previous comments on the economic duress 3.8.2.3), then a court may prefer to uphold such an agreement as a fair compromise of existing rights rather than as a diminution of the employee's rights.

Some cautionary notes First, an agreed payment *after* an invention has been made is very different to an agreed formula for compensating *future* inventions. The latter is clearly caught by s. 42(2) as an employee who cannot assess what is being bartered away (the invention is yet to be made) is in no position to value those rights. Secondly, although a court would look at the circumstances operating at the time of the contract — the invention may not have been marketed yet — one would expect the sum of money being offered to the employee to be fair, not just nominal. What is fair will depend upon a whole host of factors such as commercial convenience, avoidance of litigation, the presence of independent arbitration in the event of disagreement, and the risks of a lower level of compensation or none at all (the invention may turn out to be worthless). Perhaps, as with contractual maternity pay schemes, the overall guiding principle will be whether the scheme is demonstrably worse than its statutory counterpart.

At present, this whole debate remains hypothetical. On the one hand, it is arguable that any private deal struck between employer and employee breaks the spirit of the Patents Act 1977 (see Reid 1979, 355). The more so because there may be the threat of dismissal, or lack of promotion, hanging in the air at the time that the employee negotiates his compensation, thereby impairing his bargaining power (see the earlier comments on economic duress 3.8.2.3). On the other hand, courts are often prepared to uphold compromise agreements if to do so will avoid subsequent costly litigation. For the moment, all that one can say is that pre-assignment clauses are not the same as contracting out for compensation clauses and, therefore, one can expect them to receive different treatment in the courts.

For the above reasons, one company in the ILU survey added the following clause to staff contracts:

In respect of any invention which belongs to the company [under the provisions of the Patents Act 1977], the company shall at its discretion reward the employee

*in accordance with what the company considers fair and reasonable having
regard to the terms of the Patents Act 1977 ss. 39 to 43. Any reward paid
or offered by the company under this contract of employment shall not prejudice
the rights of the employee under the Patents Act, especially with regard to
seeking further compensation for inventions that have proved to be of
outstanding benefit to the company.*

This clause is clearly seeking to avoid costly and time-consuming litigation
by encouraging the settlement of disputes internally, whilst keeping an
employee's statutory rights intact. It would help, however, if a further payment
was possible where the benefit of a patent had proved to be unforeseeably
successful, and especially if recourse to independent arbitration was a built-
in safeguard.

3.10.2 Employee owns the invention

Section 42(2) of the Patents Act 1977 is again relevant here, attempting to
prevent an employer from pressuring his employee into a disadvantageous
contract (i.e., one that diminishes the employee's rights). Perhaps the employee
has been persuaded to assign his rights in the invention to a subsidiary of
the employer, or to a valued customer of the employer. In practice, however,
s. 42 is not as all-embracing as would first appear. For example, if the employer
occupies a dominant market position then his subsidiaries or associated
undertakings may be able to dictate terms to an employee inventor without
any need for direct or indirect intervention by the employer.

Of course, the employee may 'voluntarily' assign patent rights to a third
party for an inadequate value. Here, provided the employer has not intervened
in any way, the assignment is enforceable without any right of recourse to
the compensation provisions contained in ss. 40 and 41; that is, unless a court
is prepared to lift the corporate veil to discover whether the employer and
third party are associated employers or connected in some other way.

Employers should note, however, that any subsequent attempt to contest
ownership of the patent may be met by a defence of estoppel; i.e., that the
employer's previous conduct gives rise to the implication that the employee
owns the patent, a position from which the court will not allow the employer
to resile. For example, in the USA only the actual inventor may apply for
a patent, thus an employer would need to obtain an assignment of the rights
in any invention from his employee before applying, with the proviso that
the employee signs a form stating that for the purposes of s. 39 Patents Act
1977 the invention, as described in the US patent application, is really owned
by the employer. Only two firms in the ILU survey directly addressed this
problem. The first company used an interesting clause in a document headed
'acknowledgment and undertaking', in which the employee acknowledged that
ownership in the invention lay with the employer. It read as follows:

*Insofar as by virtue of any foreign law I may nonetheless have any rights
in the invention or to apply for patent or similar protection therefor, I hereby
acknowledge that I hold such rights in trust for the company.*

The other company preferred to claim more wide-ranging powers which, amongst other things, would cover issues of ownership and estoppel:

> *For the purposes of this clause [i.e., registering national and international patent rights] the employee agrees to the appointment of the Company as the employee's attorney in the employee's name to execute all documents and to do acts which are required to give effect to the provisions of this clause.*

What happens if an employer inserts an option to purchase clause? Clearly it will be in the employer's best interests to ensure that the employee does not assign or license his or her rights to a competitor. Recognising the dangers of constraining the employee's right to exploit his or her property an employer may insert an option clause whereby he claims the right to buy or obtain a licence on any inventions that belong to his employees, with the important proviso that:

> *in the event of the company proposing to exercise this option and if the terms on which the company shall do so cannot be agreed, the employee undertakes not to assign the letters patent or to grant a licence in respect thereof to any person, firm or company, on terms less favourable to himself than those offered by the company.*

It is arguable that the employee's rights are diminished by such a clause, in contrast to his counterparts in the Federal Republic of Germany where employers have the legal right to enforce such clauses. Why should employees not have the right to sell to anyone they choose (subject to confidentiality under s. 42(3))? Clearly if the option clause is also attempting to prevent assignment or licence to a third party on terms *more* favourable to the employee then it will be struck down, but the above clause is not attempting to do this. Moreover, the clause guarantees that the employer will offer terms identical to the most favourable offered elsewhere. The only restriction on the employee is reduced freedom of choice, without attendant pecuniary harm. The clause, therefore, may be upheld in certain circumstances owing to the following points:

(a)   The employment relationship is based on mutual trust and confidence.

(b)   The employee's training and experience received during this employment may have contributed to the invention.

(c)   Other colleagues may have given the employee important advice and assistance, short of contributing any protectable originality.

(d)   Assignment or licence to a competitor invariably places the jobs of other co-workers in jeopardy.

There are many other relevant considerations, not least the fact that ss. 40 to 42 are directed towards reasonable compensation for the employee inventor rather than unfettered exploitation of legal rights. It is submitted that a court must be convinced that the option clause is being abused by the employer before it intervenes. Such would be the case where the employer has conspired with other potential bidders to force the licence royalty down, or the invention will bring great public benefits but the employer wishes to suppress it for commercial reasons.

Employers' agreements with third parties   In a different context, if the employer enters an agreement with a third party regarding the disposition of an employee's patent rights this cannot affect his employee's rights under s. 39(2). Thus, if the contract becomes incapable of fulfilment then, subject to default provisions in contract and the assumed risk-allocation between the parties, the doctrine of frustration will settle the matter, the contract being rescinded by operation of the law.

3.10.3 Collective agreement

There is one situation where a sum of compensation, agreed with the employer, is binding upon an employee. Section 40(3) of the Patents Act 1977 renders inapplicable any right to compensation under the provisions of the Act where 'a relevant collective agreement provides for the payment of compensation' in respect of the invention, and is in force at the time of the making of the invention. Section 40(6) defines a collective agreement as one made by or on behalf of a trade union to which the employee belongs. Thus, if the employee does not belong to the relevant trade union then he will be free to claim compensation, provided he can satisfy all relevant criteria under Patents Act 1977.

The possibility arises that within a research team some members will belong to a union and others will not, the former being bound by an existing scheme of compensation whilst the latter may remain free agents. Clearly there is room for tension, especially as a court has no right to enquire into the adequacy of compensation. One way of circumventing this problem is offered by s. 1 Trade Union and Labour Relations (Consolidation) Act 1992 which defines a trade union as an organisation of workers, whether permanent or temporary. An employer might then wish to negotiate future compensation with delegated representatives of a research team regarding potential inventions emanating from a particular project. The research team would arguably, for these purposes, be considered a trade union, with any agreement binding all its members.

3.11 CHECKLIST

What procedure should employers adopt for handling employee inventions and related research activities? We have already seen that maintaining proper records, and notification procedures, is essential to establishing legal ownership over employees' inventions. But this in itself is not enough. Good industrial relations practice requires open-handedness and candour. Employees should be informed of relevant legal provisions so that they can assess their rights properly. Internal disputes result more often from the 'apparent' concealment of the truth rather than from malicious motives or personal gain. It is therefore submitted that the following points should be included in any company policy dealing with the ownership and compensation of employees' inventions.

Make employees aware of the commercial importance of patents Ensure that employees are made aware of the need to maintain the secrecy of their inventions, the contribution that such inventions can make to corporate profitability, and the manner in which patent protection will be sought. One company in the ILU survey even gave a specified sum of money for each occasion when an employee identified third-party infringement of an employer's patent — such schemes highlight to employees the importance of intellectual property rights. Finally, such comments should be backed up by proper vetting procedures designed to prevent the premature and/or unauthorised disclosure of sensitive materials at conferences or in journals.

Define inventions covered by the Patents Act 1977 As mentioned earlier, the Patents Act 1977 may well apply to company suggestion schemes and other inventions of a non-patentable nature. Such schemes must, at the very least, conform to ss. 39 and 42(2) Patents Act 1977. One company in the ILU survey stated that where a patentable invention belonged to the employee it would be 'subject to the provisions of the company's suggestion schemes laid down in company personnel policy No. 00'. Clearly this policy must not disregard the provisions of the Patents Act 1977.

Explain the effect of s. 39 Patents Act 1977 Repeating the provisions of s. 39 in a contract of employment is insufficient. Further elaboration is required which details the implications of s. 39 and its correlation with s. 42(2). One company in the ILU survey began with a preamble drawing the employee's attention to the duty of good faith, concluding that because of the employee's particular responsibilities and duties 'in certain fields any invention which he makes is by statute likely to be the property of the company'. Perhaps some practical examples in the employer's relevant statements of policy would be warranted; e.g., situations where inventions made at home by employees still belong to the employer, the general circumstances in which a special obligation will arise, or the possibility that some inventions *will* belong to the employee. Another company in the ILU survey produced a short, but detailed, manual explaining the implications of s. 39 and the rights of employees.

Explain the purpose of certain clauses For example, the idea of inserting a notification or disclaimer clause may seem obvious to a lawyer but without any further explanation it might send the wrong signals to an employee.

Update and review the contracts of employment of all company staff, especially those involved in research Section 39 assumes that an employee's normal duties, and those which have been specifically assigned, are capable of precise definition. Moreover, the expectation that an invention will result from the performance of those duties reinforces the need to identify such duties. A regular review will ensure that: (a) contractually specified duties correspond to actual duties, (b) changes in duties, perhaps not specifically assigned, are brought within the contract of employment — this prevents the possibility that the expectation criterion will be applied to the employee's original duties.

Avoid unduly wide pre-assignment clauses   Jettison the pre-1977 clauses which assumed that *all* inventions belonged to the employer. It does not make a positive contribution to staff morale and can generate unwanted litigation in the future.

Do not impose artificial duties on employee   This would include a duty to invent which was unrelated to the reasonably expected performance of the employee's normal and specifically assigned duties — it merely encourages a court to disregard other features of the employment contract!

Use compensation schemes constructively   Consider the introduction of employee compensation schemes designed to foster staff morale, encourage staff to invent, and persuade employees that litigation is the last resort, not the first. In the ILU survey one company automatically gave a sum of money for each employee invention patented, instituted a formal recognition procedure for such employees through the provision of ties (the colour depending upon the number of patents obtained!), and even had a prize for the 'annual inventor of the year'.

Where possible maintain proper records of post-invention exploitation   This should include the contribution of other employees, the costs of research and development, plant, production, marketing and advertising, sales figures, and profits from licensing. If the patent turns out to be of outstanding benefit then a court will have more information on which to assess the employee's 'fair share of the benefit'.

Consider the possibility of independent arbitration where the patent is of outstanding benefit   In these situations it will be extremely difficult to assess the employee's fair share of the benefit. A procedure which includes a set of general criteria administered by an independent arbitrator will make a positive contribution to staff morale and discourage subsequent costly litigation.

Ensure that employees receive some independent advice   It is possible that an agreed compensation sum can be rescinded by a court if there is evidence of pressure, overt or subtle, being applied to the employee inventor. Assuming that the patent has been of outstanding benefit, recourse to independent advice, perhaps a trade union official, dispels such accusations. The same should apply irrespective of whether the employee is seeking compensation or negotiating a price for the assignment of his or her patent to the employer.

3.12 BIBLIOGRAPHY

3.12.1 Books

Bowers, J. (1990), *Employment Law* (London: Blackstone Press).

Chartered Institute of Patent Agents (1990), *CIPA Guide to the Patents Acts* 3rd edn and 3rd Cumulative Supplement 1991 (London: Sweet & Maxwell).

Pearson, H. and Miller, C. (1990), *Commercial Exploitation of Intellectual Property* (London: Blackstone Press).

Phillips, J. (ed.) (1989), *Employees' Inventions, a Comparative Study* (Sunderland: Fernsway Publications).

Phillips, J. and Hoolahan, M.J. (1982), *Employees' Inventions in the United Kingdom* (Oxford: ESC Publishing Ltd).

3.12.2 Articles

Bercusson, B. (1980) 'The Contract of Employment and Contracting out: the UK Patents Act 1977' [1980] EIPR 257.

Chandler, P.A. (1989) 'Economic Duress: Clarity or Confusion?' [1989] 3 LMCLQ 270.

Chandler, P.A. (1992) 'Employees' Inventions: Outstanding Compensation?' [1992] JBL 600.

Cornish, W.R. (1978) 'Employee Inventions: the New United Kingdom Patent Law' [1978] EIPR 4.

Cox, S. (1991), 'Creative Employees and the Law' (1991) 3(1) Intellectual Property in Business 2.

Davis-Ferid, H. (1981), 'The Employed Inventor under United Kingdom and German Law' [1981] EIPR 102.

Devereux, A.N. (1985-6), 'Compensation and Awards to Employee Inventions' (1985-6) 15 CIPA 47.

Gold, T.Z. (1990), 'Entitlement Disputes: a Case Review' [1990] EIPR 382.

Hodkinson, K. (1986), 'Employee Inventions and Designs: Ownership, Claims and Compensation; and Managing Employee Inventions' (1986) 2 Co Law 146 and 183.

Hoolahan, M.J. (1979), 'Employees' Inventions: the Practical Implications: Ownership and Compensation: UK Patents Act 1977' [1979] EIPR 140.

Lloyd, R.P. (1979-80) 'Inventorship amongst Collaborators', (1979-80) 9 CIPA 16.

Reid, B.C. (1979) 'Employee Inventions under the Patents Act 1977' [1979] JBL 350.

4 Copyright and Designs

4.1 COPYRIGHT

4.1.1 Introduction

The original purpose of copyright law was to protect a person's expression of thought from unauthorised reproduction. This expression of thought was often referred to as a 'work', with enforceable rights being established once authors had recorded their thoughts, whether on paper, canvas or by some other means. With advances in technology copyright protection has been extended to other forms of 'work', recognising the originality, expense and effort involved, for example, in producing quality sound recordings, television and radio broadcasts, laser-produced video discs and so forth.

4.1.1.1 Types of work capable of copyright protection
Section 1 Copyright, Designs and Patents Act 1988 represents Parliament's most recent attempt to spell out clearly those descriptions of work in which copyright might subsist. They are:

(a) original literary, dramatic, musical or artistic works,
(b) sound recordings, films, broadcasts or cable programmes, and
(c) the typographical arrangement of published editions.

The size of this book prevents any lengthy explanation of these terms but a brief summary of the type of items which might fall under each heading is called for. Note that in sch. 1 Copyright, Designs and Patents Act 1988 there are a number of transitional provisions whereby previous statutes, such as the Copyright Act 1956, will continue to exert some influence on our understanding of existing copyright law.

In category (a) we might include the following:

(i) designs, sketches, paintings, prints, engravings, sculptures, diagrams, maps,
(ii) photographic films, graphics,
(iii) computer programs,

(iv)   musical scores, perforated rolls for reproducing sound,
(v)   labels, advertising literature, directories, football fixture lists, flow charts, brochures.

Even architectural designs are included, such as buildings or models for buildings (s. 4(1)(b)), as well as works of 'artistic craftsmanship' (s. 4(1)(c)). However, copyright will not subsist in any of the above items until they have been 'recorded' whether in writing or by some other means, such as storage on tape or in a computer database (s. 3(2)).
In category (b) the following would be included:

(i)   films on video cassette or magnetic video disc, cartoon films made from a sequence of hand-drawn pictures, home videos,
(ii)   television broadcasts (the Copyright, Designs and Patents Act 1988 does not restrict this to the BBC and IBA (now the ITC), in line with current deregulation policies), radio programmes, cable programmes (excluding private communications such as telephonic conversations).
(iii)   transmissions of computer program information in electronic form,
(iv)   cinema film soundtracks, recorded concerts.

Category (c) is merely referring to a separate copyright in the typography of published editions of literary, dramatic or musical works, distinct from the copyright in the works themselves. The general purpose of this right is to protect the publishers of new editions of work (where copyright in the original work has expired) from the photocopying pirate, although its protection will extend to the unauthorised copying of any typographical arrangement such as an article in a newspaper.

4.1.1.2 Overlapping copyrights
Interestingly, an item in one category may appear in a different guise in another category, thereby illustrating that different forms of enforceable copyright can emanate from the same activity. For example, in a televised pop concert, there may be copyright subsisting in the singer's performance (more accurately termed the singer's performer's right), the lyrics of the songs, the musical composition as distinct from those lyrics, the sound recording, and, finally, the broadcast itself. And to complicate matters, a subsequent synthesised adaption of a song that had been performed within that concert may itself create another separate set of copyrights, provided sufficient skill, effort and originality can be established!
The enormous breadth of subject-matter contained in the above categories clearly demonstrates the importance of copyright protection in a variety of important industries, not the least being publishing, music, engineering and advertising. Equally, it should be obvious that many of the works which attract the protection of copyright law will be created, in some way or other, by an appropriately skilled employee. However, subject to the concluding remarks in this chapter, there is as yet no statutory framework of employee compensation similar to that existing in patent law.

4.1.2 Ownership of literary, dramatic, musical and artistic works

The general rule, under both the Copyright Act 1956 and the Copyright, Designs and Patents Act 1988, is that the *author* of a work is the *initial* owner of the copyright. The author is normally the person who has exercised sufficient skill, labour and effort to justify being treated as the author, although, as we shall see later, special provisions will apply to certain types of work such as broadcasts, films, sound recordings and typographical arrangements (4.1.4). Once initial ownership has been established it becomes a question of fact whether ownership has been transferred by assignment or through some other means.

Under the Copyright Act 1956 there were a number of exceptions to the general rule which equated authorship with initial ownership. Under the Copyright, Designs and Patents Act 1988 the scope and number of these exceptions have been severely reduced. For the moment we will concentrate on the exception relevant to employee authors, which is s. 11(2) of the Copyright, Designs and Patents Act 1988:

> *Where a literary, dramatic, musical or artistic work is made by an employee in the course of his employment, his employer is the first owner of any copyright in the work subject to any agreement to the contrary.*

This provision is common to both the Copyright Act 1956 and the Copyright, Designs and Patents Act 1988, but the paucity of precedent on copyright ownership within an employment relationship means that the applicable legal criteria remain nebulous. A number of questions need to be asked:

(a)   What is the meaning of 'in the course of employment'?

(b)   In the light of s. 11(2) Copyright, Designs and Patents Act 1988, what use should employers make of pre-assignment clauses?

(c)   Do the provisions of s. 42 Patents Act 1977 apply to copyright, thereby preventing the use of unduly wide pre-assignment clauses?

(d)   Does the common law make a contribution to the effective policing of pre-assignment clauses?

(e)   What other clauses should an employer consider using in order to preserve the potential value and use of the copyright in employees' works.

4.1.2.1 In the course of employment

How will courts construe these words: in accordance with current principles of employment law, in which case almost anything done by an employee will be caught by this formulation, or will the intellectual property lawyer's approach dominate? Precedent suggests that the latter has prevailed, as illustrated in *Stevenson, Jordan and Harrison Ltd* v *Macdonald and Evans* (1952) 69 RPC 10, in which an employed accountant delivered lectures on a subject closely connected with his employment. These lectures were subsequently incorporated by him into a book. He used the employer's secretarial services and was paid expenses in relation to the lectures. It was held that copyright in the lecture materials (as printed in the book) resided with the employee as he was paid to advise clients, not to give public lectures. However, the copyright in another section of the book, because it originated from a written report supplied to a client, was held to belong to the employer.

The above analysis is derived from the earlier decision in *Byrne v Statist Co.* [1914] 1 KB 622 in which an employee of a newspaper was held to be the owner of the copyright in a translation, made for his employer outside normal hours for a separate fee, as he was not employed to translate.

As with the Patents Act 1977, questions will arise as to whether work done at home by an employee will be considered to have been produced in the course of employment. Relevant factors will include the relationship between the 'work' and the duties of the employee, whether the employer has paid for the installation of facilities in the employee's home for continuity of work to be preserved (e.g., computer, workstation terminal), whether employees are expected to complete outstanding work at home and are paid overtime for this work, and how this work is supervised. Perhaps even the position occupied by the employee within the employer's business will be relevant. In *Nichols Advanced Vehicle Systems Inc. v Rees* [1979] RPC 127 the employee designed racing cars. As chief designer he worked in his own office, an extension within his own home. It was accepted that he stayed at home for the purposes of peace and quiet. As the work represented the particular project upon which his employer required him to work the employee did not own the copyright in the ensuing designs.

The most recent decision in this area is found in *Noah v Shuba* [1991] FSR 14. The employee was expected to research and contribute to scientific journals. However, the writing of books and monographs was 'not expected to be done in working hours' and was done 'in addition to official duties'. The employee wrote a book in his spare time specifically related to his employer's business, using his employer's official notepaper when communicating with outside sources as well as using available secretarial services. Although the book was published by the employer it was held that copyright resided with the employee as it had not been written in the course of employment; i.e., he was not contractually bound to write a book (see also *Byrne v Statist Co.* discussed above). Alternatively, as the employer had acquiesced in the long-standing practice that the copyright in articles and books resided with the employee author, a term to that effect would be implied into the employee's contract of employment.

A similar problem arises in connection with 'moonlighting'. Assuming that there is no breach of contract, are such activities within the course of employment? Pertinent factors might include: the similarity of duties performed by the employee for the full-time and part-time employers, whether the employee carried out tasks for the latter during normal working hours, the competitive rivalry between the two employers, and the use that the employee made of the employer's facilities in fulfilling these extracurricular activities. Breach of contract aside, one would normally expect the overlap of duties and spheres of operation to be crucial to any decision. This issue was touched upon in *Missing Link Software v Magee* [1989] FSR 361, in which the first defendant was employed by the plaintiffs as a software development manager until October 1987, whereupon he took up employment with the second defendant. In April 1988 the latter sought to market a rival system to the plaintiffs' 'personnel management system'. It was claimed that the appearance of a rival system so soon after the employee's departure demonstrated that a substantial part of the system had been written by him before October 1987, a view supported by expert evidence to that effect. Even if the defendant had written the system out of company time he was still employed by the plaintiffs as software development manager in charge of a small team of programmers. It was held therefore, to be arguable that as the defendant was employed to write programs of this nature there was sufficient evidence to suggest that while writing for a competitor he was still acting in the course of employment.

In drawing together the various strands by which the ownership of copyright in employees' work can be determined a number of concluding remarks can be made. First, an employee's duties and the work accomplished during normal working hours are not necessarily coextensive. The architect who draws a simple cartoon sketch during a lunch break and sells it to the local newspaper should be entitled to claim ownership. Conversely, an employee cannot simply assert ownership over work produced at home. The existing conditions of employment, the method of payment, the status of the job, are all considerations which may prove useful in determining the real scope of the employee's duties and the place where they are expected to be performed.

Secondly, copyright protection relates to a recorded expression of thought, not to the idea which underlies that expression (e.g., *Donoghue* v *Allied Newspapers Ltd* [1938] Ch 106). The employee who has an idea on holiday but writes it up on returning to work will be taken to have created the work during normal working hours.

Thirdly, employers will encounter difficulties in pinpointing the exact time when a work was produced — ex-employees may claim that they did not consign their thoughts to paper until after the termination date! This is one reason why copyright should not be viewed in isolation. Its interrelationship with confidentiality is essential as departing employees may still be using their ex-employers' confidential information in writing up reports for their new employers, as well as developing new products and drawing up new designs (see the interesting arguments advanced by counsel in *Missing Link Software* v *Magee* [1989] FSR 361).

Finally, there is one interesting difference between s. 11(2) Copyright, Designs and Patents Act 1988 and s. 39 Patents Act 1977. The latter stipulates that an invention must reasonably be expected to result from the performance of the employee's duties, whereas s. 11(2) Copyright, Designs and Patents Act 1988 contains no similar provision for copyright works. This simplifies matters by focusing attention on the outcome, rather than the intended consequences, of performing those duties.

Directors   The position of directors in copyright and patent law is identical. The vital question is whether the director is being employed under a contract of service or a contract for services; the latter negating any employer–employee relationship. In *Antocks Lairn Ltd* v *I. Bloohn Ltd* [1971] FSR 490 a managing director was not considered to be an employee as there was no formal or informal service agreement to produce the sort of work under consideration. Conversely, in *Gardex Ltd* v *Sorata Ltd* [1986] RPC 623, the managing director's general duty was to make all the designs of the company; a contract of employment was therefore created.

The traditional control test is clearly inappropriate as it is the director who will often be issuing instructions and supervising the manner in which other employees carry out their duties. But this is not an insuperable obstacle. As Moccata J stated in *Whittaker* v *Minister of Pensions and National Insurance* [1967] 1 QB 156 at p. 167:

> It seems clear, therefore, from the more recent cases that persons possessed of a high degree of professional skill and expertise . . . may nevertheless be employed as servants under contracts of service, notwithstanding that their employers can, in the nature of things, exercise extremely little, if any, control over the way in which such skill is used.

By analogy this principle applies to directors: their singular professional and entrepreneurial skills put them in the position of controllers rather than those controlled. This point was reinforced in *Morren* v *Swinton and Pendlebury Borough Council* [1965] 1 WLR 576, the court recognising that the greater the skill required in an employee's work the less relevant the control test.

If an employment relationship does exist then it is highly likely that, as with s. 39(1)(b) Patents Act 1977, a court would interpret the phrase 'in the course of employment' more widely, recognising the fiduciary nature of the director's duties. In fact, it is arguable that directors who attempt to market *any* of their works in direct competition with their employers would be held: (a) to hold these works on constructive trust for their employers, or (b) to be estopped, in the light of breaching their fiduciary duties, from denying that they were produced in the course of employment (see the unreported comments of Hoffmann J cited in *Missing Link Software* v *Magee* [1989] FSR 361 at p. 367).

Partners   Where a work is made by one partner in the ordinary course of the partnership business and for the purposes of the partnership, the copyright in the work will form part of the partnership property (see generally *Coffey's Registered Designs* [1982] FSR 227). As the contract of partnership is based on notions of good faith it is also arguable that any other work which may be useful to the partnership should not be used by the partner in any way detrimental to the running of the partnership.

In the absence of a written assignment the legal title to any work will remain with the partner-author although other partners will have the right to claim that any copyright is applied for the benefit of the partnership generally (e.g., *O'Brien* v *Komesaroff* (1982) 150 CLR 310). Apart from any agreed pre-assignment clause, it is also preferable to insert a clause by which, on the death or retirement of a partner, his or her share in any copyright vests in the surviving partners. This prevents any copyright share devolving to outside parties such as general heirs and personal representatives.

Lecturers in higher education   The traditional approach has been that persons employed to compose and deliver lectures will, in the absence of clear terms in the contract of employment to the contrary, be entitled to copyright in those lectures (see *Stevenson, Jordan and Harrison Ltd* v *Macdonald and Evans* (1952) 69 RPC 10 especially at p. 18, *Waites* v *Franco-British Exhibition Inc.* (1909) 25 TLR 441). That being the case, the copyright in other, more scholarly, works should vest in the lecturer concerned. This latter point is reinforced by the general lack of instruction to staff as to what research they should undertake and the marked absence of any obligation to reduce their writings to a particular copyright form (see Cornish 1992: at p. 15). However, there are two reasons why this approach should nowadays be treated with some scepticism.

First, if lecturers in higher education are employed to research and, in particular, *receive some recognised timetable relief* for their efforts, it is arguable that copyright in their work will belong to their employers. The fact that certain employers have agreed voluntarily to some other arrangement merely reinforces the point that s. 11(2) Copyright, Designs and Patents Act 1988 is subject to contrary agreement (the issue of higher-education pre-assignment clauses will be considered later).

Secondly, statements issuing from the University Funding Council (merging with the Polytechnic and Colleges Funding Council) suggest that a specified proportion of higher-education funding in future will be allocated for the purposes of research and the production of scholarly work. If this is implemented then logic dictates that the ensuing work of staff in designated 'research institutions' will have been produced in the course of employment. This position is supported by current Inland Revenue practices which allow certain research expenses to be set against taxable income (i.e., the expenses have been incurred in the course of employment), with consequential tax relief. Admittedly, this must be contrasted with the decision in *Noah* v *Shuba* [1991] FSR 14, especially at p. 26, which implies that the duty to research must be contractually binding before copyright will vest in the employer. But here again note should be taken of the 1992 HEFC Research Selectivity Exercise in which certain university departments entered all their staff, with or without publications, on grounds that they had a contractual duty to research.

Joint authorship and ownership   Section 10 Copyright, Designs and Patents Act 1988 refers to works of joint authorship; that is, works produced through the collaboration of two or more authors in which the contribution of each author is not *distinct* from that of the other author or authors. For example, if two people claim joint authorship of a play then: (a) both must have contributed to the writing of the dialogue, helpful criticism and advice being insufficient (*Wiseman* v *George Weidenfeld and Nicolson Ltd and Donaldson* [1985] FSR 525), and (b) their respective contributions must be incapable of separate identification (e.g., collaborating on the writing of *each* chapter in a book rather than writing *separate* chapters).

Although the Copyright, Designs and Patents Act 1988 is slightly ambiguous, it would seem that all joint authors must be employees before s. 11(2) can vest first ownership in the employer. However, it is probable that the relevant employees can be employed by distinct employers, in which case ownership vests jointly with these employers under s. 11(2). If so, the agreement of all joint owners will be required before, for example, a licence can be granted to third parties or some other exploitation is contemplated (s. 173(2) Copyright, Designs and Patents Act 1988). It is therefore advisable for joint venture partners to determine by contract, before any work begins, the manner in which possible future copyright interests will be divided in order to avoid subsequent contentious proceedings over ownership and the exercise of exclusive rights by one or other party.

Yet again we see the need to insert appropriate pre-assignment clauses so that, for instance, if any copyright work is produced jointly by a company and an independent consultant, ownership rights will be clearly settled beforehand.

Commissioned works and independent contractors and consultants   Under ss. 4(3) and 12(4) Copyright Act 1956 the copyright in commissioned photographs, portraits, engravings and sound recordings belonged to the commissioner although in all other situations it remained with the author unless otherwise stipulated in the contract. The 1988 Act rationalises the law by ensuring that in future the ownership of copyright in most commissioned works will reside in the author of the work (but see s. 85 Copyright, Designs and Patents Act 1988: restrictions on the subsequent use of private domestic photographs). The only important exception to this is where for some reason an employment relationship subsists between the author and the person commissioning the work (i.e., s. 11(2) Copyright, Designs and Patents Act 1988 applies).

The industrial practice of commissioning work has grown steadily in recent years in line with the increasing complexity of technology. In most cases the commissioner is merely augmenting the skills of his workforce by bringing in outside contractors who exhibit specialist talents. Thus, generally, the person commissioned will be an independent contractor employed under a contract *for* services, not *of* service. In the words of Denning LJ:

> . . . under a contract of service, a man is employed as part of the business and his work is done as an integral part of the business: whereas under a contract for services his work, although done for the business, is *not integrated into it but is only accessory to it* (*Stevenson, Jordan and Harrison Ltd* v *Macdonald and Evans* (1952) 69 RPC 10, emphasis added).

This places a premium on ensuring that all confidential materials supplied to that person, for use in the designated programme of work, will be returned on completion of the project. For example:

> *All information, advice, descriptions, flow charts, diagrams, drawings, data, tables, instructions, listings, tapes, photographs, cinematographs, know-how and the like supplied to you by this Company in connection with your programme of work, together with the copyright therein, shall remain the property of this Company and shall be returned to this Company on completion of the work under the programme of work.*

4.1.2.2 Section 11(2) Copyright, Designs and Patents Act 1988 and pre-assignment clauses

Section 11(2) Copyright, Designs and Patents Act 1988 does not discourage the use of pre-assignment clauses in contracts of employment, although the phrase 'subject to any agreement to the contrary' cannot be construed grammatically as advocating the use of clauses covering works made by employees outside the course of their employment. Nor does the Copyright, Designs and Patents Act 1988 appear to offer employees any correlative right to compensation (but see 4.3 on the applicability of ss. 39 to 43 Patents Act 1977). Even an employee's right to be identified as author, as opposed to owner, of a work has been removed by s. 79(3)(a) Copyright, Designs and Patents Act 1988 where copyright has vested in the employer by virtue of s. 11(2); although this is subject to possible 'moral rights' where the employee has already been publicly identified with the work (s. 82 Copyright, Designs and Patents Act 1988, discussed later).

Current practice and the ILU survey   It is therefore not surprising that less than half the companies in the ILU survey dealt specifically with the ownership of copyright; especially as any pre-assignment of copyright would be subject to para.11(1), sch. 5, Copyright, Designs and Patents Act 1988 (amending s. 39(3) Patents Act 1977) which prevents employers from using copyright in any way which might interfere with an employee inventor's own rights of exploitation under s. 39(2) Patents Act 1977. Furthermore, the majority of pre-assignment clauses dealing with the ownership of inventions also, by implication, covered aspects of copyright by referring to such things as 'know-how, designs, improvements, processes, trade secrets, techniques' and so forth.

Those companies that did include specific clauses adopted, in some shape or form, the following examples:

> *Copyright and other similar rights in all work undertaken by you in the course of your employment will belong exclusively to the Company.*

> *The copyright in all articles, designs, drawings, programs, calculations, specifications, photographs and other similar documents and written materials produced by you in the course of your duties with the Company shall belong to the Company.*

For the purposes of good personnel management the insertion of such clauses is to be encouraged as it ensures that employees are made aware of their legal position. It can also reduce future embarrassment, if not costly litigation. For instance, one company reported that two employee draughtsmen had left their jobs and set up in competition, using drawings and sketches alleged to have been made during their employment. The firm was put to the trouble of identifying the relevant proprietary materials, proving that such materials were produced during the period of employment, and applying for an injunction to stop further unauthorised use.

But there is one practical defect associated with the above two clauses:

neither offers a fuller explanation of how copyright can arise in the course of employment. As copyright refers to the recorded expression of thought, confusion can arise in the eyes of an employee who, for example, thinks of an idea at work but writes it up outside normal working hours. To cover this eventuality it is submitted that one should follow the example of one firm in the ILU survey which added the following clause:

> *The employee assigns to the Company by way of future assignment all [proprietary] rights . . . if any for the full term thereof throughout the world in respect of all copyright works . . .* **originated, conceived, written or made by the employee** *(except only those works originated conceived written or made by the employee wholly outside his normal working hours and wholly unconnected with his appointment) during the period of employment hereunder* (emphasis added).

Commissioned works Assuming the absence of any employment relationship, s. 11(1) Copyright, Designs and Patents Act 1988 will reserve first ownership of any copyright for the author. However, in dealing with an independent contractor, considerable room exists for negotiating the future ownership of relevant property rights. The resolution of any disagreement will owe more to the bargaining leverage of the respective parties rather than to any legal niceties. In particular, the interests of the commissioning body are best served by inserting a clause which ensures that all copyright in works vests in that body. For example:

> *All documents, models, computer software and other items prepared by you in connection with or relating to the specified project will be the property of the Company and you hereby wholly assign to the Company any intellectual property rights including the future copyright in such items as and when such copyright comes into existence.*

Naturally, where a work is commissioned (from a non-employee) *first* ownership will still reside in the author, unless the written formalities required under s. 91 Copyright, Designs and Patents Act 1988 have been fulfilled. If not, the above clause will only give the client an equitable right to call for the assignment of the legal interest. Until that assignment is effected a sale of the copyright by the author to a bona fide purchaser will override the equitable interests of the client, with the latter's only remedy being against the author.

If the assignment of prospective copyright cannot be agreed upon then the client will need to secure, at the very least, a free licence to use the work for whatever purposes required, perhaps with an exclusivity clause preventing the author from exploiting the work for these designated purposes. Even if ownership of copyright vests in the independent consultant the latter should still be reminded that the use of such rights must not contravene any obligation of confidentiality to the client.

Higher education: use of pre-assignment clauses In general, few would now argue that lecture hand-outs, seminar questions and examination papers are produced in the course of employment (cf. the comments of Evershed MR regarding the ownership of lecture notes in *Stevenson, Jordan and Harrison Ltd* v *MacDonald and Evans* (1952) 69 RPC 10 at p. 18).

Previous comments have also suggested that articles and books may also be seen, in the future, as being included in this approach — subject to the decision in *Noah* v *Shuba* [1991] FSR 14 and, for example, the possibility of acquiescence by the employer. How should higher-education institutions react? Well, for a start, claiming ownership over all lecturers' work will have a negative impact on research output, with a consequential adverse effect on research funding for that institution. A compromise must therefore be reached whereby the legitimate interests of institutions are respected (a departing lecturer can cause severe disruption if no guidance is given to the new incumbent) whilst preserving the integrity of specialist scholarly work.

The Polytechnic and Colleges Employers' Forum (PCEF) has addressed this issue by advocating the insertion of the following clauses, recommended to it by the Lecturers' Common Interest Group, into the Standard National Contract (most member institutions have acted upon the proposal):

> *The copyright in any work . . . compiled, edited or otherwise brought into existence by you as a scholarly work produced in furtherance of your professional career shall belong to you; 'scholarly work' includes items such as books, contributions to books, articles and conference papers, and shall be construed in the light of the common understanding of the phrase in higher education.*
>
> *The copyright in any material produced by you for your personal use and reference, including as an aid to teaching, shall belong to you.*
>
> *However, the copyright in course materials produced by you in the course of your employment for the purposes of the curriculum of a course run by this company [i.e., higher-education institution] and produced, used or disseminated by this company shall belong to this company, as well as the outcomes from research specifically funded and supported by this company.*

It is submitted that these clauses represent a fair-minded and even-handed approach to this controversial issue. They would also influence a court's mind when interpreting s. 11(2) in the context of lecturers' contracts. For instance, the clauses clearly imply that the production of scholarly works in furtherance of professional career development is not considered by the employer generally to form part of a lecturer's normal duties. This conforms with the approach taken by Evershed MR in *Stevenson, Jordan and Harrison Ltd* v *Macdonald and Evans*, especially as the quality of publications reflects upon an institution as a whole. Conversely, the PCEF clauses claim copyright ownership over lecture materials produced for courses run by the particular institution, the very business of higher education. In this new era of 'independent learning' can one truly suggest that lecturers are paid to lecture but not to produce course outlines and associated course materials?

The pre-assignment of future copyright Why bother to insert a pre-assignment clause when s. 11(2) already covers the issue of ownership? The reason is simple: the average employee will own the copyright in any work made outside the course of employment, however useful that work is to the business of the employer. The possibility that the employee might still hold the copyright in trust for the employer would be remote unless the employee was a senior manager with special fiduciary obligations towards the employer. Thus a formal assignment will be required (complying with s. 90 Copyright, Designs and Patents Act 1988) in order to vest legal ownership in the employer. If s. 90 conditions are fulfilled then the property right will be transferred from the employee to the employer at the moment of its creation (i.e., at the time of its recording in writing, or by some other means).

Alternatively, if the agreement does not comply with these formalities (e.g., was oral rather than written) then the employer will still have a contractual right to call for the subsequent transfer of copyright. However, this right will fail if the employee has sold the copyright to a bona fide purchaser, without notice of the contract, in advance of the assignment being executed in favour of the employer (though such action by the employee would clearly constitute a breach of contract justifying his or her dismissal).

Note also that, in the absence of any pre-assignment clause, and assuming ownership by the employee of any copyright in the work, an employer must be aware of the dangers of pressuring the employee into assigning the copyright in an existing work for anything less than a fair market price (see the comments on economic duress in 3.8.2.3).

An employer can circumvent such difficulties by inserting a clause which effectively assigns all *future* copyright in works produced by employees in the course of their employment. The agreement must be incorporated in a written, signed document, complying with s. 91 Copyright, Designs and Patents Act 1988. The following clause illustrates this possibility:

All materials produced by the employee during the term of his employment, in the course of such employment or with the use of the Company's time, material or facilities, or relating to any subject-matter with which the employee's work for the Company is or may be concerned, shall be the property of the Company.

A further safeguard would be to ask each employee to sign a written undertaking regarding the assignment of future copyright, with an irrevocable power of attorney. This agreement would operate as an effective assignment, provided it complied with s. 91 Copyright, Designs and Patents Act 1988, and, generally, would allow the employer, or nominee, to execute all necessary instruments for the transfer and vesting of rights without further cooperation from the employee.

But this begs a separate question: What is the legal enforceability of pre-assignment clauses (such as the one above) which purport to cover works created outside the course of employment? The answer will depend upon the applicability of s. 42 Patents Act 1977 and the common law restraint of trade doctrine.

4.1.2.3 Section 42 Patents Act 1977 and copyright pre-assignment clauses

The question can be put simply: Does s. 42 Patents Act 1977 represent a statutory bar on the insertion of pre-assignment clauses which purport to cover all of an employee's copyright works, irrespective of whether they were produced in the course of employment or not? Consider an example taken from the ILU survey:

> *I agree that all . . . data , writings and drawings* which are related to or **useful in the business of the Company** *or result from tasks assigned to me by the Company . . . shall be the sole property of the Company and the Company shall be the sole owner of all rights (including copyright) in connection therewith.* (Emphasis added.)

It would be a mistake to assume that this clause is merely seeking to confirm s. 11(2) Copyright, Designs and Patents Act 1988. The highlighted phrase would encompass work which has been, for example, produced (a) outside the employee's assigned tasks, or (b) by an employee who has not been employed in any creative capacity, or (c) by an employee in one division (e.g., accounts) but transferred temporarily to a completely different division (e.g., research and development). Nor, unlike s. 39 Patents Act 1977, would an employee be entitled to argue that the work was not reasonably expected to result from the performance of his or her duties. If s. 42 Patents Act 1977 applied to such clauses then they would be rendered ineffective insofar as they diminished an employee's rights (i.e., exceeded the remit of s. 11(2) Copyright, Designs and Patents Act 1988). But does s. 42 Patents Act 1977 apply?

Section 42 Patents Act 1977 and copyright First, it should be emphasised that s. 42 does not refer exclusively to patents or patentable inventions. Subsection (1) applies to 'any contract (whenever made) relating to *inventions* made by an employee', whilst subsection (2) mentions not only patent and patent application rights, but also 'rights in inventions of any description'. In chapter 3, three points were made about the meaning of 'invention'. First,

(a) The word can encompass any new idea with a useful practical application in industry (see ss. 1(1)(c) and 4 Patents Act 1977).

(b) Section 39 Patents Act 1977 applies irrespective of whether a patent application has been filed or not (see generally, *Rawlplug Co. Ltd* SRIS 0/145/88).

(c) The word 'invention', in the context of s. 8 Patents Act 1977 (which concerns applications for proprietorship of pending patent applications), embraces subject-matter which is unpatentable whether because, for example, novelty has been destroyed or because it is inherently unpatentable (see *Norris's Patent* [1988] RPC 159; *Viziball Ltd's Application* [1988] RPC 213).

Secondly, s. 39(1) Patents Act 1977 determines the ownership of employee inventions for the purposes of the Patents Act 1977 'and all other purposes'. The latter phrase is not defined but an employee's 'ownership' of an unpatented or unpatentable invention has few advantages unless that person possesses other enforceable property rights which can be deployed to prevent unauthorised use of the invention.

Thirdly, s. 39 is entitled 'Rights *to* employees' inventions' whereas s. 42(2) refers to 'rights *in* inventions'. The word 'in' is wider in its effect than the word 'to'. 'In' suggests that the right refers to all matters relating to the invention, a point re-emphasised by the wording of s. 42(1): 'This section applies to any contract . . . *relating to* inventions made by an employee'. As such, the said right is not limited to the ownership of an invention but can encompass a right *associated with* that invention. This would confirm the importance of s. 43(4) Patents Act 1977, as amended by sch. 5 para. 11(2) Copyright, Designs and Patents Act 1988, which states that the word 'patent' as used in ss. 39 to 42 Patents Act 1977 refers to 'patent or other protection' (discussed later).

We submit, therefore, that in principle s. 42 Patents Act 1977 applies to issues of copyright ownership provided the employee who owns the invention under s. 39(2) Patents Act 1977 *also* produces the copyright materials which describe or refer to that invention. The reason for the latter limitation is that s. 42(2) only refers to rights 'in inventions of any description *made by*' the employee. So to put the matter simply: the employee inventor who is able to use s. 42 to protect rights of ownership under s. 39(2) can *also* use s. 42 to protect any associated copyright rights under s. 11(2) Copyright, Designs and Patents Act 1988. This has particular reference to research teams where it might be difficult to establish precisely which team members contributed to the making of the invention and which produced the associated drawings and designs. This novel application of s. 42 Patents Act 1977 is reinforced by statements in *Norris's Patent* [1988] RPC 159 to the effect that a court, in determining the ownership of an invention, should look at all aspects of an 'invention', patentable or otherwise, that contribute 'a significant part in the viability' of that invention. Does this not encompass an aesthetic design with functional utility?

The effect of this analysis would be that any pre-assignment clause which claimed ownership over copyright works produced *outside* the course of an employee's employment would be unenforceable to the extent that such works referred to an 'invention'. But this merely begs the question: In what circumstances will copyright attach to an 'invention'? Two general examples can be put forward. First, if a patent application fails to achieve grant status then any drawings which have been attached, illustrating the invention in two-dimensional form (written, computer enhanced, graphics etc.), may still retain copyright protection and should thus be regarded as embodying a 'right in an invention' (see below for limits to this principle). For instance, if the patent application lacked novelty this might not adversely affect the originality of the drawings for copyright purposes (see generally, *Interlego AG* v *Tyco Industries Inc.* [1989] AC 217). What should be emphasised is that copyright protects the recorded form rather than the metaphysical idea. Equally, patent protection attaches to the written patent specification, in which an invention is described in terms of its practical embodiments, rather than any abstract idea.

Thus considerable overlap exists between the two types of rights, such as two-dimensional copyright and three-dimensional patent protection covering different aspects of the same invention. This possibility of dual protection in intellectual property is not unusual and has been supported by the courts (e.g., *Wham-O Manufacturing Co.* v *Lincoln Industries Ltd* [1982] RPC 281 (NZ); *Gardex Ltd* v *Sorata Ltd* [1986] RPC 623; cf. *Catnic Components Ltd* v *Hill and Smith Ltd* [1978] FSR 405).

Secondly, a similar approach can be adopted for any other drawings, written materials, or even three-dimensional 'mock-ups' (assuming 'artistic' quality) which relate to an 'invention' (see generally, *Viziball Ltd's Application* and *Norris's Patent*). For example, consider an agrochemicals company that develops a new herbicide. Assuming that patent protection failed or was not sought, the formula for producing the herbicide, the instructions given to consumers for use of the herbicide, and any other written explanations contained within the patent application (all comprising part of the invention) might still attract copyright protection: see *Elanco Products Ltd* v *Mandops (Agrochemical Specialists) Ltd* [1979] FSR 46. This analysis, *subject* to the comments in the next paragraph, is no different from a finding of copyright in the drawings of simple engineering components (*British Northrop Ltd* v *Texteam Blackburn Ltd* [1974] RPC 57), or the simple design drawings for a pulley wheel (*Solar Thomson Engineering Co. Ltd* v *Barton* [1977] RPC 537). Such points are reinforced by s. 17 Copyright, Designs and Patents Act 1988 which provides that copyright infringement will be established where a two-dimensional *artistic* work (see s. 4 Copyright, Designs and Patents Act 1988) is reproduced in a three-dimensional form.

Practical limits to s. 42   It appears therefore, that copyright protection can *sometimes* extend to the unauthorised reproduction of physical artefacts in much the same way as patent law. *However, there are crucial limits.* Prior to 1988 copyright was often found to exist in industrial design drawings or simple engineering drawings on the basis that they represented artistic works, even if the three-dimensional products manufactured from these drawings were of a purely functional nature. Since 1988, if copyright subsists only in a drawing or other design document for an article which is not in itself an artistic work or a typeface then s. 51 Copyright, Designs and Patents Act 1988 prescribes that the copyright cannot be used to protect articles made from the drawing. Instead, protection for these non-artistic items is reserved for the new 'design right'. Thus the theoretical application of s. 42 to copyright issues is severely reduced in practice. Rather, we will need to look to the various forms of design rights in order to assess the real impact of s. 42 upon employees' drawings and design-related activities (discussed in 4.2).

Two companies in the ILU survey recognised the possible application of s. 42 Patents Act 1977 to certain types of employees' inventions which attracted copyright rather than, or as well as, patent protection. The consequent pre-assignment clause was formulated along the lines of s. 39 Patents Act 1977 (or s. 11(2) Copyright, Designs and Patents Act 1988), with no attempt to claim ownership of copyright over works produced outside the 'normal or specifically assigned duties of the employee' except where, because of the employee's position within the company, a 'special obligation' arose to further the interests of the company. Bearing in mind the limited definition of 'artistic work' in s. 4 Copyright, Designs and Patents Act 1988 it is perhaps advisable that this type of restricted copyright pre-assignment clause should only target employee inventions which also qualify for copyright protection as some form of artistic work. See, however, 4.2 and the transitional provisions contained within the Copyright, Designs and Patents Act 1988 relating to copyright protection in design documents.

Naturally, if the employee owns the copyright in certain works which have a direct bearing on the employer's business then the employer will need to negotiate a transfer of such rights. Clearly the latter will be in a strong negotiating position and may even be the sole bidder; for example, the employee may be bound by confidence, and possible fiduciary obligations, not to disclose the drawings to a competitor. But swift action is still advised because (a) a duty of confidence need not always arise (see *Electrolux Ltd* v *Hudson* [1977] FSR 312), (b) even if confidence subsists, if the employee sells to a bona fide purchaser then the employer's remedy against the purchaser will be of no practical value if the latter has already disclosed or used the information publicly.

In conclusion, it is arguable that s. 42 can reduce the impact of blanket copyright pre-assignment clauses where the work in question refers to an 'invention'. But if that was the end of the matter an employer could still assert ownership over *all* employees' copyright works, safe in the knowledge that s. 42 would merely reduce the impact of such a clause *to the extent* that the employee's rights had been diminished (i.e., went beyond s. 11(2) Copyright, Designs and Patents Act 1988). But there is another danger.

4.1.2.4 Common law restraint of trade and pre-assignment clauses
It is possible that a pre-assignment clause which attempts to cover all of an employee's work, irrespective of its relevance to the employee's duties, may be considered in restraint of trade and thus *completely* unenforceable. In *Electrolux Ltd* v *Hudson* [1977] FSR 312 it was held that an employer's claim over *all* of his employee's inventions, irrespective of where they were conceived, was too wide and therefore in restraint of trade. The employee was an ordinary storekeeper, not employed or expected to invent. The case has been criticised as applying restraint of trade principles during the continuance of an employment contract rather than post-termination. Nevertheless, it is a salutary reminder to employers that a catch-all assignment clause which applies to all employees, irrespective of their status, creative expertise, technical ability or general employment duties, can attract unfavourable judicial scrutiny (see generally *Clifford Davis Management Ltd* v *WEA Records Ltd* [1975] 1 WLR 61, *O'Sullivan* v *Management Agency and*

Music Ltd [1985] QB 428, *Watson* v *Prager* [1991] 1 WLR 726). We submit, therefore, that employers should insert pre-assignment clauses which are formulated along the lines of s. 11(2) Copyright, Designs and Patents Act 1988 (or s. 39 Patents Act 1977).

4.1.2.5 Clauses which prevent unauthorised disclosure

Other than the normal pre-assignment clause, certain companies in the ILU survey adopted other clauses to safeguard their interests. Most bear a striking resemblance to those which regulate the disclosure of employee's patentable inventions.

Notification clauses   An employer's best interests are served if an employee is encouraged promptly to notify the employer of any new designs, drawings or similar materials, that have been created in the course of employment. Moreover, an employer will want to make an independent assessment of whether the 'work' is related to the employee's duties, especially as premature unauthorised disclosure by an employee might give the employer's rivals a competitive advantage. Thus firms in the ILU survey adopted the following type of clause:

> *I will promptly make available to the Company all writings, documents and data (whether or not original copyright works) made by me or to my order (either alone or jointly with others) during the period of my employment with the Company provided the same were made or produced in the course or arising out of my employment with the Company.*

Perhaps one should add, for the sake of form rather than substance, that the employer, in operating the notification procedure, will respect the subsequent confidentiality of an employee's work where ownership is recognised by the parties as vesting in the employee.

Post-termination   The majority of problems occur when employees leave their present employment, taking with them certain confidential materials which they use in their next employment. Copyright materials are an obvious victim as they are normally recorded in some easily copiable format. For this reason, three firms in the ILU survey adopted the following type of clause:

> *In the event of any termination of my employment, however caused, I will deliver to the company all documents and data of any nature pertaining to my work and I shall not take with me any documents or data of any description or any reproduction of any description containing or pertaining to any proprietary information.*

There seems nothing wrong with such clauses, although their implementation is best effected by arranging an informal appointment between the departing employee and a member of staff in which legal liability is clarified. For example, the above clause does not offer a proper explanation of the words 'proprietary information'. For this reason, two of the companies which used this type of clause attempted to give more practical examples of the type of materials in question:

> *Forthwith upon his ceasing to be employed by the Company the employee or his personal representatives as the case may be shall deliver to the Company all books documents paper records memoranda lists and other written information relating to the business of the Company which may then be in his possession or under his control.*

> *The copyright in all articles, designs, drawings, programs, calculations, specifications, photographs and other similar documents and written materials produced by you in the course of your duties with the Company shall belong to the Company and all such matters (including but not limited to customer lists, correspondence and any other records) and copies thereof in your possession shall be returned to the Company on termination of your employment.*

The first clause even covers the possibility that an employee may not so much leave the company as depart the world entirely! On a more serious note, placing the word 'copyright' on company materials can also serve as a useful warning to departing employees wishing to appropriate classified or sensitive materials. But as *Missing Link Software* v *Magee* [1989] FSR 361 demonstrates, proof that an employee has appropriated important copyright materials, or produced them during his period of employment, may be difficult to establish.

4.1.3 Ownership: Crown and Parliamentary copyright

The usual provisions on ownership, whether by reference to the author or the rules regarding employment relationships, are excluded in relation to works subject to Crown or Parliamentary copyright.

4.1.3.1 Crown copyright (s. 163(1) and (4) Copyright, Designs and Patents Act 1988)
Section 163 of the Copyright, Designs and Patents Act 1988 applies to any work made by a servant of the Crown within 'the course of his duties'. This is narrower than the pre-1988 position whereby the Crown could claim copyright in *any* work (i.e., literary, dramatic, musical or artistic) which had been first published by or under its direction or control (s. 39(3) Copyright Act 1956). Where the rule applies, the Crown is recognised as being the first owner of the copyright in the work. One should treat 'in the course of duties' in the same way as 'in the course of employment'. The latter merely represents the historical position that servants of the Crown were not considered to have contracts of employment, a view from which the courts and Parliament are beginning to resile (e.g., *R* v *Lord Chancellor's Department ex parte Nangle*

[1991] ICR 743 and s. 42(4) Patents Act 1977 as amended by s. 22 Armed Forces Act 1981).

In addition, any work created by a Crown employee in breach of the Crown's confidence is likely to vest in the Crown: see *Attorney-General* v *Guardian Newspapers Ltd* [1990] 1 AC 109 and *Attorney-General* v *Barker* [1990] 3 All ER 257. See generally ss. 106, 163 to 165 and 175 Copyright, Designs and Patents Act 1988 for the duration of Crown copyright.

4.1.3.2 Parliamentary copyright (s. 165(1) Copyright, Designs and Patents Act 1988)

Section 165 of the Copyright, Designs and Patents Act 1988, which overrides Crown copyright (s. 163(6)), applies where any work (see s. 1) has been made 'by or under the direction or control' of the House of Lords or the House of Commons. Here, it is the House by whom, or under whose direction or control, the work is first made which is the first owner. Equally, the principles of joint authorship will apply where both Houses are acting jointly (s. 165(5)).

Relevant works covered include those produced by officers or employees in the course of their duties (e.g., *Hansard* and other works produced by librarians and researchers employed by Parliament) as well as any sound recording, film, live broadcast or live cable programme of the proceedings within either House. As for the position of researchers employed by MPs and peers, it is unlikely that their work would fall within this category. Moreover, work commissioned by either House is not automatically considered to be made by or under their direction or control.

Where the work is one of joint authorship, and not all the authors make the work under the direction or control of either House, then s. 165(1) only applies to those authors affected by the section, and the copyright subsisting by virtue of their contribution to the work as a whole (this provision also applies to Crown Copyright (s. 163(4)). This contradicts the general rules of joint authorship which assume that the various contributions of the joint authors are not distinct. In particular, can one state that the provision applies only to part of the copyright, subsisting by virtue of a particular contribution? Whatever else, it is clear that Parliament (or the Crown) cannot merely appropriate the entire copyright in such circumstances.

Under s. 166(1) Copyright, Designs and Patents Act 1988 copyright in any Bill belongs to both Houses jointly, although at the initial stage of its introduction it may be owned solely by one or other House, depending upon whether it is a private or public Bill.

4.1.4 Ownership of other works

Section 11(2) of the Copyright, Designs and Patents Act 1988 only applies to 'literary, dramatic, musical or artistic works'. It does not, for example, apply to sound recordings, films and broadcasts. Thus, an employer who desires unfettered ownership of such copyright items must insert a pre-assignment clause to that effect in the relevant employee's contract of employment.

4.1.4.1 Sound recordings and films (s. 9(2)(a) Copyright, Designs and Patents Act 1988)

The person who undertakes the arrangements necessary for the making of the recording or film will be considered the author of the work and, therefore, the first owner. In either case one would assume that the provision applies to the person with overall financial responsibility for the arrangement (*Re FG (Films) Ltd* [1953] 1 WLR 483). The problems of ownership by the employed camera operator or studio technician are thereby resolved without recourse to s. 11(2) Copyright, Designs and Patents Act 1988 (see generally *Adventure Film Productions* v *Tulley* (1982) *The Times*, 14 October 1982)

See also s. 12(4) and (8) Copyright Act 1956 for sound recordings made between June 1957 and August 1989, and sch. 1, para.11(3) Copyright, Designs and Patents Act 1988 for sound recordings which were commissioned before August 1989 but produced thereafter. As for films made between 1957 and 1989, see s.13(4) and (10) Copyright Act 1956.

4.1.4.2 Broadcasts and cable programmes (s. 9(2)(b) Copyright, Designs and Patents Act 1988)

The person who makes the broadcast is the author and, therefore, under s. 11(1) will be the first owner of the ensuing copyright. This refers to the television broadcast companies involved rather than, for example, the newscaster! Moreover, in the case of a broadcast which relays another broadcast by reception and immediate transmission, the person who made that other broadcast will be the author and therefore first owner of the copyright (see also s. 14(4) and (10) Copyright Act 1956).

Regarding cable programmes, the person who created the work, and who is thus the author of it, is taken to be the person providing the cable programme service in which the programme is included (see also s. 14A(3) and (11) Copyright Act 1956 inserted by the Cable and Broadcasting Act 1984, and sch. 1, para.9(b) Copyright, Designs and Patents Act 1988).

4.1.4.3 Typographical arrangements (s. 9(2)(d) Copyright, Designs and Patents Act 1988)

The person who makes the typographical arrangement of a published edition (i.e., the publisher) is the author. Thus the employed typesetter has no rights in the work (see also s. 175(1) for a definition of publication, and s. 15(2) Copyright Act 1956).

4.1.5 Mixing copyright works and patentable inventions

If the test in s. 11(2) of the Copyright, Designs and Patents Act 1988 is interpreted more widely than 'duties' in s. 39 Patents Act 1977 then difficulties will arise where the act of invention creates rights in patent, design and copyright and the latter two pass to the employer but the former stays with the employee. The problem is partially remedied by sch. 5, para. 11 Copyright, Designs and Patents Act 1988 which adds a new subsection (3) to s. 39 Patents Act 1977. This prevents an employer, who finds that his employee owns an invention under s. 39(2), from using other intellectual property rights (e.g., copyright) to sue that employee for infringement of any copyright (or design right) to which: 'as between him and his employer, his employer is entitled in any model or document relating to the invention'.

Thus, for example, the employer will be prevented from suing an employee for copyright infringement merely because the latter had inserted drawings into a patent application. This leaves the employee, or successors in title, free to exploit the invention more fully.

However, para. 11 does not extend to documents prepared by other employees as this would not be a right 'between him [i.e., employee] and his employer'. So, where the employee has worked with colleagues who themselves individually own copyrights in specific drawings, the employee will require their permission, presumably by licence or assignment, before, for example, using such materials in a patent application.

4.1.6 Employees' moral rights

Section 80 Copyright, Designs and Patents Act 1988 allows authors to object to derogatory treatment of their work. Employee authors must have been identified with the work at the time of the relevant act, or have been previously identified in published copies of the work (s. 82 Copyright, Designs and Patents Act 1988). An appropriate disclaimer at the time of treatment would prevent an employee author from invoking these rights. Moreover, an employer can still protect his position by asking for a waiver of the 'moral rights'. Interestingly, only one company in the ILU survey considered this issue worth covering:

> *The employee hereby irrevocably and unconditionally waives in favour of the company any and all moral rights conferred on him by Chapter IV of Part I of the Copyright, Designs and Patents Act 1988 for any work in which copyright or design right is vested in the company.*

4.2 DESIGNS

In order to avoid unnecessary repetition we will assume that the phrase 'in the course of employment' has the same meaning as in copyright. Thus similar considerations will apply to designs created by employees in their spare time, outside normal working hours, or peripheral to their duties.

4.2.1 Registered designs

Design registration protects the appearance of an article, the protectable features referring to 'shape, configuration, pattern or ornament applied to an article by any industrial process'. Examples would include moulded plastic furniture, etched patterns on cut-crystal glasses, and sculpted lampstands! Registration provides protection for up to 25 years against unauthorised copying, each five-year period within that time requiring a renewal application. Only the design owner may apply to register the design.

As with patent law, a registrable design must be new at the date of application. Novelty in this context is limited to the UK, rather than the worldwide novelty required under patent law.

When comparing a 'new' design to its older equivalent, registration is only permissible if the former produces a materially different 'appeal to the eye' when compared to the latter (excluding any difference commonly used in the trade as a variation).

The design proprietor must have applied for registration before selling or offering for sale in the UK articles incorporating the design.

Certain types of designs are specifically excluded from registrability. First, where the shape is dictated *solely* by the function of the article (s. 1(1)(b)(i) Registered Designs Act 1949). In the words of Lord Reid in *Amp Inc.* v *Utilux Pty Ltd* [1972] RPC 103:

> There must be a blend of industrial efficiency with visual appeal. If the shape is not there to appeal to the eye but solely to make the article work, then this provision [i.e., functionality] excludes it.

However, such designs may still obtain protection under copyright legislation; for example, medals, book jackets, certificates, greetings cards, maps, stamps, and so forth. It is more debatable how one views features of an article which are partly functional and partly decorative (see generally, *Vernon and Co. (Pulp Products) Ltd* v *Universal Pulp Containers Ltd* [1980] FSR 179).

Registration is not available if the appearance of the article is not material; that is, if aesthetic considerations are largely ignored by purchasers or users (s. 1(3) Registered Designs Act 1949).

By s. 1(1)(a) Registered Designs Act 1949, 'design' does not include a method or principle of construction. Thus in *Moody* v *Tree* (1892) 9 RPC 333 an application to register the design of a picture of a basket, woven in a particular way in order to produce a pattern, was rejected as simply a method of construction (see also *Re Bayer's Design* (1906) 24 RPC 65 and *Stratford Auto Components Ltd* v *Britax (London) Ltd* [1964] RPC 183).

Any document affecting the proprietorship of a design, such as an agreed disposition of rights, which has not been entered in the register of designs will not be admitted in any court as evidence of title or interest unless the court directs otherwise.

Ownership of registered designs No one can be the owner of a registered design unless an application for registration has been made and the registration granted. Only the proprietor of such a design can apply for registration. Assuming this, under s. 2(1A) and (1B) Registered Designs Act 1949, where a design is created in pursuance of a commission or in the course of employment, for money or money's worth, the person commissioning the design, or the employer, shall be treated as the original proprietor of the design. Note the difference from copyright where first ownership of commissioned works remains with the author.

Naturally, if it can be established that the employer produced the work then the problem of showing that the employee acted in the course of employment will not arise. Although relevant to copyright as well, this issue arises more often in registered designs where the overlap between such rights and patents is more obvious. In particular, an employer may be regarded as the 'author' of a design where precise instructions have been given to an employee about how, and in what manner, a design should be executed. Although there may be some scope for artistic freedom, sufficient for a different employee to have produced a recognisably different design, nevertheless the employer may still assert authorship. In the words of Bacon VC in *Stannard* v *Harrison* (1871) 19 WR 811 at p. 813:

> . . . there is nothing in the circumstance . . . that Mr Stannard cannot draw. He never said he could. Mr Stannard can invent, which is more valuable a great deal, and as happens in 99 out of every 100 inventions, the inventor generally is a man who cannot perfect the machinery by which the invention is to be carried into effect.

Although this statement was referring to ownership of employer-inspired inventions there is little reason to doubt that it is of general application in design cases as well, provided the employer's instructions are not so vague that an employee is expected to evolve an independent, unsupervised design (see *A. Pressler and Co. Ltd* v *Gartside and Co. Ltd* (1933) 50 RPC 240).

If the employer fails to establish 'authorship' then reliance can still be placed on s. 2(1B) Registered Designs Act 1949, assuming that the employee created the design in the course of employment.

The possibility that s. 42 Patents Act 1977 applies to pre-assignment clauses involving registered designs will be discussed in 4.2.2. For the moment two points should be noted. First, an article may incorporate patentable and registrable design features (see *Wingate's Registered Design No. 768,611* (1934) 52 RPC 126 and *Werner Motors Ltd* v *A.W. Gamage Ltd* [1904] 1 Ch 264). Secondly, if s. 42 applies, the Registered Designs Act 1949, as amended by Copyright, Designs and Patents Act 1988, does not contain any reference to the pre-assignment of future rights (unlike s. 91 Copyright, Designs and Patents Act 1988 and the assignment of copyright). At present it is difficult to interpret the importance of this omission. It is arguable that a pre-assignment clause, in these circumstances, will only transfer the equitable ownership in a registered design right, thereby requiring a subsequent legal assignment to effect a proper legal transfer.

Notwithstanding the above, it is clearly advisable to use such clauses, where work has been commissioned from an independent consultant (i.e., non-employee) in order to avoid undue doubt over the disposition of rights when they finally materialise. This is in spite of s. 2(1B) Registered Designs Act 1949 which assumes that first ownership in such designs resides in the commissioning body. Thus, one company in the ILU survey adopted the following clause when dealing with independent contractors:

> *All designs . . . (whether or not capable of being registered or patented) made by you in connection with or relating to the programme of work which are or may be of value to the Company shall promptly be disclosed to the Company which shall have the right to acquire, free of charge, all the rights therein and in this regard you will sign all documents and do all things necessary to enable the Company to become the registered proprietor to such . . . designs . . . in any country of the world.*

Section 42 Patents Act 1977, as applied through s. 39 Patents Act 1977 to s. 2(1B) Registered Designs Act 1949 and the ownership of registered designs, cannot apply to independent contractors as there is no subsisting employment relationship. Nor is it likely that the restraint of trade doctrine would be used by courts to strike down an all-embracing pre-assignment clause unless it clearly went beyond the protection of the employer's legitimate business interests.

4.2.2 Design rights

Under the Copyright Act 1956 copyright protection was afforded to a defined category of artistic works irrespective of their artistic quality! This category included most types of drawings, ranging from engineering blueprints through to simple cartoon sketches. The effect was to create the ludicrous situation in *British Leyland Motor Corporation Ltd* v *Armstrong Patents Co. Ltd* [1986] AC 577 that design drawings for motor car exhaust systems qualified as artistic works and therefore were capable of copyright protection — although the right could not be exercised to prevent other manufacturers from making and putting such spare parts on the market.

Protection for these design drawings lasted for the life of the author plus 50 years and covered not merely the unauthorised copying of such drawings but also the copying of the design from another article which had been made to that design. However, whereas this protection applied to drawings of functional articles, if the drawings referred to articles designed to appeal to the eye (i.e., were registrable under the Registered Designs Act 1949), and had been publicly marketed, then protection was reduced to 15 years.

Section 51 Copyright, Designs and Patents Act 1988 deals with the above anomaly by excluding the majority of industrial designs, as opposed to artistic designs, from copyright protection. Specifically, although copyright will remain in drawings, there will be no infringement of such drawings where an article is manufactured to a design, contained within a *design document or model which records or embodies that design*, or where that manufactured article is itself copied, unless the *article is classifiable as an artistic work*. For example, if one produced an industrial drawing of a new type of plastic moulded drainpipe then copyright might subsist in that design document but as drainpipes are rarely artistic works s. 51 would apply.

However, there is a transitional 10-year period of copyright protection for industrial articles made from drawings produced before 1 August 1989. This is especially important as previous comments have suggested that s. 42 Patents Act 1977 could be used to strike down all-embracing pre-assignment clauses covering the disposition of copyright in works which related to inventions. In particular, until August 1999, the scope of s. 51 Copyright, Designs and Patents Act 1988, as applied to drawings and design documents from which 'non-artistic' articles can be reproduced, will be severely curtailed by the transitional provisions (see sch. 1, para. 19 Copyright, Designs and Patents Act 1988).

Subject to this, the Copyright, Designs and Patents Act 1988 introduces as a replacement the new 'design right' which basically covers: (a) an article made to the design, such as a 'design model', and (b) any design document, such as a drawing or photo, which records the design (s. 263(1) Copyright, Designs and Patents Act 1988). This new right may subsist in 'any aspect of the shape or configuration (whether internal or external) of the whole or part of an article (s. 213(2)) — note the emphasis upon shape or configuration of the article rather than any surface pattern or ornamentation. As 'eye appeal' is not a prerequisite of protection the right applies both to functional and aesthetic designs such as machine tools and furniture. However, the right will only subsist in *original designs*; i.e., those which are not *commonplace* in the design field in question (see s. 213(4) Copyright, Designs and Patents Act 1988). This raises doubts over the applicability of such rights to purely functional items as their level of originality is generally considered to be low. 'Design right' protection lasts for a maximum of 15 years from creation and 10 years from first marketing.

The Copyright, Designs and Patents Act 1988 specifically excludes from design protection 'must fit' and 'must match' designs. These are features of shape which *enable* an article to fit with another article so that either article can perform its function (e.g., car exhausts, carburettors), and features of an article which is intended to form an integral part of another article which are *dependent* upon the article they must fit (e.g., car panels, facias for kitchen equipment). Emphasis on the highlighted words is important. For example, the size and shape of a removable oven roasting tray will be dependent upon (a) the dimensions of the oven it is intended to 'fit', and (b) the receiving indentations for the tray, located on either side of the oven's interior walls. The above exemptions allow another manufacturer to sell separate oven trays which correspond with these two design parameters, but it does not mean that they can copy other design features of the oven tray unrelated to the 'must fit' specification (e.g., the configuration of the steel rungs or webbed interlace of the tray).

It is probable that the effect of all these changes will be to encourage designers to seek protection of their works through the registered design system, with the design right operating as a residual form of protection for a limited category of new, non-aesthetic, functional items.

4.2.2.1   Ownership of design rights
Section 215 of the Copyright, Designs and Patents Act 1988 provides:

> *(1)   The designer is the first owner of any design right in a design which is not created in pursuance of a commission or in the course of employment.*
> *(2)   Where the design is created in pursuance of a commission, the person commissioning the design is the first owner of any design right in it.*
> *(3)   Where. . . a design is created by an employee in the course of employment, his employer is the first owner of any design right in the design.*

Whereas s. 215(3) mirrors its counterpart in copyright, maintaining the test of 'course of employment', s. 215(2) follows the registered design scheme of placing ownership in the commissioner's hands. This may represent a potential source of dispute where the creation of a design also involves the creation of a copyright (artistic) work although the Copyright, Designs and Patents Act 1988 incorporates special provisions to resolve this issue. For example s. 236 states that where copyright and design rights subsist in the same work or design then it will not be an infringement of the design right to do anything which constitutes an infringement of the copyright in that work.

4.2.2.2   Pre-assignment clauses: registered designs and design rights
No type of design right can subsist in a method or principle of construction (s. 1(1) Registered Designs Act 1949; and s. 213(3) Copyright, Designs and Patents Act 1988), although the new design right may subsist in the shape of a functional article irrespective of eye appeal to the ultimate consumer or user. The general exclusion cuts down the potential overlap of design and patent rights, especially if s. 213(3) Copyright, Designs and Patents Act 1988 is construed as impeding design protection in the features of an article resulting from the method or principle employed in its construction.

However, design right and patent protection are not *per se* mutually exclusive (*Werner Motors Ltd* v *A.W. Gamage Ltd* (1904) 21 RPC 621 at p. 629). Consider an example based on the facts in *Tetra Molectric's Application* [1977] RPC 290. An employee, outside the course of employment, has designed a new cigarette lighter. The design has an aesthetically pleasing appearance, although not materially different from other lighters being sold (i.e., Registered Designs Act 1949 protection is unavailable). It also has considerable utility because the design would be considered inventive in the way that it ensures that the working parts of the lighter's igniting mechanism are protected from dirt. A patent application covering aspects of the lighter fails as it is found that the lighter was accidentally marketed beforehand. However, an enforceable unregistered design right remains. Surely this design right subsists *in an invention* (s. 42 Patents Act 1977) so any pre-assignment clause which attempts to transfer this right to the employer will be void; note that on the facts s. 215 Copyright, Designs and Patents Act 1988 would vest initial ownership in the employee as the design was created outside the course of employment.

Thus, it is perfectly possible to envisage situations where, for example, employees would want to use s. 39(2) Patents Act 1977 to claim ownership over inventions which had failed to secure patent protection on grounds of obviousness, using current design rights to buttress their rights of ownership over those inventions.

More importantly, if our interpretation of s. 42 Patents Act 1977 is correct, then any employee who owns an invention under s. 39(2) Patents Act 1977 cannot be prevented by an employer from asserting ownership over any designs relating to that invention which the employee also made. The same would apply to a team of employees who all contributed in some way to the making of the invention, the drawings and ancillary designs. Thus, it may be advisable to adopt the following type of clause (emphasis added):

> *The employee hereby assigns to the company by way of future assignment all copyright, design rights and other proprietary rights for the full terms thereof in respect of all works and designs which were originated, conceived, written or made by the employee during the course of his or her normal duties or during those duties specifically assigned to the employee whether on a temporary or permanent basis.*

Finally, section 223 Copyright, Designs and Patents Act 1988 provides for an agreement assigning future design rights. As for design rights that fell outside this clause, the employer would presumably wish to negotiate a fair settlement with the employee which provided for an assignment or, at the very least, an exclusive licence (see ss. 222 and 225 Copyright, Designs and Patents Act 1988).

4.2.3 TOPOGRAPHY RIGHTS

The Design Right (Semiconductor Topographies) Regulations 1989, as amended by the 1992 Regulations (SI 1992/400) protect the topography of a 'semiconductor product'. This refers to articles which perform an electronic function, consisting of layers of which at least one is made of semiconductor material (e.g., silicon, germanium or gallium arsenide) and at least one of which has a pattern, that pattern relating to the electronic function of the chip. The topography right protects the pattern of a layer of the end-product, the arrangement of the layers in relation to each other, and the pattern of a layer which is an intermediate pattern created during the course of manufacture (including the design of each photographic mask).

The rights of an employer with regard to ownership of topography rights in semiconductor devices made by employees is identical to their position with regard to design rights. The pre-assignment of future design rights is permissible, with s. 223 Copyright, Designs and Patents Act 1988 stipulating the need for the employee's signature along with the normal conditions required for an effective assignment of legal ownership. However, as mentioned earlier, if the topography right relates to an 'invention' then s. 42 Patents Act 1977 may prevent employers asserting ownership insofar as it extends beyond reg. 5 of the 1989 Regulations; i.e., the chip was made outside the employee's course of employment.

4.3 EXTENDING THE COMPENSATION PROVISIONS OF THE PATENTS ACT 1977 TO COPYRIGHT AND DESIGNS

Under the Copyright Act 1956 there was only one important situation in which an employee could claim copyright over work prepared in the course of employment. Section 4(2) provided that where the employee was a journalist, copyright vested in the employee to the extent that the employee's work was used for any purpose other than publication in a newspaper, magazine or similar periodical. During the Parliamentary debates on the Bill which became the Copyright, Designs and Patents Act 1988, a concerted effort was made by a number of MPs to extend this exception in a rather novel way. Specifically, all copyright would vest in an employer where the work was produced in the course of employment but an employee would have a right to seek arbitration in order to secure a fair share of the profits realised by the employer through the exploitation of the work in ways not contemplated by the parties at the time when the contract between them was made. At first sight s. 11(2) Copyright, Designs and Patents Act 1988 would suggest that this move towards some form of compensation failed — with even the journalist's exception being removed. However, it is arguable that a minor amendment within the Copyright, Designs and Patents Act 1988 to s. 39 Patents Act 1977 may have brought the principle of compensation in through the back door. The relevant amendment is an obscure provision in sch. 5, para. 11(2) Copyright, Designs and Patents Act 1988:

In section 43 of the Patents Act 1977 (supplementary provisions with respect to employees' inventions), in subsection (4) (references to patents to include other forms of protection, whether in UK or elsewhere) for 'in sections 40 to 42' substitute 'in sections 39 to 42'.

The question arises: Does this extend the compensation scheme to other forms of intellectual property such as copyright and designs? The answer remains unclear but the effects of an affirmative response would be profound indeed, although employees would still have the same hurdles to surmount in order to claim compensation: proof of ownership, establishing that the right has been of outstanding benefit to the employer, and that it is 'just' that compensation be awarded.

Originally, s. 43(4) stated that any references in s. 40 to 42 to a 'patent or to a patent being granted' were respectively references to a patent 'or other protection'. Although one could argue that 'other protection' extended to ancillary intellectual property rights there was always the problem of establishing ownership under s. 39 before the compensation provisions could come into play.

Has the Copyright, Designs and Patents Act 1988 amendment, by which s. 43(4) Patents Act 1977 has been extended to s. 39 ownership, changed things? It is arguable, for instance, that a liberal interpretation of s. 43(4) might allow an employee to claim compensation where an employer had deliberately chosen not to patent the invention, provided some other protection was conferred.

For example, copyright or design protection over any designs, drawings or other documents, or through the law of confidentiality (e.g., *Weir Pumps Ltd v CML Pumps Ltd* [1984] FSR 33). It is doubtful whether one would extend this to trade secret protection, outside the realms of confidence or contract, as no *separate* legal protection is offered.

In Chartered Institute of Patent Agents 1990, the authors clearly feel that ss. 39 to 42 can be extended in this way although an employee would still need to prove that an 'invention' had been made. The difficulty with this approach is that s. 43(4) states that 'patent or other protection' must have been '*granted* whether under the law of the United Kingdom or the law in force in any other country' (emphasis added). Undoubtedly the words 'other protection' would include petty patents, utility models and inventors' certificates granted in other countries. It is submitted that it would also include registered designs (assuming relevance to an existing invention) as this right is 'granted'. It is less likely to apply to UK copyright, topography and design rights which are not 'granted', although here again the USA does 'grant' copyright whilst topography rights are granted in the USA and some EC countries.

Insofar as the above analysis proves to be correct, the employee seeking compensation will need to prove, amongst other things:

(a)   that he or she not only made the invention but also created the work for which ancillary protection is being sought,

(b)   that it is the 'rights in the invention' (e.g., registered design right, patent grant) which have been of outstanding benefit, rather than the invention itself.

Other than this, the comments made in chapter 3 will apply equally to this situation. At present there are no authoritative statements concerning this issue but employers should be reminded that if the Patents Act 1977 compensation provisions apply to forms of intellectual property other than patents then appropriate adjustments to in-house suggestion and compensation schemes may be necessary.

4.4 CHECKLIST

(a)   *The copyright in all literary, dramatic, musical or artistic works produced in the course of employment belongs to the employer*. This does not necessarily mean that all works produced during an employee's normal working times belong to the employer, nor does it mean that all works produced outside the workplace belong to the employee. Special clauses will need to be considered to ensure that the copyright in other works (e.g., broadcasts) is spelt out in the contract of employment.

(b)   *The Copyright, Designs and Patents Act 1988 acknowledges an employer's right to insert pre-assignment clauses covering future copyright and design rights* (though not registered designs), but it is important that the written formalities are complied with in order to vest an immediate legal title in the employer.

(c) *It is difficult to predict whether s. 42 Patents Act 1977 and/or the restraint of trade doctrine will apply to copyright and design pre-assignment clauses,* but, for the purposes of good personnel management, employers generally should confine pre-assignment clauses to works produced in the course of employment. Additional clauses may be necessary where specific employees occupy a special position in the employer's management hierarchy.

(d) *As copyright resides in the recorded expression of thought rather than the idea which generated the whole process,* it would be best to insert a pre-assignment clause covering work which has been generated, conceived, written or made by an employee in the performance of his or her duties.

(e) *Where a work is commissioned* (i.e., from a non-employee) *first* ownership of copyright will reside in the author, unless an agreed pre-assignment clause conforms with the written formalities required under s. 91 Copyright, Designs and Patents Act 1988. Conversely, ownership of any type of design right will vest initially in the commissioning body (s. 2(1A) and (1B) Registered Designs Act 1949); the need for pre-assignment clauses therefore being less urgent.

(f) *An employer's best interests are served if an employee is encouraged promptly to notify an employer of any new materials, designs, drawings* and so forth, that have been created in the course of employment. Equally, measures should be instigated to prevent employees from using confidential information, copyright or design documents in their next employment — this could include appropriate warnings, contractual clauses, pre-termination meetings with superiors and written undertakings concerning the return of materials.

(g) *Schedule 5, para. 11 Copyright, Designs and Patents Act 1988* inserts a new provision into s. 39 Patents Act 1977 whereby an employer, who finds that an employee owns an invention under s. 39, is prevented from using other intellectual property rights (e.g. copyright) to sue that employee for infringement of any copyright (or design right) where 'as between him and his employer, his employer is entitled in any model or document relating to the invention'.

(h) *In determining the rights of ownership in employees' copyright and design work it is possible that s. 42 Patents Act 1977 performs an important role.* An employee will need to prove that he or she made the invention *and* produced the ancillary copyright and design materials which *relate* to that invention. Employers should be aware of this and the possible compensation claims that could be made by employees.

4.5 BIBLIOGRAPHY

4.5.1 Books

Chartered Institute of Patent Agents (1990), *CIPA Guide to the Patents Acts*, 3rd edn (London: Sweet & Maxwell).
Dworkin, G., and Taylor, R.D. (1989), *Copyright, Designs and Patents Act 1988* (London: Blackstone Press).

Lester, D., and Mitchell, P. (1989), *Joynson-Hicks on UK Copyright Law* (London: Sweet & Maxwell).

Pearson, H., and Miller, C. (1990), *Commercial Exploitation of Intellectual Property* (London: Blackstone Press).

Phillips, J., and Hoolahan, M.J. (1982), *Employees' Inventions in the United Kingdom* (Oxford: ESC Publishing Ltd).

Skone James, E.P., et al. (eds) (1991), *Copinger and Skone James on Copyright*, 13th edn (London: Sweet & Maxwell).

4.5.2 Articles

Bercusson, B. (1980), 'The Contract of Employment and Contracting out: the UK Patents Act 1977' [1980] EIPR 257.

Cornish, W.R. (1978), 'Employee Inventions: the New United Kingdom Patent Law' [1978] EIPR 4.

Cornish, W. R. (1992), 'Rights in University Innovations: The Herschel Smith Lecture for 1991' [1992] 1 EIPR 13.

Hodkinson, K. (1986), 'Employee Inventions and Designs: Ownership, Claims and Compensation; and Managing Employee Inventions' (1986) 2 Co Law 146 and 183.

Hoolahan, M.J. (1979), 'Employees' Inventions: the Practical Implications: Ownership and Compensation: UK Patents Act 1977' [1979] EIPR 140.

Lloyd, R.P. (1979–80), 'Inventorship amongst Collaborators' (1979–80) 9 CIPA 16.

Reid, B.C. (1979), 'Employee Inventions under the Patents Act 1977' [1979] JBL 350.

PART III

PERSONAL INFORMATION

Control over personal information signifies to most people a sense of power over the individual to which that information refers. It also conveys a feeling of unease as regards security: who has access to the information, what use will they make of it, and who will they tell? The dramatic changes in computer technology and communications equipment have merely served to heighten these fears by offering expanded opportunities for efficient, high-speed automatic information processing and unparalleled data retrieval facilities.

In the employment sphere, companies have made considerable use of this technology in recording personal information regarding their employees. In this context, it is imperative that any regulatory informational framework requires employers to maintain accurate employee data records, use the information contained therein for the right reasons, and maintain tight security in order to prevent unauthorised access to, and misuse of, personal data files.

This part will concentrate on recent statutory innovations which regulate the control of and access to certain types of personal information, as they affect individual employees; in particular, the Data Protection Act 1984, the Access to Medical Reports Act 1988, and the Access to Health Records Act 1990. However, readers should be aware of a patchwork of common law and statutory controls in this area. These can be grouped into five categories:

(a)   The tort of negligence which compensates for the reasonably foreseeable losses resulting from breach of an established duty of care — this might arise from the negligent mishandling or processing of personal data (see generally, *Hedley Byrne and Co. Ltd* v *Heller and Partners Ltd* [1964] AC 465).

(b)   The law of defamation which prevents the disclosure of any *untrue* statements liable to hold up the subject of the information to 'hatred, ridicule or contempt'.

(c)   The law of confidence which could be extended to any improper disclosure of confidential information obtained by employers from their employees (see generally, *Coco* v *A.N. Clark (Engineers) Ltd* [1969] RPC 41 and the discussion in chapter 6).

(d)   An assortment of statutes which focus on specific fields of activity: the Interception of Communications Act 1985, the Post Office Acts 1963 and

1969, the Official Secrets Act 1989, the Computer Misuse Act 1990, and even the Consumer Credit Act 1974 in which ss. 157 to 159 provide for limited access to credit reference agencies and the removal or amendment of inaccurate data.

(e) Either party may be bound by an express or implied contractual obligation not to divulge certain information acquired during the currency of employment (e.g., *Attorney-General* v *Barker* [1990] 3 All ER 257).

One should not underestimate the importance of the above. For example, the Data Protection Act 1984 generally does not apply to manually recorded information. Consider the employee who is aggrieved by the circulation of a memo, written by his employer, in which details of his past and present shareholdings are disclosed. If the information is inaccurate a remedy may lie in the tort of negligence; if the information originally was disclosed in confidence then an action for breach of confidence may exist; whilst if the memo wrongly suggested that the employee had anonymously held shares in a pro-Nazi German armaments company during the Second World War then an action in defamation might appear the most appropriate.

5 Data Protection

The passing of the Data Protection Act 1984 was a direct result of the United Kingdom becoming a signatory in May 1981 to the Council of Europe Convention on Data Protection. This Convention attempts to regulate the trans-border flow of automatically processable personal data. As the Convention invokes the mutuality principle, ratification is a prerequisite for maintaining an uninterrupted flow of data between one country and any other signatory State. The Data Protection Act 1984 itself establishes new rights for an individual about whom information is recorded on computer or on other forms of automatic processing equipment. In particular, individuals are given a right of access to the information stored about themselves, as well as the right to challenge any inaccuracy and claim compensation for ensuing injury. Finally, the Data Protection Act 1984 initiates a registration scheme for those who record and use personal data, imposing specific obligations on such users to follow sound and proper procedures.

This chapter will consider these aspects in the following order:

5.1 Introduction and definitions
5.2 Registration requirements
5.3 The principles of the Data Protection Act 1984
5.4 Powers of the Registrar
5.5 Criminal offences under the Data Protection Act 1984 and non-disclosure exemptions
5.6 Employees' rights
5.7 Checklist
5.8 Bibliography

5.1 INTRODUCTION AND DEFINITIONS

The Data Protection Act 1984 applies to information classified as 'personal data'. This is information which:

    (a)   is stored in computer-readable form;
    (b)   relates to an identifiable living individual;
    (c)   is part of a collection of data;

(d)   is processed or intended to be processed by reference to that individual;
(e)   is processed for a purpose other than simply preparing the text of documents;
(f)   is other than simply an indication of the data user's intentions.

Clearly the Data Protection Act 1984 has affected the running of personnel administration in the majority of companies. The computerisation of records, including the names of employees, their addresses, payroll information, pension arrangements, training schedules, personal work sheets and so forth are all regulated by the provisions of the Data Protection Act 1984. This chapter will explain the basic principles of the Data Protection Act 1984 and its impact upon personnel administration. In particular, it will draw upon two sources of information: (a) an ILU survey on the type of computerised data stored by employers, the purposes for which they hold such data, and their employees' right of access to such data, and (b) the 1989 guidelines (Nos. 1 to 8) produced by the Data Protection Registrar in order to clarify the effects, implementation and enforcement of the Data Protection Act 1984.

However, s.1 of the Data Protection Act 1984 employs certain terminology which must be understood before the Act can be meaningfully applied to employment law in general and personnel administration in particular.

5.1.1 Data

Section 1(2) of the Data Protection Act 1984 defines data as information which is capable of being automatically processed in response to instructions given for that purpose. The Data Protection Act 1984 does not apply to information which is recorded and processed *manually* unless that information was originally in an automatically processable form and the intention is that it will be converted back to that form for processing on a subsequent occasion (s. 1(5)). Thus, information recorded manually from a VDU, the computer file subsequently being deleted, *may* still be covered by the Data Protection Act 1984 (e.g., where the manual records will be keyed into a new software package).

5.1.2 Personal data

The Data Protection Act 1984 is only concerned with personal data. This means information which relates to a living individual, identifiable from that information or from that and other information in the possession of the data user; for example, data containing employees' payroll reference numbers where the data user maintains a separate list, in *any* form, from which named employees can be identified. It includes any expression of opinion about the individual but excludes any indication of intentions of the data user in respect of that individual; for example, the opinion that an employee is lazy constitutes 'personal data' but not the intention of the employer to commence dismissal proceedings.

In this context, 'intention' should be contrasted with 'fact': if employer A expresses an intention to institute criminal proceedings against an employee and this is communicated to employer B then the latter is in possession of a fact which may be personal data. Equally, employers should not attempt to disguise their opinions by phrasing them as intentions, as subsequent use of the information may disclose the true purpose for recording the data.

5.1.3 Data user

A data user is the person or organisation who 'holds' data. The term 'holding' relates to data which form part of a collection of data processed or intended to be processed. The user in question must have the ability to 'control' the use and content of the data, whether by processing the data on in-house equipment or making use of another's processing facilities, i.e., a computer bureau.

Control signifies the power of the user, jointly or exclusively held, to decide what information on an individual is to be recorded, whether that information should be added to, amended or deleted, and the use to which it will be put — powers which are unlikely to be wielded by the employee charged with mere storage of the information. Thus, company auditors who are given access to the computer system, *verifying* the recorded data, would not be considered data users; but an auditor who is given additional powers to *amend* faulty data would be a data user.

Sometimes it will be difficult to identify who is the data user in a particular situation. For example, what happens if a company has services provided to it by another firm and, in the course of that relationship, information is automatically processed by the service provider? The Registrar's Guideline No. 1 cautions against any 'sham' allocation of responsibilities under the Data Protection Act 1984. In particular, if one of the parties has accepted full responsibility as a data user under the Act then that party must be free to make decisions on some of the following matters, irrespective of the instructions received from the other party:

(a) the extent to which records containing information about individuals should be kept;
(b) the type of information recorded;
(c) the sources of such information;
(d) the method and timing for processing this information;
(e) the means by which the information is checked for inaccuracies and, where appropriate, updated;
(f) the potential availability of this information to third parties;
(g) the retention of the information after the contract has ended.

What is important is that the data user has a reasonable amount of discretion which can be exercised in relation to the recorded personal data, otherwise it will be difficult to see how such a person can claim to 'control' the use and contents of that data (i.e., be a data user).

5.1.4 Computer bureau

A computer bureau provides data services to others, either by processing data for others by equipment operating automatically or by allowing others to use equipment in its possession to carry out such processing (s. 1(6)). The bureau need not be a profit-making business; for instance, a reciprocal back-up arrangement with another user in case either of their computers fails will be covered by the definition.

5.1.5 Data subject

The data subject is the living individual referred to in the data — companies are therefore excluded. The individual need not be a United Kingdom national or resident.

5.1.6 Processing

Processing means amending, adding to, deleting or rearranging the data or merely extracting the information constituting the data and, in the case of personal data, means performing any of those operations by reference to the data subject (s. 1(7)). As the information must be automatically processable, it will include data stored on mainframe, mini and microcomputers, word processors, or even machine-code and punch-card processors. Nevertheless, the Data Protection Registrar has suggested that other types of equipment, not normally associated with computers, may possess some ability to process information automatically. These might include electronic flexitime systems, telephone logging equipment and automatic retrieval systems for microfilm and microfiche, provided, of course, that individuals can be identified.

Section 1(8) provides that operations 'performed *only* for the purpose of preparing the text of documents' do not constitute 'processing' as covered by the Data Protection Act 1984; thus, using the editing facilities on a word processor does not make you *per se* a data user. However, using processing equipment in order to analyse or select from the personal data would be an additional purpose which would fall outside s. 1(8). For example, employing the mailmerge functions of a word processor in order to address standard circulars to employees would be covered by s. 1(8), but the employer who periodically updates employees' addresses would become a data user as updating is a purpose distinct from text preparation.

5.1.7 Disclosing

Section 1(9) states that 'disclosing', in relation to data, includes disclosing information extracted from the data. However, where the identification of the data subject depends partly upon other information in possession of the data user, the data are not regarded as being disclosed or transferred unless this other information is also disclosed or transferred. Interestingly, the manner in which the information is extracted appears irrelevant; for instance, a handwritten memorandum copied from a VDU or computer printout would constitute a 'disclosure' under s. 1(9).

5.1.8 Territorial scope of the Data Protection Act 1984

The Act applies to all data users who control the contents and use of personal data from within the United Kingdom. Even if control of the data is exercised through an employee (i.e., data user) who is employed mainly overseas the data user's control is still being exercised from within the UK.

Equally, the Data Protection Act 1984 will apply to personal data processed wholly overseas where the data are used or intended to be used in the UK. This intention would be established if the information is produced overseas but then sent to the UK for use here, irrespective of whether the information arrives in an automatically processable form.

If a company is not resident within the UK but exercises control of the data through a UK employee then that person will be considered a data user and will need to apply for registration. For example, if a UK subsidiary of an overseas company maintains computerised records of its employees then the person responsible for directing operations in the UK office would be the data user.

5.2 REGISTRATION REQUIREMENTS

5.2.1 Registration and the register

The Data Protection Registrar is required by the Data Protection Act 1984 to keep a register of:

(a) data users who hold personal data,
(b) computer bureaux which provide services in respect of personal data.

This register must be open to public inspection, free of charge, at reasonable hours. Although data subjects will not be named, the register will show the relationship which such people have with the data user (e.g., employer-employee). Interestingly, the law does not assume that individuals know the contents of the register, so data users cannot avoid giving information to a data subject purely on the pretext that the information is on the register.

Every data user who holds personal data must, unless all the data are exempt, apply for registration. A data user's register entry is compiled from information given in the application. The entry will describe:

(a) who the data user is and where an individual may make a 'subject access request' (see 5.6.1);
(b) the personal data held and the purposes for which they are held or used (e.g., the birth dates of employees in order to compute early retirement eligibility);

(c) from where the data user may obtain the information contained in the data (e.g., employment references at the time of appointment);

(d) to whom the data user may disclose the information (e.g., selling mail-shot lists);

(e) any overseas countries or territories to which the data user may transfer the personal data (e.g., offices abroad).

Having registered, the data user must operate within the terms of the entry. The data user may apply to alter the descriptions whenever necessary. Registration lasts three years although a lesser period of one or two years may be chosen. A computer bureau which provides services in respect of personal data must, unless the data are exempt, apply for registration. The register entry for the bureau will contain only its name and address.

Under s. 13(1) there is a right of appeal where the Registrar refuses an application for registration or alteration of existing registered particulars. This appeal will take place in the Data Protection Tribunal (discussed later), with further appeals on points of law being entertained in the High Court in England and Wales, or the Court of Session in Scotland.

5.2.2 Registered purposes: employment

The use of data for employment purposes will normally be covered by two of the standard purposes defined by the Data Protection Registrar for registration purposes. These are:

P001 The administration of prospective, current and past employees, including, where applicable, self-employed or contract personnel, secondees, temporary staff or voluntary workers.

P002 The planning and management of the data user's workload or business activity.

5.2.3 Exemptions from registration

If personal data fall within one of the following exemptions they do not have to be included in the data user's register entry, there is no individual right of access to the data, and the Registrar has no powers in respect of the data. Moreover, if the exemption covers *all* the personal data held by the data user then that user need not register at all under the Data Protection Act 1984. Nevertheless, a court may inspect data if an individual makes a formal application claiming that the data are not exempt.

The following items represent the most important exemptions for our purposes, in each case the exemption applying to Parts II and III of the Data Protection Act 1984:

5.2.3.1 Payroll, pensions and accounts purposes (s. 32)
This exemption will be lost in its entirety if the personal data are held or used for any other purpose.

Payroll and pension purposes, as defined by s. 32(1)(a), include such things as:

(a)   calculating wages (net or gross), salaries, or the amount payable as pensions for service in employment — including pensions payable to the widow or other dependants of a former employee;

(b)   paying salaries, wages and pensions (e.g., relevant data might include details of bank accounts) or making payments of sums deducted from remuneration or pensions (e.g., National Insurance contributions, trade union membership, private health insurance premiums).

Accounts purposes, under s. 32(1)(b), refers to:

(a)   the keeping of accounts relating to any business carried out by the data user;

(b)   keeping records of purchases, sales or other transactions, thereby ensuring necessary payments to and by the data user as well as facilitating financial and management forecasts helpful to the conduct of the data user's business.

For these exemptions to apply, two conditions must be met. First, any disclosure for accounts purposes or for both accounts and payroll purposes must be:

(a)   for the purpose of audit, or for the purpose of giving information about the data user's financial affairs — use of the word 'or' in s. 32(4)(a) may widen this exemption to include the disclosure of other matters unintended by the draftsman of the Act such as the publication of an employee's salary within an annual 'financial affairs' report;

(b)   in circumstances covered by one of the exemptions from the non-disclosure provisions of the Act (s. 32(4)(b) — see 5.5).

However, if personal data are held *only* for the exempt payroll purposes, then, under s. 32(3), they may *also* be disclosed to:

(a)   any person, other than the data user, by whom the remuneration or pensions in question are payable (s. 32(3)(a));

(b)   in order to obtain actuarial advice (s. 32(3)(b));

(c)   for research into occupational disease or injuries (s. 32(3)(c));

(d)   when the data subject (or his agent) has requested or consented to the disclosure, whether the consent is given generally or limited purely to the circumstances (s. 32(3)(d) — or even where the person making the disclosure has reasonable grounds for believing the disclosure is so authorised (s. 32(3)(e)).

Secondly, the data must only be used for the above purposes. This is particularly important as much of the personal data held in the payroll file is useful for wider personnel administration purposes unconnected with calculation and payment (s. 32(2)).

Guideline 6 states that the above exemptions are only likely to be of use to very small businesses. In particular, it is questionable whether the following uses, amongst others, fall exclusively within the exemptions:

(a) time-keeping records and absences used to calculate pay, but which are also used to evaluate an employee's performance;

(b) records of trade union membership used to deduct dues from salaries (and transferred to the union) which are also used to monitor which employees belong to trade unions;

(c) records held by pension fund trustees in order to pay pensions but which are also used by the employer in considering a possible programme of early retirement;

(d) records of employees' addresses kept for accounts purposes which are also used to distribute information unconnected with the accounts (e.g., advertising literature for a personal accident insurance scheme subsidised by the employer).

Moreover, one cannot simply determine the breadth of the exemptions from the actual information recorded. The uses and purposes of disclosure are equally important. For example, a date of birth may be relevant in calculating pay, but if it is used to calculate the retirement age then the full exemption is lost.

5.2.3.2 Other exemptions

Personal data held for domestic or recreational purposes (s. 33) This exception covers personal data held by an individual which solely concerns the management of personal, family or household affairs, or is held for purely recreational purposes. This exemption applies to an 'individual' and therefore excludes from its ambit personal data held by companies, clubs or other organisations.

Information that the law requires to be made public (s. 34(1)) This is information which the data user is 'required' by law (Act of Parliament or statutory instrument) to make available to the public, whether by publishing it, making it available for inspection, or otherwise, irrespective of whether payment is required or not. For example, the Companies Act 1985 requires every registered company to make its register of members available for public inspection.

National security (s. 27) Personal data are exempt if exemption is necessary for the purposes of safeguarding national security. A Cabinet Minister, the Attorney-General or the Lord Advocate may make the necessary decision on this matter. A signed certificate provides conclusive evidence of this fact which cannot be questioned by the Registrar or by the courts.

Mailing lists (s. 33(2)(b)) This exemption refers to mailing lists held for the purpose of distributing, or recording the distribution of articles or information to individuals. But four conditions must be met:

(a) The lists must only include the names and addresses of the individuals, unless the method of distribution requires other details such as telephone numbers or telex numbers. Recording other information such as the occupation of the individual loses the exempt status.

(b) If the information is used for any other purpose the exemption is lost.

(c) The individuals concerned must be asked whether they object to the personal data relating to them being held by the data user. If an objection is lodged then the personal data must be deleted from the computer (manual processing can still occur) or the data user must register in respect of the personal data, in which case the data may continue to be held irrespective of any individual's opposition. Clearly, as an employer requires the names and addresses of employees for other purposes it is very unlikely that this exemption will have any real practical appeal in employment circles.

(d) Disclosure of the personal data is only permitted where the individual (or agent) has requested or consented to the disclosure and the disclosure falls within one of the 'non-disclosure exemptions' (see 5.5).

5.3 THE PRINCIPLES OF THE DATA PROTECTION ACT 1984

At the centre of the Data Protection Act 1984 lie eight principles around which the Act is structured, enforced and interpreted (Sch. 1, Parts I and II). There is an obligation on all data users to observe these principles; and, in addition, an obligation on computer bureaux to observe the eighth principle. The principles are more than a mere declaration of good practice. The powers of the Registrar to issue enforcement notices, requiring compliance with the Data Protection Act 1984, or even to de-register a data user, thereby preventing any further processing of data, are dependent upon one or more of these principles being infringed.

5.3.1 The first principle

The information to be contained in personal data shall be obtained, and personal data shall be processed, fairly and lawfully.

Central to the acquisition of information is the knowledge of the person from whom it is obtained. It is vital that there is no deception as to the purpose or purposes for which the information is to be held, used or disclosed. The Registrar will need to be assured that the supplier of information can, in the particular circumstances, reasonably appreciate the identity of the data user and the intended purposes. If any explanation is necessary then it must be forthcoming prior to the information being transmitted.

The Data Protection Act 1984 gives a special dispensation from the first principle for personal data held for historical, statistical or research purposes. Information will not be regarded as obtained unfairly merely because its use for those purposes was not disclosed when the information was obtained. This dispensation applies only if the personal data are not used in such a way that they are likely to cause damage or distress to any data subject.

Employees or potential employees should not be induced or unnecessarily pressurised into providing information. Nor should they be led to believe that a failure to supply information might disadvantage them unless this can be justified by the needs of the employer's personnel administration requirements. Employers should recognise that they may be required to justify the collection of particular items of data, especially where it is questionable whether the proposed uses truly fall within the purposes stated in the employer's data registration details. Moreover, the provisions of the Data Protection Act 1984 do not assume that employees will know the contents of their employers' register entries; thus, unless the information is being requested in circumstances where the reasons for its collection, and the purposes to which it will be put, are abundantly clear, one would expect proper explanations to be forthcoming.

5.3.1.1 Fair uses
The following are typical uses of personnel data which might reasonably be expected by employers:

(a)   recruitment;
(b)   recording of working time;
(c)   administration of wages and salaries, pensions and other benefits;
(d)   employee assessment and training;
(e)   manpower and career planning;
(f)   compliance with safety legislation;
(g)   job scheduling or workshift planning;
(h)   provision of references.

Undoubtedly, employers should only collect personal information that is required for legitimate or legal reasons, whilst ensuring that employees are aware of current data protection policies and are held accountable for any transgressions. In particular, one should emphasise the confidentiality of any data collected and their use in personnel administration only. Do not follow the example of one employer who sold lists of his employees' addresses to local advertising companies! On this point see also the comments in chapter 6 on *Dalgleish* v *Lothian and Borders Police Board* [1991] IRLR 422.

5.3.1.2 Assumed fairness
Personal data will be regarded as obtained fairly if they are obtained from a person who (a) is authorised by statute to supply it or (b) is required to supply them by any convention or other instrument which imposes an international obligation on the UK. Any disclosure of information which is

so authorised or required must be disregarded when considering whether information was obtained fairly. For instance, information disclosed by employees about themselves to their employer is not obtained unfairly merely because the former have not been informed that the employer is bound by statute to disclose some of that information to the Inland Revenue.

5.3.1.3 Legal considerations
Personal data are not obtained lawfully if they are received from an unregistered source. Personal data are not processed lawfully if they are used, or intended to be used, for unlawful purposes; for example, recording data on the racial origins of employees would be contrary to the Race Relations Act 1976 if used for the purposes of determining promotion prospects adverse to the interests of the applicants.

The Registrar cannot enforce the first principle in any case in which enforcement would be likely to prejudice the prevention or detection of crime, the apprehension or prosecution of offenders, or the assessment or collection of any tax or duty.

5.3.1.4 Checklist
Under your in-house data protection policy:

(a)   Are employees only expected to provide personal information that is required for your legitimate business needs or in order to comply with your current statutory obligations?

(b)   Are employees responsible for access to, use and disclosure of employees' personal data aware that they must avoid any use of employees' data falling outside the above legitimate reasons without the individual employee's knowledge and consent?

(c)   Is the data protection policy, written in readily understandable form and, communicated to all employees — preferably with the rider that all personal data are treated with the strictest of confidence and for the purposes of personnel administration only unless prior approval of relevant employees has been sought and obtained?

5.3.2 The second principle

Personal data shall be held only for one or more specified and lawful purposes.

A specified purpose is one described in the register entry relating to the personal data. Data users are advised, therefore, to comply with this principle by registering all their lawful purposes and by establishing procedures that ensure that new purposes are added to the register entry as and when they arise. Clearly this is best done at the time of applying for registration as multipurpose registrations incur a standard charge identical to that of single-purpose registrations whereas any later amendment or registration of a new purpose is charged a separate fee.

Part II of the Data Protection Act 1984 exempts certain data held from the need for registration. However, although the Act provides for a narrowly defined exemption for payroll processing applicable to personnel administration (5.2.3.1), it is recommended that payroll data should be registered in the same way as other personal data.

5.3.2.1 Checklist
Under your in-house data protection policy:

(a)   Are persons responsible for access to, use and disclosure of employees' personal data within your firm fully conversant with your register particulars, thereby preventing the use of data for unregistered purposes?

(b)   Where problems arise on the above issue, is there an employee of sufficient seniority to deal with the matter?

(c)   Is the employee charged with overall supervision of your data protection needs fully acquainted with the provisions of the Data Protection Act 1984; for example, the need to review existing registered particulars and apply for renewal or even amendment where appropriate?

5.3.3 The third principle

Personal data held for any purpose or purposes shall not be used or disclosed in any manner incompatible with that purpose or those purposes.

Whereas the second principle stresses the need for registration of purposes, the third principle emphasises the prohibition on using personal data outside such registered purposes.

The term 'incompatible' should be read in the light of *all* the principles. For example, the disclosure of personal data to any person is permitted provided data users have registered that they intend, or may wish, to disclose those personal data to people of that description (second principle).

Disclosure that falls outside the registered intentions of the data user may be permitted if it is covered by one of the 'non-disclosure exemptions' (see 5.5.2). Conversely, a data user may register additional disclosure purposes with the Registrar, provided an additional fee is paid for amended particulars to the original register or a fresh registration application is made.

In practice, it is vital that any company data protection policy respects the privacy of employees, and the importance of employee confidence and good employee relations. As the NCC Codes of Practice (NCC 1990) state:

With due regard to the resources available to a given organisation, personnel administrators should endeavour . . . wherever possible, to obtain an employee's written consent, even if the disclosure in question has been registered. Alternatively employers should advise employees of likely disclosures at the time the data are collected . . . It is good personnel practice to define clearly the internal restrictions on access to personal data in order to enhance confidentiality. Personnel administrators should have a clear policy to ensure that data about employees can be accessed only where there is a legitimate 'business need to know'.

5.3.3.1 Checklist
The points made in the checklists for the first and second principles (5.3.1.4
and 5.3.2.1) apply also to the third principle.

5.3.4 The fourth principle

*Personal data held for any purpose or purposes shall be adequate, relevant
and not excessive in relation to that purpose or those purposes.*

The adequacy, relevance and sheer weight of the personnel data stored will
clearly depend upon the circumstances. Employers should seek to identify
the minimum amount of information about each individual employee which
is required in order to ensure the smooth running of their businesses. This
might include personal details such as the address, marital status, job details,
details of payments, benefits, training, qualifications, disciplinary matters and
assessments of performance. Naturally, any such information can be
supplemented by manual information which is not covered by the Data
Protection Act 1984.

Employers may then wish to identify special cases where additional
information will be required and seek to ensure that such information is only
collected and recorded in those cases. Moreover, each data file must not be
excessive in relation to the avowed purpose for its existence. A direct mailing
list incorporating employees' addresses which can be used by an affiliated
pension company may also require the age of each employee, whereas a mailing
list in connection with a charity appeal would not.

In the ILU survey, employers were asked to identify the type of personal
information on their employees which was recorded in computerised form.
The breakdown of responses was as follows:

	(%)
Name	100
Age	100
Salary	90
Position	90
Sickness absences	85
Marital status	80
Qualifications	75
Disabilities	50
Professional body membership	40
Trade union membership	38
Previous employment	35
Number of Children	30
Disciplinary offences	25
Medical reports or notes	10
Opinions (supervisor or interviewer)	10

Other information that was specified by respondents included: addresses, hours of work, next of kin, car details, maternity information, starting and leaving dates, pension details, appraisal dates, training courses attended and holidays. Even driving licence details were recorded, presumably where the employee was required to drive company vehicles, or owned a company car. Rather more worrying was the admission by a small number of respondents that details of ethnic origin and nationality were also recorded. One would expect these employers to encounter some difficulty in justifying the need to record such information for the purposes of business organisation.

Interestingly, all respondents recognised that additional information was kept in non-computerised form. The most popular items were: original application form, references, relocation expenses, benefits, opinions of supervisors, bank details, medical reports, grading claims, car parking and season ticket loan facilities.

As will be seen, there are obvious links between the fourth, fifth and sixth principles. Personal data which are not kept up to date may be deemed inadequate and, if kept longer than is necessary, may become both irrelevant and excessive.

5.3.4.1 Checklist
Under your in-house data protection policy:

(a)   Is only the minimum amount of information about each employee maintained, consonant with your legitimate business needs and other legal considerations?

(b)   Are senior personnel administrators equipped to provide suitable explanations and justifications as to why each item of data is requested and kept?

5.3.5 The fifth principle

Personal data shall be accurate and, where necessary, kept up to date.

Section 22(4) of the Data Protection Act 1984 defines 'accurate' as being correct and not misleading as to any matter of fact. However, s. 22(3) adds the proviso that it is a defence to show that reasonable care had been taken at the material time to ensure the accuracy of the data, whilst s. 22(2) confers a limited immunity where the inaccuracy of the information stems from the data subject supplying the wrong information.

Guideline 4 poses the question whether the Registrar will take any formal action against the data user in order to remedy a breach. Matters which may be considered include:

(a)   the effect of the inaccuracy in terms of its likelihood to cause damage or distress to the data subject;

(b)   whether the source from which the data user obtained the information was reliable and/or required further verification from a different source;

(c)   whether it would have been reasonable to ask the data subject, either at the time that the data were collected, or at some other convenient opportunity, whether the information was accurate;

(d) the existence of other in-house fail-safe procedures for preventing inaccurate data being recorded;

(e) the time it took to remedy the inaccuracy and inform third-party data recipients once the error had come to light;

(f) whether the inaccuracy produced any consequences before it was corrected and, if so, what remedial action the data user has taken.

Many of these issues can be resolved by the simple expedients of: (a) providing employees, at periodic intervals, with a copy of their computerised records with an opportunity to examine them, raise queries and correct the record where appropriate (without prejudice to their rights under the Data Protection Act 1984), (b) encouraging employees to notify changes in their current circumstances as soon as possible, (c) ensuring that wherever possible all information received, especially from outside sources, is verified by reference to documentary evidence.

5.3.5.1 Updating

Regular updating is clearly in the interests of all the parties concerned. Acting on outdated information will be costly if it leads to an employee suing for damages in negligence. Consider the employee who has been convicted of a criminal offence but whose conviction becomes 'spent' during the course of employment under the provisions of the Rehabilitation of Offenders Act 1974. The personal data file is not updated so when a job application is made elsewhere the employer includes within the requested employment reference information regarding the conviction. Clearly the employer is in breach of the fifth principle and may face being sued by the employee whilst simultaneously having an enforcement notice (see 5.4.2) served upon him by the Registrar.

Apart from instituting a procedure which incorporates regular updating, an employer should also ensure that the date when an employee's personal file was last revised should be recorded and that all interested employees (e.g., departmental managers, supervisors) are aware of any changes in the data.

In the ILU survey, 80 per cent of respondents stated that employee files were routinely updated. The specified responses were as follows:

	%
Daily	30
If changes occur	55
Annually	15
Two yearly	–

Finally, there will be situations where updating is a pointless exercise. For example, the data may be used merely as a historical record of meetings between the employer and employee — changing the data, as opposed to adding the content of new meetings, would defeat the purpose of maintaining this historical record.

5.3.5.2 When is updating necessary?
In many ways this will depend upon the type of data concerned and the purposes for which they are being kept. If the data are not particularly sensitive and any inaccuracy is unlikely to cause damage or distress then the need for regular updating is not so important. Equally, if specific data are maintained for historical reasons then the question of updating will rarely arise. Perhaps the most important point is that the employer is seen to be making a genuine attempt to avoid inaccuracy in personnel files by recording, for example, the date when each file was last updated or making those concerned with use of the data aware that certain files require periodic updating.

5.3.5.3 Checklist
Under your in-house data protection policy:

(a)   Are employees periodically provided with a copy of their personnel record and an opportunity to make appropriate amendments where necessary in order to rectify errors and update personal changes in circumstances?

(b)   Are all employees informed (e.g., through notices on boards, induction courses etc.) of the need to notify any changes in personal circumstances to the personnel office?

(c)   Is information received about employees from third-party sources properly verified? For example, newspaper reports about an employee's extracurricular activities should be treated with caution!

5.3.6 The sixth principle

Personal data held for any purpose or purposes shall not be kept for longer than is necessary for that purpose or those purposes.

This principle emphasises the need for a continuous data processing audit which deletes obsolete data. Guideline 4 offers some useful assistance on in-house policies regarding the systematic removal of data:

This might involve setting a standard 'life' for records of a particular category. At the end of that life the record should be reviewed and deleted unless there is some special reason for keeping it. The length of the review period will depend upon the nature of the record. If the data have only a short-term value to the data user, it may be appropriate to delete them within days or months.

The real problem is in identifying the point at which information is no longer required. For instance, should an employer delete 'stale' disciplinary warnings? This particular issue arises most often when employees resign or leave their job. Superficially, the employer will have little or no reason to maintain most of the relevant personal file. However, employers should be cautioned against wholesale deletion. It may be necessary to keep some types of information in the event of subsequent litigation until the relevant limitation period has expired. One need look no further than the claims made by employees suffering from asbestosis long after their employment terminated. On more routine issues, perhaps the opinions of other colleagues and supervisors may be relevant where ex-employees seek further work references.

As with the fifth principle, an employer is allowed to retain indefinitely records for historical, statistical or research purposes provided the data are not used in such a way as is likely to cause damage or distress to any employee. Nevertheless, in order to reduce the damage caused by accidental leaks, employers would be well advised to depersonalise such records, wherever possible, in order to prevent identification of a particular individual.

5.3.6.1 Checklist
Under your in-house data protection policy:

(a)   Are the time-limits for maintaining records regularly reviewed and amended where appropriate? For example, changes in legal limitation periods may require a review of the appropriate standard life of ex-employees' personnel records.

(b)   Are personal data files regularly reviewed in order that out-of-date and unnecessary information is deleted?

(c)   Where data are held for historical, statistical or research purposes (e.g., for predicting future changes in manpower trends) are such data depersonalised where practicable?

5.3.7 The seventh principle

An individual shall be entitled—
(a)   at reasonable intervals and without undue delay or expense—
(i)   to be informed by any data user whether he holds personal data of which that individual is the subject; and
(ii)   to access to any such data held by a data user; and
(b)   where appropriate, to have such data corrected or erased.

This principle will be dealt with more fully in 5.6. For the moment, four points should be made:

(a)   Employers will need to comply with the conditions set out in s. 21 of the Data Protection Act 1984 (rights of access to personal data).

(b)   The Registrar will only enforce para. (a) if satisfied that the employer has failed to supply information to which the employee is entitled and which has been requested in accordance with that section.

(c)   The phrase 'reasonable intervals' will depend upon the nature of the personal data, the purpose for which they are held and how often they are altered.

(d)   The correction or erasure of personal data is only 'appropriate' where it ensures compliance with the data protection principles (e.g., the data is inaccurate); there is no general right for an employee to have data deleted merely on grounds of personal preference.

In the ILU survey, respondents were asked about the efforts that they made to inform employees of personal data held about them. The breakdown of responses was as follows:

	%
Letter to employee	38
Induction sessions	19
Handbook	19
Briefing meetings	10
Training sessions	10
Articles in house journal	5
Newsletter	5
Workplace notices	5
Video	5
Other	33

In the 'other' category, over one-third of those respondents stated that they sent a copy of records to each employee. Interestingly, one company sent an annual print-out of records to each employee, whilst another company adopted an open file policy.

The ILU survey also asked employers to specify the type of information which had some form of restricted access placed upon it. The examples given were of files containing: promotion suitability, recommendations for transfers, courses and posting restrictions, grading appeals, disciplinary notes, career plans and succession plans.

5.3.7.1 Checklist
Under your in-house data protection policy:

(a)   When employees request access to their data files, are *all* requested data (covered by the Data Protection Act 1984) which are held on different systems within your organisation supplied?

(b)   Are persons responsible for responding to these access requests properly trained in order, for example, that information which refers to identifiable third parties suitably depersonalised or, if that is not possible, that appropriate authorisation from such individuals is obtained prior to disclosure to the requesting employee?

(c)   Are suitable standard access request forms available which are written in a helpful manner which facilitates rather than obstructs the processing of requests, and are identification procedures established which prevent disclosure to unauthorised persons?

(d)   Is information supplied to the requesting employee in an easily understandable form, with any coded information fully explained?

5.3.8 The eighth principle

Appropriate security measures shall be taken against unauthorised access to, or alteration, disclosure or destruction of, personal data and against accidental loss or destruction of personal data.

This principle applies to data users and computer bureaux and is concerned with data security. Schedule 1, Part II Data Protection Act 1984 indicates that regard should be had to where the personal data are stored, the security measures programmed into the relevant equipment and to other measures taken for ensuring the reliability of staff having access to the data. Thus, amongst other things, the following points will be encompassed by the principle:

(a)   Unauthorised access to the information, either physically or through 'hacking'.
(b)   Destruction, amendment or disclosure of data without the employer's authority.
(c)   Unintended yet negligent loss or adulteration of sensitive information, including the possibility of unreliable hardware, faulty software, or the absence of sensible back-up procedures.

'Appropriate' security will depend upon the nature of the recorded data and the harm that would result from a breach of security. For example, the health and financial records of employees are likely to demand a higher standard of security than would be appropriate for a list of addresses of those employees, the latter being available from publicly available sources such as the electoral register. Interestingly, the Data Protection Act 1984 specifies four categories of data which are deemed to be particularly 'sensitive', presumably requiring special attention:

(a)   racial origin
(b)   political opinions or religious or other beliefs
(c)   physical or mental health or sexual life
(d)   criminal convictions.

The Secretary of State can modify or supplement the principles in order to provide additional safeguards in relation to these categories. Although this power has not yet been used, it would be as well that employers recognise such data as requiring special precautions.

5.3.8.1 Checklist: storage security

The type of questions which should be asked here concern the adequacy of the premises where the data is stored:

(a)   Are there suitable precautions against burglary, fire or natural disasters such as floods?

(b)   Is access to the premises controlled? For example, is it reasonable to expect security badges, security combination codes or electronic key cards to be issued in order to reduce the chances of unauthorised access?

(c)   Can persons outside the premises read data off screens or printouts?

But the problems do not end here. Computer terminals connected to a mainframe computer effectively breach the physical boundaries of 'secured' premises. For this reason, it is essential that the employer not only regulates access to personal data but also employs software packages and checks procedures which effectively monitor this access.

5.3.8.2 Checklist: software access security
Assuming access to the premises where data are stored, or access to a terminal outside the physical confines of this space, further security measures will be needed, depending in part upon the sensitivity of the data.

(a)   Is access to the relevant software dependent upon passwords, known only to authorised personnel? Are these passwords changed regularly, or at other appropriate times such as when an authorised employee changes job responsibilities? Should there be audit facilities for checking who is accessing the data and for what purpose?

(b)   Does the software incorporate checks that ensure, for example, that data are valid? Are there backup and restore facilities which allow for recovery of data and the production of backup copies? Is any duplicated data, such as storage of backup files on floppy disk, kept separate and secure?

5.3.8.3 Checklist: employees' reliability and other procedures
Employers should ensure that all authorised employees are properly trained in the use of all relevant procedures. The responsibility for data security training and procedures should be placed in the hands of an employee occupying a high status within the firm, or, if the organisation is large and complex, in the hands of a separate personnel unit. Such details will reassure employees about the continuing integrity of their own personal data files whilst highlighting the importance attached to general data security. Apart from this, an employer should consider the following points:

(a)   Has sufficient consideration been given to those necessary characteristics which an employee must possess, such as honesty and integrity, before access to data is authorised?

(b)   Do the internal disciplinary procedures take account of the Data Protection Act 1984? For example, are employees made aware that any unreliability, negligence, or laxness in abiding by current security procedures will lead to an immediate withdrawal of their data access authorisation?

(c)   Are shredding facilities available for hard copies? Moreover, is withdrawal of printouts from the secured premises properly monitored or regulated, if not prohibited? Should the employer consider imposing 'read-only' safeguards, thereby preventing any printed hard copy?

Clearly, security is expensive and the Registrar will not apply the same standard to every employer. Equally, no security policy yet devised is completely foolproof. However, the Registrar has stated that formal action will be taken against any data user where a breach of security has occurred unless he is 'satisfied that the computer user has done everything which could *reasonably be expected* in order to avoid the breach'.

5.4 POWERS OF THE REGISTRAR

5.4.1 Role of the Registrar

The duties of the Data Protection Registrar are:

(a) To establish and publish the register of data users and computer bureaux.

(b) To disseminate information on the Data Protection Act 1984 and its operations.

(c) To promote the observance of the data protection principles.

(d) To encourage, where appropriate, the development of codes of practice to assist data users in complying with the principles.

(e) To consider complaints about breaches of the principles or other provisions within the Data Protection Act 1984.

5.4.2 Enforcement and appeals

To ensure compliance with the Data Protection Act 1984 the Registrar can serve three types of notices:

(a) *Enforcement notice (s. 10)*. This is directed against a registered user who is contravening any of the data protection principles. It requests the user to take, within a stated period of time, such steps as are specified for compliance with the principle in question.

(b) *De-registration notice (s. 11)*. This cancels from the register the whole or part of a register entry. For example, it is possible that only certain details will be removed from the register such as a specified source of personal data. The notice will only be served if the Registrar believes that an enforcement notice will not adequately ensure compliance with the principles, taking account of whether any breach has caused or is likely to cause any person damage or distress (s. 11(2)).

(c) *Transfer prohibition notice (s. 12)*. This prohibits the transfer of personal data overseas. The actual powers of the Registrar, and the circumstances in which they may be exercised, are determined by whether the country to which the data are to be transmitted has ratified the European Convention on Data Protection.

Normally none of the above notices will take effect for 28 days and if an appeal is lodged within that period then the notice will be suspended. However, if the Registrar requires certain steps to be taken urgently a seven-day period may be put into operation, with no suspension by appeal.

Appeals against notices will be taken to the Data Protection Tribunal (s. 13(1)). This body acts as a court of appeal for data users unhappy with the Registrar's decisions, such as the issue of an enforcement notice. The tribunal may decide that a particular notice was unlawful, or that the Registrar ought to have used his discretion differently. If so, it may allow the appeal or substitute its own notice for that of the Registrar's. Interestingly, the Data Protection Act 1984 contains no appeals procedure for data subjects who feel that the Registrar should have issued a more stringent notice.

5.4.3 Ancillary powers of the Registrar

If the Registrar has reasonable grounds for suspecting that a criminal offence has been committed under the Act (see 5.5), he may apply to a circuit judge for a warrant to enter and search premises on which he suspects evidence of the offence is to be found. Equally, he may apply for a search warrant if he suspects a breach of any of the data protection principles. The judge will need to be assured in most cases that the Registrar has demanded access to the premises at a reasonable hour, which was unreasonably refused, by giving seven days' notice to the occupier. If a warrant is forthcoming then any occupier who intentionally obstructs a person in the execution of the warrant or fails in some other way, without reasonable excuse, to cooperate with anyone executing the warrant, will be committing a criminal offence (see sch. 4).

Furthermore, if the Registrar considers that a criminal offence has been committed under the Data Protection Act 1984 then the offender may be prosecuted in the criminal courts.

5.5 CRIMINAL OFFENCES UNDER THE DATA PROTECTION ACT 1984 AND NON-DISCLOSURE EXEMPTIONS

5.5.1 Introduction

An unregistered data user who holds personal data which are not exempt from the Data Protection Act 1984 commits a criminal offence (s. 5(5)). This is an offence of strict liability, not requiring any specific intention or knowledge by the data user or computer bureau, and can therefore be committed quite innocently.

Moreover, a registered data user commits a criminal offence if he or she knowingly or recklessly:

(a)   holds personal data of any description other than that specified in the register entry;

(b)   holds or uses any such data other than for purposes described in the register entry;

(c)   discloses personal data to a person not described in the register entry (subject to exemptions outlined below);

(d)   transfers, directly or indirectly, personal data to an overseas country or territory other than those described in the register entry;

(e)   obtains personal data, or information to be contained in personal data, from a source not described in the register entry (or from an unregistered processable source).

These offences can also be committed by agents or employees of a data user if such acts are committed 'knowingly or recklessly'. The maximum penalty for any of these offences is an unlimited fine, so it is important that data users regularly review the contents of their register entries and respond to changes in data-handling operations by applying for appropriate modifications to current register entries.

Disobeying a Registrar's notice also constitutes a criminal offence under ss. 10(9) and 12(10), although both provisions offer a defence of 'due diligence' in attempting to comply with, or not to contravene, the notice in question. As we shall see, this brings a data subject's right to compensation under the Data Protection Act 1984 broadly into line with a claim for damages based on negligence.

Finally, government departments are not liable to prosecution under the Data Protection Act 1984 but there are limited situations where specific civil servants who personally commit particular acts can be prosecuted. For further details, see the very useful summary provided at the end of Guideline 7 on the criminal offences that the Data Protection Act 1984 creates.

5.5.2 Avoiding criminal prosecution: the non-disclosure exemptions

When registering under the Data Protection Act 1984 a data user must describe, in the register entry, the people to whom he or she intends or may wish to disclose the registered personal data. A disclosure to such a person is perfectly lawful, irrespective of whether it falls within any of the non-disclosure exemptions discussed below.

Two further points should be made. First, as we shall see later, these non-disclosure exemptions do not prevent a court awarding compensation for damage suffered because of an unauthorised disclosure, even if the disclosure falls within one of these exemptions. Secondly, unless one of the registration exemptions applies (see 5.2.3), the personal data should be registered even though *all* disclosures fall within the non-disclosure exemptions. If not, although no criminal offence has been committed, the Registrar can issue an appropriate notice.

5.5.2.1 Disclosure with consent
The following disclosures by an employer will always be permitted:

(a) to the employee who is the subject of the data;

(b) to an agent authorised by the employee, who is the subject of the data, although 'adequate security measures' should be taken (e.g., verification of identity) so as to ensure that information is not disclosed in violation of the employee's wishes (see eighth principle and Sch. 1, Part II, para. 6(b));

(c) with the consent of the employee concerned — it would be good practice to ensure that written consent is received from the employee and that disclosure to external sources was kept to a minimum and always under secure regulated circumstances.

A disclosure is exempt provided that the person making it has 'reasonable grounds' for believing that it falls within one of the above categories. This might encompass a disclosure to a third party whom the employer has 'reasonable grounds' for believing is acting on behalf of an employee. For example, one might give details of an employee's annual salary to a building society which is considering a possible mortgage advance, although one would expect the production of some form of suitable documentary authorisation from the employee.

5.5.2.2 Disclosure within employment
A disclosure of personal data to an employee (i.e., other than the data subject), or an agent of the employer (e.g., company solicitor) will be exempt provided it is made for the purposes of enabling that employee, or agent, to perform his duties.

However, disclosures for different purposes will not be exempt. For example, the disclosure of employees' addresses and telephone numbers to a trade union representative who wishes to organise a football match between the employer's workforce and the local police constabulary will not be exempt. It is preferable that employers restrict internal access only to information which promotes business organisation and efficiency.

5.5.2.3 Disclosure for legal purposes
Disclosure is exempt if:

(a) required by statute, by any rule of law or by order of the court (s. 34(5)(a)), or

(b) made for the purpose of obtaining legal advice or for the purpose of, or in the course of, legal proceedings in which the person making the disclosure is a party or a witness (s. 34(5)(b)).

For example, disclosures which an employer is legally required to make to the Inland Revenue or the Department of Social Security would be exempt. In many ways the exemption is merely a wider application of the principle stated in *Tournier* v *National Provincial and Union Bank of England* [1924] 1 KB 461 that a bank which holds confidential information about its customers is not permitted to disclose it to third parties save under compulsion of the law.

5.5.2.4 Disclosures for the prevention of crime, and for taxation purposes
This exemption covers disclosures made for the purposes of:

    (a)   preventing or detecting crime (s. 28(1)(a)),
    (b)   apprehending or prosecuting offenders (s. 28(1)(b)), or
    (c)   assessing or collecting any tax or duty (s. 28(1)(c)).

The exemption only applies where failure to make the disclosure would be likely to prejudice one of those purposes. Although data users may not be obliged under the provisions of the Data Protection Act 1984 to make such disclosures they may be subject to other statutory duties in this regard. The data user should always verify the credentials of the enquirer.

If the data user is misled about the intended use of the information the exemption does not apply. However, data users will not be prosecuted under the Data Protection Act 1984 provided that they have reasonable grounds for believing that failure to disclose would be likely to prejudice one of the purposes mentioned above.

5.5.2.5 Emergency disclosures (s. 34(8))
Disclosures of personal data are exempt if they are urgently required for preventing injury or other damage to anyone's health. For example, if an employee has an epileptic fit then the disclosure of certain details to his GP may be a prerequisite for receiving timely assistance and advice. If the disclosure was not actually required then the person making the disclosure can still avoid criminal prosecution provided that there were reasonable grounds for believing that the disclosure was urgently required for the above purpose.

5.5.2.6 National security (s. 27)
The same exemption applies here as described in 5.2.3.4. The central issue is whether the disclosure is made to safeguard national security.

5.5.2.7 Modification of the exemptions (s. 2(3))
The Data Protection Act 1984 gives the Secretary of State the power to modify or supplement the non-disclosure exemptions for the purposes of additional safeguards in relation to personal data consisting of information about:

    (a)   racial origin,
    (b)   political opinions or religious or other beliefs,
    (c)   physical or mental health or sexual life, or
    (d)   criminal conviction.

5.6 EMPLOYEES' RIGHTS

An employee, as a data subject, has certain rights under the Data Protection Act 1984. These can be broadly categorised as:

    (a)   the right of access to personal information held on computers,
    (b)   the right to compensation for inaccuracy of data,
    (c)   the right to compensation for loss or unauthorised disclosure,
    (d)   the right to have inaccurate data corrected or deleted,
    (e)   the right to complain to the Registrar that the data protection principles or any other provisions of the Act have been broken.

5.6.1 The Right of access (s. 21)

An individual who makes a subject access request to a data user is entitled:

    (a)   to be told by the data user whether he holds any personal data relating to that individual, and
    (b)   to be supplied by the data user with a copy of all of the information constituting any such personal data held, with appropriate explanations where the information is not presented in a readily intelligible form (see s. 21(1)).

In the employment context, it is not just current employees who have a right of access. Previous or even prospective employees, job applicants, next of kin and many others will have the same right to gain access to personal data held about them on a computerised system.

In the ILU survey respondents were asked to state the approximate number of employees' personal files held and the approximate number of times that employees had asked to inspect their personal files:

Estimated number of files	Percentage of respondents to survey	Estimated number of access requests as a percentage of the estimated number of files (Average)
Under 1,000	25	Less than 0.02%
1,000–9,999	50	Less than 1.1%
10,000 and above	10	Less than 0.07%

15 per cent did not hold information on the numbers of requests received.

Requests should be made in writing and sent to the data user at the address for subject access requests given in the register entry. The data user may charge a fee for dealing with the request, the maximum fee prescribed being £10. Moreover, the data user who has more than one register entry is entitled to ask the data subject to supply sufficient information to identify the register entry or entries to which the request relates.

A separate fee is payable where the data user has separate entries in the register in respect of data held for different purposes (i.e., a separate request must be made — see s. 21(3)). As Guideline 5 states:

> Data subjects may find it helpful to check the data user's requirements before submitting a request for access. The data user's reply to the request need only reveal personal data covered by that register entry. If the individual is interested in more than one register entry a data user may insist that a separate written request be made and a separate fee paid for each entry to be searched.

Naturally, an employer could discourage access requests by registering multiple entries for personal data held for different purposes and then charge £10 for each response. Employees should be forewarned of the possible costs of making a series of access requests to an employer who has multiple registrations, although in the ILU survey only one respondent admitted to charging for access requests, that fee being £10!

Conversely, individual employees may cause considerable administrative inconvenience if frequent access requests are submitted. For this reason, employers are advised to preserve the right to charge a fee where the frequency of requests rises above a certain level, or ex-employees submit access requests.

Usually the data user must respond to the subject access request within 40 days of receiving it. However, the 40-day period does not start until the data user has, where necessary, received the information which is reasonably required to identify the data subject and locate his or her data. If consent is required from other individuals (e.g., the information identifies other individuals) then the 40 days runs from the time of their consent. What if this third-party consent is not forthcoming? On the one hand, if the data referring to that individual cannot be depersonalised and are not of a type where consent to their circulation amongst other data subjects can be implied then the data user is not obliged actively to seek that person's consent. In such circumstances, it would be sensible for the data user to explain to the data subject why some or all of the information requested cannot be given. On the other hand, if reference to third parties can be deleted or concealed by some other means then the information will have to be supplied, albeit in a suitably amended form.

5.6.1.1 Response procedure
A data user must always reply to a subject access request. If no personal data is held about the individual, or the information is subject to a statutory exemption then the data user should reply on the lines of 'The data held do not include personal data (a) to which your access request relates or (b) which I am required to reveal to you'. There is no need to specify which reason applies in any specific case (see Guideline 5).

Where personal data are not covered by an exemption then the data user must supply a copy of the information to the data subject. This copy must be supplied unless the manner in which the access query is made clearly shows that such a copy is not wanted. The information can be supplied in any suitable manner such as typescript, handwritten document, computer printout, fax; even an oral delivery would be acceptable, provided the details required are relatively short. However, in whatever form this information is communicated, it must be intelligible and accompanied, where necessary, with appropriate explanations of any coded phrases.

Data users are advised:

(a) not to tamper with any personal data in order to make it more acceptable to the data subject;

(b) not to withhold access to information merely because it is inconvenient or expensive to produce, or is difficult to locate or extract;

(c) not to refuse to respond to an access request merely on grounds that insufficient time has been given by the data subject to locate the requisite personal data (the data user must make this problem known to the individual).

In particular, data users should not make any amendments or deletions to the personal data, after a request has been made, unless such activities are merely routine adjustments (e.g., monthly updates). This prevents data users relying upon data subject enquiries to trigger data updating processes. However, if interim amendments and updating are a regular part of an ongoing data processing audit, unrelated to the access request, then the data user has the *option* of supplying the amended data.

Failure to reply to a subject access request is not a criminal offence. However, the data subject may apply to a court or complain to the Registrar that there has been a breach of the seventh principle. In particular, the right of access is limited by the seventh principle to 'reasonable intervals', taking account of the nature of the data, the purpose for its collection and the frequency of its alteration (Sch. 1, Part II, para. 5(2) and s. 21(8)). Frivolous or malicious requests will not be looked on with favour by the courts. If a court upholds the claim it may order the data user to comply with the request. As regards a complaint to the Registrar, we have already seen that this official has the power to serve an enforcement or de-registration notice, the former requiring compliance with the original request with continued refusal constituting a criminal offence. As with the courts, the Registrar will consider the general merits of the case, attempting to act reasonably and apply a fair degree of common sense to the facts of each case.

5.6.1.2 Response and security

If the information held is not very sensitive and the reply is being sent to the data subject's recorded address, then the normal signature of the individual should be sufficient proof of identity. But what if the information is more sensitive? Perhaps an accidental disclosure to an individual impersonating the data subject would be likely to cause damage or distress to the real data subject. In these circumstances, it is reasonable for the data user to require better proof, although impersonators should be warned that false identification may constitute an offence under the Forgery and Counterfeiting Act 1981.

Guideline 5 offers the following possible methods of verifying the identity of the person making the request:

(a) asking the person making the request to divulge personal information which can be tested against information recorded in the employee's file, for example, the bank account number to which monthly salary cheques are credited;

(b) requiring the signature of the person making the request to be witnessed, with any witnesses providing their full names and addresses and certifying that to the best of their knowledge the applicant has been identified correctly;

(c) asking for the production of a certain document expected to be in the applicant's possession; for example, a driving licence or passport.

5.6.1.3 Subject access exemptions

If personal data are covered by one of the exemptions mentioned below then the data subject has no right of subject access to the personal data and neither the courts nor the Registrar can order the data user to give subject access. However, the data must still be registered unless specifically exempt from the registration requirement (n.b. if the personal data are exempt from registration then no right of subject access arises — see 5.2.3).

The first set of exemptions deal with personal data which:

(a) are held for the purposes of preventing or detecting crime, the apprehension or prosecution of offenders, the assessment or collection of any tax or duty, and allowing any subject access would prejudice one of these purposes (s. 28(1));

(b) are held for the purpose of carrying out statutory functions where the data was obtained from a person who held them for one of the purposes mentioned in paragraph (a) and allowing any subject access would prejudice one of these purposes (e.g., ss. 28(2) and 30(1));

(c) are held by a government department and consist of information received from a third party and considered to be relevant to the making of judicial appointments (s. 31(1));

(d) consist of information in respect of which a claim to legal professional privilege could be maintained in legal proceedings — in Scotland the claim would refer to the confidentiality as between client and professional legal adviser (s. 31(2));

(e) are held *solely* for the preparation of statistics or the carrying out of research (with no disclosure for any other purpose), the resulting statistics or research being set out in a form that does not allow the identification of the data subjects (s. 33(6)).

In all the above cases, an exemption will still remain in force where the disclosure is to the data subject (or agent), or at the request or with the consent of the data subject, or to any employee or agent for the purpose of performing their duties. Moreover, it includes any of the above situations where the person making the disclosure has reasonable grounds for believing that the exemption applies, or where the sole purpose of the disclosure is for the preparation of statistics or the carrying out of research.

There are three other exemptions from subject access: (a) data kept purely for the purposes of backup replacement of existing data, provided there is no opportunity of consulting the backup data (archive data would not be exempt); (b) data held by a credit reference agency consisting of information covered by s. 158 of the Consumer Credit Act 1974; (c) under s. 34(9) Data Protection Act 1984, data which might expose the data user to proceedings for a criminal offence (excluding offences under the Data Protection Act 1984).

Finally, the Data Protection Act 1984 does not cover manual records so an individual will have no right of access to such records. However, if computerised records incorporate a coded sign indicating that further information is held in manually processed files then the employee has a right to know the meaning of these codes even if the employer has a right to restrict access to the manual files.

5.6.1.4 Modification of the right to subject access

Four modifications have been made by way of statutory instrument which have introduced a further group of subject access exemptions. These are: (a) health data under the Data Protection (Subject Access Modification) (Health) Order 1987; (b) social work data, based on whether disclosure would be likely to prejudice the carrying out of social work by causing serious harm to the physical, mental or emotional well-being of the data subject or any other person (see Data Protection (Subject Access Modification) (Social Work) Order 1987); (c) disclosures prohibited by law, concerning information held in adoption records and records of the special educational needs of children (see Data Protection (Miscellaneous Subject Access Exemptions) Order 1987); (d) data held by financial regulatory bodies where subject access would be likely to prejudice the discharge of functions relating to the regulation of financial services (see Data Protection (Regulation of Financial Services etc.) (Subject Access Exemption) Order 1987).

5.6.2 Compensation for inaccuracy

The fifth principle requires that personal data be accurate and, where necessary, kept up to date. Section 22(1) reinforces this position by giving individuals a right of compensation where they suffer damage resulting from the inaccuracy of personal data held about them by data users. This statutory remedy is in addition to other common law remedies that the data subject may possess such as an action for breach of contract, in negligence or for defamation. An application for compensation must be made by the individual to the court. The Registrar cannot award compensation. No compensation is payable if the data user can prove that all reasonable care was taken to ensure the accuracy of the personal data.

Data are inaccurate if they are incorrect or misleading as to any matter of fact. A mere opinion, which does not purport to be a statement of fact, cannot be the subject of an action for compensation unless it is based on a statement of fact. Nor will any right to compensation arise where the personal data are exempt from registration.

'Damage' includes financial loss or physical injury but does not include distress suffered by an individual. If the individual can establish that some type of damage or injury was sustained then a court may award compensation for any distress which has *also* been suffered by reason of the inaccuracy. But if the individual has only suffered distress and not damage, no compensation is payable.

5.6.2.1 Inaccuracy of third party sources

Interestingly, s. 22(2) absolves data users from the onerous task of enquiring about the accuracy of all received data, either received from the data subject or a third party. However, two conditions must be met.

First, the data must indicate that the information was received from a third party, or the data subject. If the information has been extracted from the data then the extracted information (e.g., computer printout) must also contain the same indication. How one indicates such an origin is rather more questionable. Perhaps use of the letter 'R' displayed next to an item of information would be a sufficient indication that the information had been received from the data subject or a third party (provided the meaning of 'R' has been explained).

Secondly, where the data subject indicates that he considers the data to be incorrect or misleading, then the data (extracted or otherwise) must contain this indication.

The above concession has become known as the 'received status' provision. Its applicability will be severely limited because one would expect a data user who is informed by a data subject of such a problem to amend the appropriate data entry. Moreover, the fifth principle requires regular updating of data. If data are accurate when received but, owing to changed circumstances, become misleading or out of date then the received status provisions will not apply. This is emphasised by s. 22 which focuses on the accuracy of the data rather than the accuracy in recording the data.

Finally, s. 22(2) has no application where the information is rendered inaccurate by the data user or his staff at the time at which the data are being entered. A cautious data user may therefore wish to retain a separate record of the information received and its source in case of any later dispute as to the validity of the origin marker (e.g., 'R'). This is especially useful in the light of s. 22(3) which provides the data user with a defence of 'reasonable care'.

5.6.3 Loss and unauthorised disclosure

Employees may be entitled to claim compensation if there is a breach of security which causes damage on the part of either: (a) a data user who holds personal data about them, or (b) a computer bureau which is involved in the processing of personal data which relate to them. In particular, s. 23

provides a cause of action where damage has resulted from a breach of the eighth principle. The remedy is particularly useful to employees whose personal data are disclosed negligently by their employers where the data are accurate and are not of a type that could be classified as confidential.

5.6.3.1 Compensation

Section 23 compensation is available for damage *caused* by the loss or destruction of data without the data user's authority, or the unauthorised disclosure or access to data (excluding persons to whom disclosure is specified in the register entry — see s. 4(3)(d)). The section concentrates on unauthorised actions and, therefore, does not apply to deliberate disclosures by the data user for which the data subject's only available remedies may be breach of confidence or breach of contract. The data user can effectively defend the action only by establishing that all reasonable precautions were taken to prevent this loss.

5.6.3.2 Application

In an employment context one could readily imagine s. 23 applying to the destruction of personal data by dissatisfied or malicious employees, the disclosure of personal data to unauthorised personnel (i.e., persons not described in the register entry) and the negligent supervision of access to employees' personal data.

These examples merely serve to underline the purpose of s. 23. This section is not really concerned with the wanton or intentional disregard of the interests of the data subject. Rather, it emphasises the importance of effective security measures. Thus, no compensation is payable if reasonable care has been taken to avoid the unauthorised loss, disclosure or destruction of data, nor if the personal data are exempt from registration.

5.6.4 Rectification and erasure of data

The seventh principle offers to individuals the right to have personal data corrected or erased where necessary for ensuring compliance with the other data protection principles. For example, in accordance with the sixth principle, data should be deleted if held for longer than is required to meet a declared aim.

If personal data are inaccurate, the data subject may apply to a court for an order that the data user should correct or erase the data. 'Inaccurate' means incorrect or misleading about any matter of fact. However, although opinions will not be considered as facts, an order for an opinion to be corrected or erased will be made where it has been based upon inaccurate data. Correction or erasure can be ordered by a court even if the information has been received from the data subject or a third party (see discussion of s. 22(1) above) and even though the court is unable to award compensation to the individual for damage caused by the inaccuracy of the data.

The Registrar also has the power to order correction or erasure, except where the personal data are governed by the 'received status' provision contained in s. 22(2).

Current evidence suggests that employers are normally prepared to amend files having been informed of any errors by employees. This is merely a recognition that no information system is perfect. For example, in response to the question, 'How often have employees' personal files had to be amended after inspection' (ILU survey), the answers were as follows:

	%
Never	40
Occasionally	45
Often	0

15 per cent did not have any statistics available on this point.

5.6.5 Complaints to the Registrar

An individual who considers that there has been a breach of the data protection principles, or any other provision of the Data Protection Act 1984, may complain to the Registrar. The Registrar must consider the complaint if it appears to raise a matter of substance and has been made without undue delay by a person directly affected. However, the Registrar need not take any formal action beyond considering the complaint itself.

The right to complain exists whether or not the individual also has a right to bring proceedings through the courts. In practice, unless compensation is being sought, many individuals may prefer to have their complaints investigated by the Registrar rather than to incur the expense and trouble of court proceedings (s. 36(2)).

Guideline 5 states that the Registrar's general approach to investigating complaints will be:

(a) to seek an agreed solution where this achieves a result in accordance with the Data Protection Act 1984 and is satisfactory to all parties;

(b) to assist data users and computer bureaux to comply properly with the Data Protection Act 1984 by guidance if there is genuine lack of knowledge or confusion;

(c) to use available powers to issue notices where an agreed solution is inappropriate or unattainable;

(d) to use the powers to prosecute for criminal offences where the Data Protection Act 1984 is being ignored or flouted.

5.6.6 Court proceedings

As we have seen, whereas data users have a limited right of appeal to the Data Protection Tribunal, this cost-effective, informal appeals procedure is not available to data subjects. If the data subject is unhappy with the response of the Registrar then he or she must initiate appropriate court proceedings.

In particular, under ss. 21 to 24 Data Protection Act 1984 only a county court or the High Court (Court of Session in Scotland) can direct compliance with a subject access request and award compensation for the effects of data inaccuracy and the loss or unauthorised disclosure of data.

5.7 CHECKLIST

Instigating access procedures   Although the Data Protection Act 1984 places the burden on the employee to instigate a subject access request there are good reasons for providing each employee at regular intervals with a copy of any personal data without waiting for a specific request. First, there are economies of scale associated with sending out a whole batch of data printouts — savings on time, manpower and administrative inconvenience. Secondly, by taking the initiative, employees will feel reassured that the employer is not trying to conceal important information. Thirdly, regular printouts will ensure that personal data are properly updated and existing inaccuracies corrected. This may prove useful when an employer is defending a claim to damages made by an employee injured as a result of inaccurate data being maintained.

Manual or computerised   As an individual has the right to examine *all* relevant personal data (i.e., data in automatically processable form), subject to any legal exemptions, each employer must consider what information should be kept on computer and what information is recorded manually. Sensitive areas would include current performance ratings, opinions of supervisors (even colleagues?) and promotion prospects.

Guidelines for staff   The right of individuals to claim compensation for damage caused by inaccurate or misleading data and a correlative right, in many situations, to press for suitable amendment or deletion of specific data, highlights the need for proper guidelines to be issued to staff. These guidelines must explain the reasons for adhering to a proper updating procedure, the need for proper verification of subject access applicants, and the effective supervision and control over access to and disclosure of personal data.

5.8 BIBLIOGRAPHY

5.8.1 Books

Chalton, S. and Gaskill, S. (eds) (1988a), *Encyclopedia of Data Protection* (London: Sweet & Maxwell).

Charlton, S. and Gaskill, S. (1988), *Data Protection Law* (London: Sweet & Maxwell).

Evans, A. (1984), *The Data Protection Act: a Guide for Personnel Managers* (London: Institute of Personnel Management).

Evans, A. and Korn, A. (1986), *How to Comply with the Data Protection Act: Policies, Practice and Procedures* (Aldershot: Gower).

Gulleford, K. (1986), *Data Protection in Practice* (London: Butterworths).

NCC (1990), *Data Protection Codes of Practice* (NCC Blackwell).

Savage, N. and Edwards, C. (1985), *A Guide to the Data Protection Act 1984*, 2nd edn (London: Financial Training).

Sizer, R. and Newman, P. (1984), *The Data Protection Act: a Practical Guide* (Aldershot: Gower).

6 Access to Confidential Files and Medical Reports

The issue of access to information took on greater social and legal significance throughout the 1980s. The advent of the real 1984 seems to have signalled the opening of (small) floodgates in this area so that, together with the Data Protection Act 1984, which was considered in chapter 5, an increasing amount of information is being made available for access by individuals. This is not to say that we have moved towards any general law of privacy; and even if we were to do that many of the constraints seen elsewhere in this book, and noted below, would probably apply.

The dissemination of 'information' in its loosest sense has been the subject of statutory intervention for some time. For instance, s. 1 of the Employment Protection (Consolidation) Act 1978 states that an employee should receive a written statement of terms and conditions after 13 weeks' employment. When redundancies are proposed or a business is to be transferred information regarding selection procedures etc. has to be given to recognised trade unions affected by such moves. Information also has to be supplied for the purposes of health and safety matters and occupational pension schemes. These are some of the wider issues. For the purposes of this chapter we will concentrate on the following points:

6.1 Access to confidential files
6.2 Access to Medical Reports Act 1988
6.3 Access to Health Records Act 1990
6.4 Checklist
6.5 Bibliography

6.1 ACCESS TO CONFIDENTIAL FILES

Other than files held on computer (to which the provisions of the Data Protection Act 1984 will apply), companies may keep a large number of files in manual format. In the ILU survey *every* company stated that this was their policy. These confidential files may be kept for a number of reasons in employment, ranging from factual details of salary, qualifications, car parking permits, previous employment details and the like through to more subjective assessments used for promotion and disciplinary purposes. A variety of sources are available: application forms, interviews, references, appraisal interviews, disciplinary warnings, grievance procedures, and medical records. Eighty per cent of these files were updated routinely; usually when the personnel department was notified of changes.

The restrictions placed on 'management' access within the organisation, together with the keeping of duplicate or supplementary files, varies considerably between companies. In assembling this information the employer takes on moral and legal responsibilities. Even at the initial stage of collation the questions an employer asks may be classed as discriminatory so that great care should be exercised in this area.

Otherwise than in the course of litigation, however, an individual employee has no *specific* right to see reports and records kept in manually recorded format by an employer. Thus there is no right to inspect files to check their accuracy; nor is there any right of access to references supplied by an employer. For that matter, there is no legal right to be given references.

The ILU survey found that some companies did have a policy of allowing access to personnel files and permitted employees to challenge the information, particularly information concerned with managerial assessments. The report also showed that it was not common practice for employees to request such access. Seventy per cent of the respondents also noted that there existed personal information on file to which employees were *not* allowed access. These matters covered assessment for promotion, career plans, grading appeals, information supplied from other sources (e.g., references) and, in some cases, *all* information kept in manual form other than very basic material such as address or bank account numbers for salary purposes. A number of companies' policies stated that medical records are kept separate from other personnel files and are subject to particularly limited access.

Many policies stated that disciplinary matters such as warnings would become 'stale' after certain periods; which indeed would be assumed in matters such as unfair dismissal actions anyway. However, just because a warning etc. has become stale does not mean that the details have consequently been removed from employees' records. Occasionally, disciplinary procedures are drafted so as to include a right of 'removal', but this is not common practice.

Information assembled by the employer, such as disciplinary records, most likely belongs to the employer and not to the employee. Except where the information is derived from the employee's own submissions, it is debatable whether the employee strictly has any right of confidentiality in that information (though attempting to identify the particular source of any piece of information might prove a hazardous experience). Where information is supplied by the employee, however, the position alters. In the same way that an employee owes an employer a duty of confidentiality there will be a corresponding obligation for the employer to maintain employees' confidences. Failing any express clause to this effect the duty will nevertheless arise where the employee has made disclosures to the employer; the duty being that use can only be made of the information within the limited purposes of the disclosure.

References supplied by previous employers or education establishments are more difficult to classify in that the information never belonged to the employee. Inasmuch as the references have become part of the employee's 'file' and access was gained through the employee's permission it is submitted that they could be covered by the duty of confidentiality. Where the employer supplies references for the employee any action based on those references would have to relate to defamation, injurious falsehood or negligent misstatement (see *Lawton* v *BOC Transhield Ltd* [1987] ICR 7), not breach of confidentiality, if permission for full disclosure has been given. As with confidences belonging to the employer, the information must of course not already be in the public domain and must have come to the employer directly or indirectly from the employee. There will also be a duty owed to the recipient of references to ensure their accuracy.

The most vivid example of the principle of confidentiality in operation arose recently in *Dalgleish* v *Lothian and Borders Police Board* [1991] IRLR 422. The police board was asked by Lothian Regional Council to provide the names and addresses of police board employees. The aim was to establish which 'council employees' were in arrears with community charge payments. The employees were all civilians working for the police board. They sought to prevent the disclosure.

The Court of Session, Outer House, granted an interim interdict (injunction) restraining the employers from disclosing the contents of the staff records. The decision was based on the alternative grounds of an express term incorporated in the employees' contracts via a collective agreement or by the general duty of confidentiality. On this second ground the court applied the principles of *Robb* v *Green* [1895] 2 QB 315 so that, although the list of names *could* be discovered by reference to telephone books etc. the list itself was protectable in the form assembled by the employer. The same information was also held on computer disks, which, it was accepted by the employer, could not be disclosed under data protection legislation.

Thus there is protection available to employees regarding disclosure by employers to unauthorised parties. But the files themselves, other than those falling under the Data Protection Act 1984, are not necessarily available to the *employees* themselves for inspection and correction. As a natural adjunct to legislation such as the Data Protection Act 1984, however, certain files are now open to scrutiny by employees, notwithstanding any company policy. The two Acts detailed below, the Access to Medical Reports Act 1988 and the Access to Health Records Act 1990, exemplify this. These Acts came into force on 1 January 1989 and 1 November 1991 respectively. It should also be noted that, where litigation is undertaken, disclosure of medical records and other documents may also be made available under ss. 33 and 35 Supreme Court Act 1981.

6.2 ACCESS TO MEDICAL REPORTS ACT 1988

Under the provisions of this Act a person may apply to gain access to medical reports relating to that person which are to be, or have been, supplied by a medical practitioner for employment or insurance purposes. The Act thus has a wider scope than employment relationships as it applies to any individuals and to a variety of situations. However, we will only be concerned in this work with the position of employees and prospective employees under the Access to Medical Reports Act 1988 and Access to Health Records Act 1990 and therefore we will address the issues only from this standpoint; hence wherever the Act refers to 'persons' or 'individuals' we shall simply use the term 'employee'.

The BMA supported the introduction of this Act and perceived its provisions as putting into a set of administrative procedures what is in any case good medical practice. The administrative consequences of this Act fall to a great extent on the employer; and the employee may seek access to the report(s) at several stages in the process. Prior to the Access to Medical Reports Act 1988 doctors would not normally submit information without the employee's consent; now to this has been added an employees' statutory 'right of inspection and veto'.

Medical reports may be sought in a variety of situations. Most commonly, employers will wish to obtain reports: to assess the state of health of prospective employees; for those employees applying to take early retirement; when dismissals are contemplated on the grounds of ill health; for entry to pension schemes; where promotions occur to senior positions; for employees travelling abroad; for canteen workers; and for workers operating in hazardous areas. In the ILU survey 5 per cent of companies stated that all current employees are required to undergo medical examinations at some time in their employment; 50 per cent said that this applied to particular groups of employees such as those noted above; 60 per cent required medical examinations for new prospective employees. All companies envisaged medical examinations occurring in particular circumstances. The circumstances specified included: after an accident; when employees returned to work after a long absence; to determine fitness; if requested by the employee; after attendance at the company surgery; for those over 40; all senior managers. All companies stated that they bore the cost of such examinations.

6.2.1 The basic right

An employer may request a medical report concerning an employee. Any request raises two discrete issues. The first is whether the employer has the contractual right to demand that the employee undergoes a medical examination. Express clauses allowing for this are the safest procedure for employers to follow. In the absence of express terms it is unlikely that any obligation would be implied for the employee to accede to a medical examination. The second issue is that an employee who agrees to a report being supplied now gains certain rights over that report.

The medical report must be for 'employment purposes', but no distinction is drawn in the Act between employees and prospective employees; or for that matter with those undertaking a contract *for* services. The Act allows an employee or prospective employee to give or withhold consent regarding an application being made for a medical report relating to that person. This will apply whatever the express term states. Further, under s. 3 the employer seeking a medical report *cannot* do so unless the employee has been notified of this *and* the employee notifies the employer that consent is given. Any notification by the employer must inform the employee of the relevant rights which apply at various stages in the procedure. These are noted below.

The report itself can relate to physical or mental health matters. Perhaps more importantly it also allows the employee the right in most cases to see the report and, to a limited extent, challenge it. The major effect of this is that employees will be allowed to correct inaccuracies that may be present in any report. The right to withhold consent is a fine theoretical right but, in the end, of less practical significance than it first appears because the employer will still have to make a decision (e.g., to employ or even to dismiss) on the evidence available. And what the Act does not permit is the suppression of *particular* items of information by the employee.

The Access to Medical Reports Act 1988 does not apply to medical reports prepared before 1 January 1989.

6.2.2 Who is covered by the Act?

The Act concerns reports made by 'medical practitioners', and this term is defined as meaning a person registered under the Medical Act 1983. That list is extensive. It includes those persons holding a UK bachelor of medicine degree, licentiates of the Royal College of Physicians and members of the Royal College of Surgeons.

Despite this definition most commentators have perceived that there is still some difficulty with the Act. A 'medical report' is defined in the Act as a report prepared by a medical practitioner who is or has been responsible for the clinical care of the individual. The use of the word 'responsible' seems to connote a continuing relationship between doctor and patient. The use of the word 'care' also causes difficulties. In most cases company medical departments will not be responsible for the 'clinical care' of the employee; nor will independent doctors who are being consulted over a specific issue. It is thought, therefore, that the Act is likely to apply only to people such as the employee's general practitioner or a psychiatrist or perhaps a particular consultant who has treated that employee on more of a continuing basis.

The Act was designed to allow employees to gain access to reports prepared by persons holding their medical records. At the same time, however, the Act does not apply to medical records but to *reports*, which may well have to be prepared from existing medical records but may equally arise from a one-off examination. Furthermore, the word 'care' is defined in s. 2(1) only as *including* 'examination, investigation or diagnosis for the purposes of or in connection with any form of medical treatment'.

There are two points which can be raised in relation to s. 2(1). The first is that the wording of the definition can just as easily apply to a single meeting with a doctor as to a course of treatment. The second is that we have stressed the word 'including' in the definition because the word can either mean that the definition is exhaustive or that it merely provides examples to a list that is not necessarily closed. In *Coltman* v *Bibby Tankers Ltd* [1988] AC 276 the House of Lords noted this duality of meaning and proposed a method of interpretation. Lord Oliver noted that, if other definitions in the statute have lists which are obviously meant to be complete in themselves, e.g., where the introductory words read 'This means. . . .', then any use of 'includes' in other definitions most likely signifies that that particular list can be added to. This is exactly what happens in s. 2 Access to Medical Reports Act 1988. All other definitions in s. 2 are governed by the words 'This means'. So, if the examples given of 'care' are open to additions then it is possible that company doctors who *attend to*, *monitor* or generally *advise* employees could be covered by the definition.

Running the definitions of 'medical report' and 'care' together one finds a sentence which reads:

a medical report means a report. . . prepared by a medical practitioner who is or has been responsible for the clinical. . . [*examination*] [*investigation*] [*diagnosis*] [for the purposes of, or in connection with, any form of medical treatment]. . .of the individual.

Read in this manner it is arguable that any one-off examination etc. by a company or independent doctor will be covered by the provisions of the Act, especially if this examination reveals problems previously undetected leading to further references to the person's GP or other consultants.

The prevailing view is that the Act has the limited application already noted, but there is no case law either way at the moment. Certainly, company doctors (occupational health physicians) will be encompassed by the Act where clinical care has been provided within the employment relationship or where the doctor effectively acts as the employer's agent in obtaining information from other medical practitioners. Further, occupational physicians have been held to be responsible for the health of employees even when they have not been consulted: *Stokes* v *Guest Keen* [1968] 1 WLR 1776 — where a duty to screen for cancer and provide health education was held to exist in relation to hazardous activities.

In the ILU survey it was found that the vast majority of medical reports (75 per cent) were normally supplied by the company doctor. The employee's own doctor was the next most popular source, and then company-nominated doctors and occupational health consultants or health screening units. The extent of the Act's definition, therefore, will clearly have ramifications on companies' policies in the future. In the ILU survey, for instance, only 15 per cent of companies stated that it was standard practice for employees to see medical reports before they are passed on to personnel departments. The same number said that employees were not allowed to see the reports; the remainder stating that permission might be given if a request was made.

If most of these companies who do not allow an *automatic* right of access to medical reports receive their information from company doctors (which seems to be the case, though this information was not cross-referenced in the survey) then, under the generally accepted view of the Act, this presents no legal problems. If these figures reveal that companies are not following the procedure of the Act (or the Act does apply to company doctors) there may be difficulties ahead for these employers.

It is also interesting to note that only 55 per cent of personnel staff had received special training on the provisions and implications of the Access to Medical Reports Act 1988.

6.2.3 Procedure before the report is supplied

As noted above the employee must be given notification of, and must consent to, the request for a report. As the person seeking the report must also notify the employee of his or her rights, many companies (70 per cent in the ILU survey) have now adopted a standard form (based on or directly following the BMA's recommendations to occupational health physicians) for obtaining consent. This form also explains the employee's position in clear words. In the ILU survey these forms followed a common pattern of giving a general explanation of the right to withhold consent and most contained a specific note to the effect that if consent was withheld the employer would make decisions on the known facts. This may be perceived as a disguised threat by the employer, but it is a statement of reality. It is difficult to envisage how industrial tribunals or courts could expect an employer to act differently. The position is in many ways no different from that where references are not forthcoming in relation to a prospective employee.

The employee is then required to complete a form granting or refusing permission for the employer to apply for a medical report. Some forms contained a specific clause whereby the employee agreed that the form would be copied to the medical practitioner and that it was agreed that the copy would be as valid as the original. Finally, the employee would be asked whether he or she wished to see a copy of the report. If such a request is made the employer must notify the medical practitioner of this.

Along with the request, employers frequently include a more detailed explanatory note on what are the various options open to the employee, with some attempt to summarise the provisions of the Access to Medical Reports Act 1988.

What the employer is obliged to tell the employee is:

(a)   that the employee has the right to withhold consent,

(b)   that the employee has the right to request access to the report both before it is supplied and up to six months afterwards,

(c)   that the employee has a right to withhold consent to the submission of the report at various stages,

(d) that the employee may request amendments be made to the report before submission.

If the employee has consented to the report and has also exercised the right to see that report then it cannot be given to the employer until the medical practitioner has been so notified. Section 4 lays down particular procedures for this. The medical practitioner must: (a) not submit the report at all if the employee so demands; or, failing this, (b) make amendments (or attach a note of disagreement with the employee's views) to the report before submission; or (c) wait 21 days without having heard from the employee. The same procedure applies if the employee did not originally request notification but the medical practitioner has since been notified by the employee of a change of mind.

The employer may therefore acquire quite different kinds of medical reports for different employees; if indeed any report is submitted. The Act does not determine what the employer has to do in such situations.

6.2.4 Access after the supply of the report

Even though the report has been supplied an employee may gain access to it up to six months later. That access may be by inspection or through a copy being made. Applications for access have to be made to the medical practitioner, not the employer. A fee may be charged.

6.2.5 Amendments to the report

The employee may seek to have amendments made to the report at any time before it is submitted to the employer (s. 5 Access to Medical Reports Act 1988). If the medical practitioner accedes to the request the employer will simply receive the amended report, and will not know of the disagreement. It may be that the medical practitioner refuses to make the amendments; and must then attach 'a statement of the individual's views in respect of any part of the report which he is declining to amend'.

6.2.6 Information excluded from the report

Information may be withheld by the medical practitioner from the employee in certain circumstances. The type of information is that which, if revealed, might cause harm to the employee or others. Similar restrictions appear in the Access to Health Records Act 1990 and also in the Data Protection (Subject Access Modification) (Health) Order 1987 in relation to computer-stored information.

Thus s. 5 of the Access to Medical Reports Act 1988 permits the medical practitioner to withhold information 'whose disclosure would in the opinion of the practitioner be likely to cause serious harm to the physical or mental health of the individual or others or would indicate the intentions of the practitioner in respect of the individual'. Further exemptions relate to the position where disclosure would be likely to reveal information about another person, or reveal the identity of anyone who supplied information unless consent has been given by that person or that person was a health professional involved in the care of the employee. If the exemptions apply then only the remaining part of the report, if any part at all, will be open to access. The employee has to be told that the whole or part of the report is not open to access and may of course refuse permission for the submission of that report. It is worth noting that it is the employee who is not allowed to see the report; the full report will still be available to the employer if the employee does not block its use.

6.2.7 The effect on employers

We have noted above that employers are required to provide certain information to employees as well as gaining their consent before requesting or receiving medical reports. Most of the administrative burden under the Access to Medical Reports Act 1988 is therefore borne by the employer.

Apart from this, however, there is little substantive change to the law relating to medical reports. For instance, the Act does not effect changes to the law of confidentiality in this area, nor does the Act alter the range of responses open to an employer when faced with the information, or the lack of it. Once the information has been gathered it should be treated in the same way as references supplied to the employer in relation to the duty of confidentiality. In the survey, 20 per cent of companies stated that medical reports do not go to the personnel department but to the employee only and copies are then held on separate files, if held at all.

But there is no separate right created, along discrimination lines, relating to the recruitment or non-recruitment of employees in response to any report submitted. Nor does this Act have any direct effect on the law relating to unfair dismissal. Where an employer is faced with information from a report which indicates that an existing employee is unable to continue in that work, the medical report alone will not justify transfer, demotion or dismissal. Nor will the failure to obtain a report mean that the employer is relieved of any further responsibility. The law relating to dismissal on grounds of ill-health incapability has always placed great stress on the procedural aspects. In particular, matters such as taking all reasonable steps to discover the true medical position, consultation with the employee and the consideration of alternative work have been emphasised by tribunals.

6.2.7.1 Requesting medical examinations

Where the request relates to prospective employees there are few restraints placed on employees save the practical one of deterring employees who might object to the examination. It will be unlikely that objections would be made, unless the form of the examination is seen as an invasion of privacy. Such might be the case with testing for HIV or AIDS, for instance. Employers must obviously take care in pursuing such a course, and to test without specifically notifying the employee of this would, it is submitted, be a dangerous course to take; at least in relation to adverse publicity.

As regards employees already in service, the value of express terms allowing an employer to demand, rather than merely request, a medical examination and report should be noted here. There is no general implied duty to participate in medical examinations (*Bliss* v *South East Thames Regional Health Authority* [1987] ICR 700), though exceptions might occur where there is a justifiable need for a report, e.g., following an accident.

Even in the case of present employees who are already subject to a clause giving the employer a right to demand medical examinations care needs to be exercised from a personnel perspective. The presence of an express clause allowing the employer to seek medical reports on employees will still be subject to the provisions of the 1988 Act.

The focus of the ILU survey was on the protection and use of information. Nevertheless some companies provided us with their complete contracts. On this small sample we found that there was no standard practice of including terms relating to medical examinations. Where terms were included they usually related to prospective employees, i.e., making any offer conditional upon the satisfactory completion of a medical examination or report. Of the remainder one example illustrates the general approach to current employees:

> *The employee, at the request and cost of the company will from time to time submit to and cooperate in the conduct of a medical examination by a duly qualified medical practitioner to be nominated by the company whose report shall be sent to the company and treated by it as confidential.*

Finally, it would seem extremely unlikely that a refusal by an employee to consent to the release of the report could be construed as misconduct which might justify a dismissal; although an employee's refusal to submit to *any* medical examination where there is justifiable concern, or a valid dispute, about suitability to perform the job may be held to constitute misconduct.

6.2.7.2 Employee's declarations

As we noted in the introduction and in chapter 1, there is no generally applicable implied obligation for employees to volunteer information about their activities. Nor will prospective employees be under any duty other than that of not misrepresenting their position. This will include, in some cases, information concerning criminal convictions under the Rehabilitation of Offenders Act 1974. However, where employees have been asked direct questions at an interview, on an application form, or during the course of their employment, they will come under a duty not to mislead or be fraudulent.

As an alternative, or in addition, to seeking a medical report more companies are making use of questionnaires on health matters. Questions raised can cover an extensive range, from medical history questions (the 'Have you ever suffered from . . .?' questions) through to questions about habits, e.g., relating to smoking or, with increasing frequency, how much alcohol the prospective or current employee consumes. Apart from questions which may be discriminatory (directly or indirectly) there is no legal bar as such on this type of investigation.

If an employee is taken on under false pretences this may well justify a later dismissal when the concealment is discovered. This principle applies to concealment of physical or mental illness, at least where such illness affects the job (*O'Brien* v *Prudential Assurance Co. Ltd* [1979] IRLR 140).

6.2.7.3 Enforcement

There is no separate right of damages created under the Access to Medical Reports Act 1988. The remedy is that, if the court is satisfied that a party has failed (or is likely to fail) to comply with the requirements of the Act an appropriate order may be made (s. 8) compelling compliance.

6.3 THE ACCESS TO HEALTH RECORDS ACT 1990

This Act again relates to records kept in manual format. The Act has much less immediate impact on the employment relationship than the Access to Medical Reports Act 1988 and therefore we will only deal with the relevant points. The Act was designed to allow individuals access to their 'health records' whether for reasons of curiosity or to seek to correct entries; though the right of access only applies to records made after 1 November 1991. However, information recorded before that date must be disclosed if it is necessary to make intelligible any part of the record for which access is given.

The Act follows very similar lines to the Access to Medical Reports Act 1988 as regards rights of access and the withholding of information, and provides the same general rights regarding health records kept in manual format as the Data Protection Act 1984 had previously established for the computerised equivalents. A fee (currently £10) may be charged by the record holder. If the record has been made or added to within the previous 40 days access must be given within 21 days of application. Otherwise the period is 40 days.

The first point of interest relates to the holder of the records. The term used in s. 1 Access to Health Records Act 1990 is a 'health professional' instead of the Access to Medical Reports Act 1988's 'medical practitioner'. Thus the 1990 Act has a wider effect than the Access to Medical Reports Act 1988. Indeed the list of 'health professionals' in s. 2(1) runs from medical practitioners through dentists and opticians and on to chiropodists, dietitians and senior scientists employed by a Health Service body. Thus health records held within a company's medical department may be open to scrutiny by employees. It is noticeable, for instance, that whereas the definition of 'medical report' in the Access to Medical Reports Act 1988 referred to 'a medical practitioner who is or has been responsible' for the clinical care of the individual, the Access to Health Records Act 1990 (s. 1(b)) merely refers to a 'health record' as having been 'made by or on behalf of a health professional *in connection* with the care of the individual' (emphasis added). The wording is therefore more extensive than the 1988 Act.

This also poses the problem that, assuming for the moment an employee could gain access to health records held by the company, these records might also include previously submitted medical reports, thus providing indirect access to these reports.

The second key element concerning the employment angle comes in s. 9 of the Access to Health Records Act 1990. This states that:

> Any term or condition of a contract shall be void insofar as it purports to require an individual to supply any other person with a copy of a health record, or of an extract from a health record, to which he has been given access under section 3(2).

This section clearly outlaws contractual terms which put an employee under pressure to make an application for access to his or her records and then provide copies to the employer. The only point of difficulty might be where a contract allows for an employer to request reports from an employee's GP (say, without an accompanying medical examination) so that the GP would effectively be producing 'extracts' from the records held. Such a situation would overlap with the Access to Medical Reports Act 1988 anyway, bringing into play both the employee's consent and rights of scrutiny.

If there is a failure to comply with these rules then, under s. 8, the High Court or a county court may, on application, order the holder of any record to comply with the relevant requirements.

6.4 CHECKLIST

Employers hold a great deal of personal information on their employees. Less attention has hitherto been given to information maintained in manual format than computerised records. That is changing. The drive that promoted greater access under the Data Protection Act 1984 has already flowed over into the area of medical documents. Equally, the duty of confidentiality, though commanding a less conspicuous role than in the case of protecting the employer's secrets, is relevant here. Employers need to be aware therefore of the following points.

The duty of confidentiality applies to information held by employers This will take the various forms noted above, such as preservation of secrecy, e.g., by limited access on a 'need-to-know' basis, and will overlap with a duty not to be negligent in storing the records.

Employees have no 'right' to access non-medical files kept on them The ILU survey revealed that there is no common policy as regards giving employees access to their files. This is a matter for employee relations; the law is silent on the point.

Medical reports cannot be taken as of right The employee's veto, based on the rights of access and assessment, means that employers are now placed under an administrative burden to obtain permission *and* explain the employee's rights to him or her. Comprehensive standard-form letters would appear to be the best solution here, such as those issued by the BMA. This has been recommended by various employers' organisations, though the survey did not reveal whether this had been adopted as universal practice.

There are no further constraints placed on employer's responses Neither the Access to Medical Reports Act 1988 nor the Access to Health Records Act 1990 created new obligations controlling employers' responses to information obtained. Such responses are still governed by the law on contracts of employment, wrongful and unfair dismissal. The same applies where an employee refuses an employer's request to obtain a medical report.

The two Acts may apply to company doctors The general understanding of the Acts is that they *do not* apply in this way, but, as we have argued, this may not be an accurate picture.

Employees' medical records should be kept separate from other personnel files As part of the general idea of best maintaining confidentiality this makes sense as part of personnel policy. If all files are kept in the personnel department limited access should be ensured rather than hoped for. If the 1990 Act does apply to employers, such a policy becomes even more important.

Medical examinations can only be demanded where there is an express term to this effect The case law is sparse in this area but the general approach seems to militate against implying terms for these purposes. Where there is a potential safety problem, or there is conflicting evidence regarding a possible dismissal for ill health, it may be easier to argue the need for an examination, even in the absence of an express power.

6.5 BIBLIOGRAPHY

6.5.1 Books

Clarke, L. (ed.) (1990), *Confidentiality and the Law* (London: Lloyds of London Press).
Gurry, F. (1984), *Breach of Confidence* (Oxford: Clarendon Press).
Mason, J.K., and McCall Smith, R.A. (1991) *Law and Medical Ethics*, 3rd edn (London: Butterworths).
Sweet and Maxwell's *Encyclopedia of Health Services and Medical Law* (latest edn 1991) (London: Sweet & Maxwell).
Wacks, R. (1989), *Personal Information: Privacy and the Law* (Oxford: Clarendon Press).

6.5.2 Articles

Cram, I. (1990), 'Access to Health Records' (1990) 140 NLJ 1382.

Howard, G. (1989), 'Access to Medical Reports Act 1988: Implications for Practitioners' (1989) 86 (13) LS Gaz 22.

Lewis, C.J. (1987), 'Medical Negligence Update' (1987) 84 LS Gaz 3089.

Prestataire (1991), 'Patients' Right of Access to Health Records' (1991) 88(10) LS Gaz 24.

Pitt, G. (1988), 'Access to Medical Reports Act 1988' 17 ILJ 239.

Index